# SOCIAL CREDIT
# AND THE FEDERAL POWER
# IN CANADA

# SOCIAL CREDIT IN ALBERTA

## Its Background and Development

A series of studies sponsored by the Canadian Social Science Research Council, directed and edited by S. D. Clark.

1. *The Progressive Party in Canada.* By W. L. Morton
2. *The Winnipeg General Strike.* By D. C. Masters
3. *Next-Year Country.* By Jean Burnet
4. *Democracy in Alberta.* By C. B. Macpherson
5. *Social Credit and the Federal Power in Canada.* By J. R. Mallory
6. *Sect, Cult, and Church in Alberta.* By W. E. Mann
7. *The National Policy and the Wheat Economy.* By V. C. Fowke
8. *The Liberal Party in Alberta: A History of Politics in the Province of Alberta, 1905–1921.* By L. G. Thomas
9. *Movements of Political Protest in Canada, 1640–1840.* By S. D. Clark
10. *The Social Credit Movement in Alberta.* By John A. Irving

# Social Credit and the Federal Power in Canada

J. R. MALLORY

UNIVERSITY OF TORONTO PRESS

Reprinted in 1976 (with additional preface)
Printed in USA

ISBN 0-8020-2254-5 (cloth)
ISBN 0-8020-6301-2 (paper)
LC A55-10300

FOR

C. W. M.

WHO LIKED POLITICS

# Foreword

It is now almost twenty years since Mr. Aberhart led his Social Credit legions to victory in the Alberta election of 1935. A long record of successful administration of the province's affairs has convinced even the most wary that the party he founded is no threat to the economic institutions of the country, that it is, indeed, one of the country's most vigorous forces of opposition to movements of radical economic reform. Conditions of economic prosperity in Alberta during the past ten or fifteen years have made unnecessary any sweeping changes in the province's economic institutions, and the increasingly conservative temper of the population has favoured the continuance in office of a party which in its economic philosophy is essentially conservative in outlook. The apparent concern of Mr. Manning, Aberhart's successor as Social Credit premier, to provide "good government" and avoid any act likely to antagonize business interests has secured the reputation of the Social Credit party as a sane, conservative political force in the community.

This shift to conservatism was in part determined by the turn of economic events with the outbreak of the Second World War and by the spectacular oil discoveries in the province since. What becomes increasingly clear, in retrospect, however, is that Social Credit never really was in its leadership a radical economic reform party. With their background of religious fundamentalism and their lack of understanding of economic processes, it could scarcely be expected that Mr. Aberhart and Mr. Manning would be prepared to undertake any fundamental reorganization of the economic system; both men had lived too long in a world of religious prophecy. Mr. Aberhart's thunderings in 1935 did create the general impression that he would balk at nothing to put into effect a programme of monetary reform, but, once he was elected to office, it quickly became evident that he was as much frightened by the radical as bored by the administrative implications of such a programme. Had his back-benchers been content, he would thus have happily forgotten the election promises he had so recklessly made. The fact that he was not permitted to forget them completely was an indication of the extent to which Social Credit had in 1935 attracted the support of people who were in principle radical reformers. It is significant, however, that the movement had appealed in particular to the small-town middle classes in Alberta, to people who, while dismayed and exasperated by economic conditions, did not really envisage or desire to see established a new economic order in the province. Conservatism could develop quickly within such segments of the movement once it became apparent, as it did not so long after Social Credit came into power, that the economic depression was coming to an end. As it turned out, Mr. Aberhart had to play at the game of introducing Social Credit for a few years; his successor, more fortunate, has had scarcely to pay lip-service to the cause which led to the movement's rise to power.

By confining attention to the economic programme of Social Credit it is easy thus to demonstrate the essential conservatism of the movement from its very beginnings. What can easily be overlooked, however, is the fact that it was not in its economic but political outlook that Social Credit was really radical. An examination of developments in Alberta from 1935 to 1942 indicates very clearly that Aberhart's attempts to introduce Social Credit were directed primarily towards the object of strengthing the political position of the province in its relations with the federal government. Monetary reform thus was a means to an end. That is not to say that some of the economic legislation which involved the Alberta Government in conflict with the federal was not desired for its own sake. But the successful implementation of his monetary reform legislation would have been acutely embarrassing to Mr. Aberhart. What was not embarrassing was the political effect of such legislation in widening the rift between the Alberta and federal governments. In seeking the increased separation of Alberta from the Canadian federal system, Aberhart was prepared to go to very great lengths. In this respect he was a true radical; crying war upon the powers of Ottawa, he could remain faithful to his chosen role of a prophet who had led his followers out of the corrupt, eastern-dominated churches and was now called upon to lead them out of the equally corrupt, eastern-dominated federal state. The new world he visioned was one marvellously simple in form and purpose; it involved no radically new principles of economic organization or of economic conduct. But to attain such a world involved a supremely radical political act, that of defying to a point which bordered on the illegal the authority of the federal governing bodies.

Something of the spirit which animated the Social Credit movement in its conflict with Ottawa is revealed in the study by Professor Mallory of the constitutional problem of dissallowance and judicial interpretation in Canada. To Professor Mallory, the developments of 1935–42 in Alberta were but an episode, though a highly significant one, in the long, unfolding story of Dominion-provincial relations. To the student of Social Credit, however, his study not only places in clear perspective the political events which occurred in Alberta after 1935 but throws much light upon the fundamental character of the Social Credit movement itself. With the cessation of political conflict in the years since the Second World War there was apparent not only a new economic and political balance within the Canadian community but a new sort of integration of Alberta into the economic and political life of Canada. Conservatism developed as a dominant characteristic of the Social Credit movement not with the abandonment of efforts to secure a reform of the monetary system but with the disappearance of any strongly felt need to secure the increased economic and political independence of the Alberta community. Professor Mallory has sought an understanding of the underlying forces determining the nature of Dominion-provincial relations in Canada. By doing so, he has contributed significantly to an understanding of those developments which took place in Alberta with the election in 1935 of a Social Credit government.

S. D. CLARK

The University of Toronto

# Preface

It has seemed to me for some time that Canadians have been looking at their constitutional development from too narrow a point of view. As Canada has grown, the old interpretations of Canadian history have become less and less satisfactory. What Professor W. L. Morton has described as the themes of survival and self-government are not adequate to account for a subtle and complex pattern of events. The time cannot be far off when, from a different point of vantage, the full pattern of Canadian constitutional development is set out on a broader canvas than was available to the historians of the 1920's.

For one thing these historians were, whether consciously or not, partisans. They assumed, like the great Whig historians of England, that the reformers, the Liberal politicians, and the apostles of Canadian autonomy about whom they wrote were marching with the destiny of Canada. Their heroes and villains were, as it were, preselected. They painted with strong lights and shadows. They provided, for their time, not only a history but an ideology.

Perhaps the two most important factors in Canadian history did not sufficiently engage their attention. Canada was their world, and they did not look far beyond it. But Canada was not a private world. It existed at all because of the demands made on it by a vast world economy, itself undergoing violent growth and change. This outer world affected Canada at every turn and in two quite separate ways. In the first place, the flow of investment overseas, changes in the pattern of world prices, and the upsetting effect of changes in technology created insistent pressures. In the second place a variety of ideologies blew and eddied about the world, modifying the intellectual climate of Canada as well as of the world beyond.

The Canadian West was more profoundly affected by these forces than was any other part of Canada, and changes in the Canadian West had their effect on the internal balance of forces in Canadian politics. It has been my intention in this book to examine, with particular reference to the relations of Western Canada with the central government, some of the stresses and strains (and the resultant modifications) on Canadian political institutions which these violent extraneous forces brought about. The rise of Social Credit in Alberta, and the larger adjustment in the politics of the Canadian West of which it was a part, became involved in a major readjustment of the whole balance of Canadian federalism. It is with the character and implications of this readjustment that this book is concerned.

Its construction has left me with many creditors. These are debts which I am happy to acknowledge, for they arise out of the endless patience of teachers and colleagues. I wish to record my unfailing gratitude to Dr. R. A. MacKay, for first directing my attention to the whole subject of Dominion-provincial relations, and for much else besides; to the late Dr. H. A. Innis, both for a new insight into Canadian history, and for his encouragement in this particular venture. There can be few Canadian scholars who have not at some time benefited by stimulus and encouragement from Dr. Innis, and I feel deeply the honour of being numbered among them. I gratefully acknowledge the help and encouragement of two former colleagues at McGill University, Professors B. S. Keirstead and F. M. Watkins. In the dreary task of revision I have received invaluable help, generously given, by Miss Mary Keller and Mrs. Muriel Armstrong.

Lastly, I am happy to record my thanks to Professor S. D. Clark, whose patient labours at every stage have been selflessly given, and to the Canadian Social Science Research Council and the University of Toronto Press, whose financial support has made this book possible. If, in spite of them all, I remain obtusely in error, the fault is mine.

J. R. M.

Montreal
September, 1954

# Preface to the 1976 edition

THIS BOOK OWES a great deal to Harold Innis. Scholars of my generation in Canada could hardly fail to be influenced by his ideas. His own work on transportation and the staple trades had demonstrated that the Canadian state was a specific response to the challenge of geography and economics. This could lead to a rather simplistic and determinist view of the nature of political development; but with Innis it did not. His own later work on the relationship between communications and social organization suggests an awareness of the importance of ideas – particularly economic and political doctrine – as factors in the process of change. What I sought to do in the book was an exercise in political economy. More particularly it was a case study which sought to illuminate the nature of Canadian federalism by linking a change in the economic environment, a significant shift in economic and political ideology, and the way in which the strains which these changes produced then affected the institutions of the Canadian state. It was, in that sense, a theory of Canadian federalism.

A quarter of a century later, it is useful to reflect on the more significant changes in the way the Canadian federal system is now reacting to the economic environment and the way in which these changes are perceived in terms of currently powerful economic and political ideas. In some respects the economic environment is the same. The Canadian economy still is heavily dependent on the need to produce both renewable and non-renewable commodities for the world market. This is essentially a world of wary oligopoly in which economic decisions are highly concentrated and in which the role of government is increasing more rapidly than the capacity for rational and effective decision-making, which seems never to be adequate to the problems at hand.

The hundred years' war in the minds of men between laissez-faire and collectivism is now largely over. Ideology, however, is no less important today in animating a continuing struggle among self-conscious social groups seeking to protect or expand their interests by gaining control over some part of the apparatus of the state. Nowhere is this more manifest than in the determination of French-Canadian élites in Quebec to control and expand the powers of what they perceive to be their own nation-state of Quebec. The strain which this has imposed on the Canadian federal system is obvious. Furthermore, it involves not only a difference of view on the definition of federal and provincial powers, but in a significant degree a difference over the nature and extent of the role of the state.

Nevertheless, it is not a simple matter in which Quebec alone is struggling for the means of expanded control over its particular destiny while the other provinces are content to accept a modest place in a federal system strongly ruled from the centre. Regionalism, in part based on apparent differences in economic interest, is producing federal-provincial conflict throughout the system. Nor are the cleavages wholly based on region and/or Lord Durham's two nations. They have class overtones as well, just as they did in the struggle between Alberta and the federal government in the 1930s. In a federal system one obvious method of defence against 'national' policies or international pressures on a regionally concentrated interest group is through a provincial government which can only with difficulty avoid being responsive. Divisions of the share of benefits and burdens when there is a serious breakdown in the system of distribution or an acute and costly shortage on the supply side as in the case of energy will cause the strains to take the form of class conflict as well. Such may well be the case in relation to the current anti-inflation program. Furthermore, as we have so often seen in the past, times of trouble tend to shift the balance of the federal system inexorably towards an aggrandizement of the role and power of the federal government. And a failure of the federal government to respond effectively is the greatest threat of all to the survival of the Canadian state.

In retrospect, it is possible to see that there were two possible ways in which the Canadian federal system might have developed after the Second World War. One way, which was set out clearly in the Report of the Rowell–Sirois Commission, was to reformulate the historic role of the federal government which had initially concentrated its energies on a policy of development based on opening up the West in a way which would at the same time strengthen the industrial base of Eastern Canada. In its newer role of economic management the fiscal and monetary powers of the central government would be used to foster growth and expansion, as well as take appropriate measures to counter the downward effects of the business cycle. At the same time the federal government would use its financial resources to equalize provincial revenues yet leave the provinces free to develop social policies as they saw fit.

This latter course was rejected. The politicians and civil servants in Ottawa, in the abounding self-confidence generated by the war years, sought instead to use their fiscal and administrative resources to initiate a broad package of social welfare policies administered uniformly across the country by the provinces with the necessary support of federal funding. The apparent unity of the war years, and the persuasive power of such well-known public documents as the Beveridge Report in Britain and the Marsh Report in Canada, produced an almost irresistible public opinion in support of such policies being carried out by the federal government.

From this initiative flowed the whole massive apparatus of federal-provincial consultation which usually goes by the name of co-operative federalism. Paradoxically, this strong central initiative had the effect of enhancing, rather than diminishing, the role and position of the provinces in the federal system. Participation in large and growing federally inspired programs impelled the provinces to create bureaucracies with considerable capabilities of their own in the field of planning and policy creation, with the consequence that almost all major policy areas – no matter which jurisdiction they fall under – must go through a reconciliation process through federal-provincial bargaining. This has produced a very different kind of federal system from the one defined by the courts under the guiding hands of Lords Watson and Haldane.

At the same time the role played by the courts as major theatres of conflict resolution in the federal system has declined markedly. Part of the reason for this has been sensitively analysed in Richard Simeon's *Federal-Provincial Diplomacy*. If one thinks of federal-provincial conflicts as being between states in the international arena, then resort to the courts involves the same kind of escalation as war since it has some of the characteristics of a zero-sum game. It is not surprising that provincial politicians prefer the diplomacy of federal-provincial conferences in which they can use whatever bargaining power they have to achieve a maximization of gains and minimization of losses. Hence the modest role of the courts in deciding the boundaries of jurisdiction.

The decline in the importance of judicial determination in Canada has been influenced by two further factors. One is the reluctance of powerful vested economic interests, both Canadian and multinational, to resort to the courts to halt the growth of government control of the economy. They now have too great a stake in stability to run the risk, as Professor Corry put it, of rocking the boat. It is not without significance that one of the few areas where such conflict now seems to be emerging involves the struggle between the almost wholly foreign-owned potash industry and the government of Saskatchewan, where the motivating force is to a considerable extent the political and strategic interests of the agricultural industry in the United States.

The second factor, no doubt, is the broader problem of the authority of the Supreme Court of Canada. As Dicey pointed out years ago, the 'legislative' role of the courts in a federal system depends on the willingness of the community to accept their decisions as objective and authoritative. The continuing discussion, as part of the process of constitutional patriation and revision, of the need to make the Court an 'entrenched' part of the constitution, standing more clearly apart from the federal government which appoints it and the Parliament of Canada which defines its role, is conclusive evidence of the nature of the problem.

Although in recent years the disposition to avoid resort to the courts in defining the boundaries of the Canadian federal system has been pronounced, the issues at stake nevertheless may be sufficiently grave to impel one or other of the protagonists to resort to this ultimate weapon. Such has been the case with the anti-inflation measures undertaken by the federal government in 1975. In the end only the courts can decide which level of government under the constitution possesses primary responsibility for the matter and, to the extent that both levels of government are involved, define the boundaries of their respective jurisdictions.

As this was being written the Supreme Court of Canada, in the Reference on the Anti-Inflation Act, was compelled to face the issue. Major questions of constitutional significance were involved. The first was whether the Act could be defended on the ground that the matter had assumed a permanent 'national dimension' as a logical outgrowth of the responsibility of the federal authorities for the defence of the currency and the national economy against international pressures which threaten them. Acceptance of this proposition would add significantly to the powers which the constitution as interpreted by the courts in the past has placed on Parliament. If the Court were hesitant to take this long step it might nevertheless uphold the Act as valid during a period of emergency. A further, and not unimportant, question was whether Ontario's adherence to the programme by executive action rather than by concurring legislation was valid.

In the last-named question the Court was unanimous – to no one's surprise – in finding that the Ontario cabinet cannot in effect alter the laws of the legislature by executive fiat. The question of legislative jurisdiction presented a more agonizing dilemma. In a lengthy reasoned opinion, which is a learned and lucid commentary on the whole corpus of judicial opinion on the matter since *Russell v the Queen* in 1882, the Chief Justice concluded that the legislation could be sustained on the long-established ground of emergency. Only two members of the Court dissented. The dissenting opinion of Mr. Justice Beetz articulated the fears of those who find even in the emergency power a lethal threat to the balance of the federal constitution. As such it must be pondered by all students of Canadian federalism.

The fact that the Court followed a familiar pattern in reaching its decision on the narrowest available ground illustrates again the tendency of constitutional courts to conserve their authority by exerting it as lightly as possible. In ruling on the constitutionality of the legislation the Chief Justice made this clear when he said, 'If it is sustainable as crisis legislation, it becomes unnecessary to consider the broader ground advanced in its support, and this because, especially in constitutional cases, Courts should not, as a rule, go any farther than is necessary to determine the main issue before them.' An attempt to lead the Court further, one suspects, might have revealed divisions of opinion which would have made it very hard to know what the Court as a whole was agreed upon.

The case raises issues of a sort which were all too familiar in the inter-war years, and with which I have dealt at some length in this book. If the response of the Supreme Court on this occasion tends to strengthen a growing federal power it will confirm trends which seemed to me to be visible over twenty years ago.

Nor is it without irony that the matter in the end was forced into the judicial arena by the determined opposition of the labour movement to the imposition of wage controls. Who, a quarter of a century ago, would have expected the trade unions to emerge as the major champions of provincial rights? It would appear that the process of constitutional change is still, in the end, a response to deep-seated conflicts between economic interests.

To some extent the authority of the Supreme Court is bound up with the legitimacy of the Canadian federal state itself, and no one will deny that its legitimacy is not universally accepted. Nor is this a wholly new phenomenon. In the past, Canadian federalism has faltered when environmental conditions severely strained the capacity of the federal government to play a large and necessary role. But, as events have unfolded, the emergence of some externally generated threat has persuaded Canadians that strong central authority over economic policy is essential to survival. The effectiveness of this role will present a challenge to the resources of political leadership in Canada. There is nothing inevitable about the survival of Canada as a political entity. It will not be easy to adjust to the present difficulties. But then, it never was.

Montreal J.R.M.
June, 1976

# Contents

# SOCIAL CREDIT
# AND THE FEDERAL POWER
# IN CANADA

CHAPTER ONE

# Dominion-Provincial Relations and Constitutional Change

WHEN THE NEWLY FORMED Social Credit party gained fifty-six of the sixty-three seats in the Legislative Assembly of Alberta in 1935 it was not realized that this landslide was a symptom of a major shift in the balance of power in Canadian federalism. Few political movements, in fact, were more thoroughly misunderstood by contemporary observers. Far from being a novel form of Bolshevism—as it was presented to the startled readers of eastern newspapers—Social Credit in Alberta was little more than a projection of forces and ideas inherent for a generation in western agrarianism. Nor did it represent a break with the party tradition, since Alberta had been lost, possibly for all time, to the major national parties in 1921. Nevertheless a chain of events had begun which was to have great consequences for the government of Canada. "Generations of Canadians yet unborn," wrote Dr. Eugene Forsey at the height of the movement, "may look back to Mr. Aberhart as a public benefactor, not because of his monetary theories or practice, but because, in spite of himself, he contributed powerfully to a revival of Dominion control over the provinces."[1] It is with the relationship of the rise of Social Credit to Canadian federalism that the present study is concerned.

It cannot be maintained that either William Aberhart or the Social Credit movement was the principal cause of the profound change in Canadian federalism which has taken place within the last twenty years. In part, that change was the reflection of a fundamental readjustment of the relations between Canada as a whole and the agrarian West, following the abandonment of the old National Policy after the First World War. In part, it was the reflection of something deeper: the adjustment of the federal constitution to industrialization and twentieth-century collectivism. An examination of the relations be-

[1]Eugene Forsey, "Dissallowance of Provincial Acts, Reservation of Provincial Bills, and Refusal of Assent by Provincial Lieutenant-Governors since 1867," *Canadian Journal of Economics and Political Science*, IV (1938), p. 47.

tween the federal government and the government of Alberta in the decade after 1935 brings out the character of the underlying constitutional adjustment. In this adjustment the Social Credit government was not prime mover but pressure gauge, not the earthquake but the seismograph.

What follows is not, as the persistent reader will find out for himself, a history of the Social Credit movement. On the whole the period with which this work deals ends in 1945, though it is necessary to follow some matters to their natural conclusion in 1948 or later. In the summer of 1935 the Social Credit party came to power in Alberta; in the summer of 1945 the Second World War came to an end. Between those two dates the whole atmosphere of Canadian politics and the Canadian economy changed. At the beginning of the period there were not many people left who believed that the twentieth century belonged to Canada. The best that could be said for the future was that it could scarcely be worse than the present. Ten years later, though it was not apparent to everyone (including many economists in Ottawa), Canada stood on the threshold of the greatest expansion in its history.

We are not here concerned with how this metamorphosis came about, but with its implications for the Canadian federal system. How did it happen that the grave and intricate problems which led to the appointment of the Royal Commission on Dominion-Provincial Relations in 1937 had almost disappeared ten years later? What had happened in this time to bring about a reassessment of its role by the federal government? It is with these questions in mind that we look at the impact of the Social Credit movement in Alberta on the federal system.

The period of activity of Social Credit in Canada coincided closely in time with fundamental changes in the constitutional balance between the provinces and the Dominion. What is more important, the struggle between Alberta and the central government involved the three major institutions of Canadian federalism: the power of disallowance, the review by the courts of the distribution of legislative power, and political parties as mechanisms of adjustment in a federal state. All three institutions are sensitive indicators of any shift in the balance of power within the Canadian federal system.

The power of disallowance and judicial review both played a prominent part in the struggle between the Dominion and Alberta over the social credit programme. In order to clarify the issues involved some examination of these institutions and the role which they play in the Canadian state is necessary. Accordingly the early chapters of this study are concerned with the nature of the power of disallowance and of judicial review as they bear upon the discussion.

For one reason or another the treatment of both disallowance and judicial review in standard works remains unsatisfactory. Historians of a generation now passing provided the historical assumptions upon which most Canadian legal, constitutional, and political studies have been founded. "Survival and self-government were the original themes of Canadian historical study. But these were narrowly political, essentialy colonial, and were not infrequently developed in a somewhat antiquarian spirit."[2] The work of Canadian economic historians, following Professor Innis, has provided a new depth and perspective to Canadian history which have not yet begun to infuse political and constitutional studies. The nature of the power of disallowance, which has never been adequately studied in the past, is particularly in need of re-examination. No attempt is made here to provide such a thorough study; the discussion of the evolution of disallowance in the next chapter is sufficient only to serve as an introduction to the detailed discussion of Alberta disallowances in subsequent chapters. Similarly, some discussion of the general lines of judicial interpretation of the division of legislative power before 1935 is unavoidable. The large body of case law since 1935, much of it directly concerning Alberta, becomes intelligible only when its roots in earlier decisions are exposed.

The number of political parties, and the distribution of their strength in different provinces, are important indices of the degree of national integration and of the extent to which this integration is modified by strong local pressures. The Social Credit party came on the political scene as a third party at a time when the fortunes of the Liberal and Conservative parties were at a low ebb in western Canada. The extent to which Social Credit was able to modify national policy in the interests of the agrarian West demonstrates the way in which third parties play the part of innovators in social policy. At the same time the failure of Social Credit to capture a national following illustrates the limits of third party action in a single province in a federal country. The history of Social Credit in Alberta reveals the way in which the national party system is affected by strong regional protests which generate third parties, and how the party structure affects the character of the federal system.

[2]W. L. Morton, "Clio in Canada: The Interpretation of Canadian History," *University of Toronto Quarterly*, XV (1946), p. 227.

The constitution of Canada is in process of continuous evolution as the balance of forces which are brought to bear on it alters. The constitutional relations between the province of Alberta and the Dominion in the years between 1935 and 1945 are a unified part of that process which is rich in examples of constitutional doctrines being strained and modified under the pressure of economic and social change. They provide a good opportunity to observe and to distinguish the factors which, in Canada, make for modification and change in the constitution.

The federal system which had taken shape by the eighteen-eighties lasted without serious strain into the inter-war period. It was designed to meet the needs of an expanding and developing capitalist economy which was being created by a vast inflow of foreign capital. In some of its parts the political structure was strongly centralized in order to safeguard the interests of creditors and to encourage rapid capital growth. These institutional arrangements were not necessarily the result of calculated intent. Any people creates its government in the image of its own needs. Numerous disparate pressures created the Canadian federalism of the nineteenth century for well understood and tacitly agreed objectives. These objectives centred on the rapid settlement and devolpment of the prairie region as a great export area and a market for eastern goods and services.

The change in world market conditions for the great prairie staple in the nineteen-twenties, together with the subsequent drought, was a body blow to the western economy. In the West itself, a new set of pressures was brought into being which aimed at the protection of debtors and the equitable modification of existing legal rights of creditors. The *laissez-faire* heritage of the past had left in the hands of the provincial legislatures an implied residuum of power which enabled the provinces to attempt defensive measures against strongly entrenched creditor groups.

At the same time the whole governmental structure, fashioned for a nineteenth-century expansion, lacked both powers and organization to deal with the actual problems of relief and reconstruction which arose. It became clear how specialized even the political institutions of federalism were. They had been created in an age of rapid capital accumulation and were clearly unsuited to the needs of an economy which seemed to be slipping into stagnation. The paralysis of the normal channels of government heightened the economic problem and made the demand for fundamental change all the more insistent.

Three separate factors were at work forcing a modification in existing constitutional relations. These factors were: (1) the impact of a hard-pressed debtor economy on a legal and governmental framework built to expedite economic expansion; (2) the effect of novel political and economic doctrines on the constitution, and the response of interest groups in using the constitution as a symbol of social order and a means of maintaining the status quo; and (3) the place of those forces in the major long-run change in the relations of the citizen and the state which was the result of the general retreat, since 1920, from *laissez-faire.*

The present study is an examination of those forces of change at work as far as the relations between eastern Canada and the West are concerned. To the westerner, eastern Canada has a monolithic appearance. It is, or was, no more and no less than St. James Street and Bay Street. In the protracted antagonism of East and West the struggle between the Dominion and Alberta is of special significance. This significance does not arise because the issues were particularly clear to the participants—for in fact they were scarcely understood at all. It stems from the fact that the struggle took place during the break-up of one long-run trend and the emergence of another, thus bringing the past and the present into focus and perspective. History viewed from any single vantage point assumes a particular perspective which is not visible from any other, and each particular perspective foreshortens and distorts the image to the eye of the viewer. It is only by the comparison of these perspectives that the full dimensions of human development may be discovered.

CHAPTER TWO

# The Historic Role of Disallowance in Canadian Federalism

DISALLOWANCE is an executive restraint on the power of a subordinate legislature. When legislative powers were given to British colonies the imperial executive retained a veto by way of disallowance over legislation validly passed by a colonial legislature. This rounded out the old imperial system of colonial government by providing a device by which imperial interest could be preserved against the encroachment of purely local interests expressed through the will of a colonial legislature. Any colonial act could, within a limited period after its enactment, be disallowed by imperial order-in-council and thus rendered null and void. This form of veto was in addition to the normal executive restraint on colonial legislation by which the governor could refuse assent outright, or by which he could reserve a doubtful bill for the signification of Her Majesty's pleasure and thus pass the responsibility for giving royal assent back to the imperial executive.

Such an elaborate system of checks on local power was in part the outcome of the nature of the old Empire and in part an elaborate effort to solve the problem of communication and span of control presented by a world in which effective military control through sea power greatly outran effective administrative control. The old Empire was conceived as an economic unit with the result that the whole range of economic policy had to be controlled from London to keep the parts of the machine in step. This centralization of economic objectives meant that practically everything was in some respect an imperial interest. The way in which the North American colonies raised their revenues, the manner in which they disposed of and exploited their public lands and natural resources, even the class structure which they fostered by their policies of settlement, were of immediate concern to the home government. Continuous control over the restless interplay of interest groups on distant frontiers was an administrative problem of great complexity.

In part the imperial interest could be maintained through the office of governor. In so far as was possible he was provided with instructions, supplemented by despatches, defining the kind of legislation for which the veto was appropriate; when in doubt (and here again guidance was provided by his instructions), he could reserve legislation for more mature consideration at home. But this was insufficient. Communication across the Atlantic was bad at the best of times, and was further interrupted by the freezing of the St. Lawrence for half the year. The governor, in his remote provincial capital, was likely to be confronted by entirely novel situations for which his instructions provided no useful guide. To this problem the solution was disallowance.

Towards the middle of the nineteenth century three things happened which greatly altered the relationship between the home government and the colonies. The gradual abandonment of mercantilism greatly reduced the area of imperial interest which anxious and often bewildered governors had been forced to defend in the past. With the granting of responsible government, the fact that the governor was in most matters to act on the advice of a ministry inhibited the open assertion of an imperial veto. Thus refusals of assent and reservations declined rapidly in number and significance. Finally, the invention of telegraphic communication made negotiation easier, so that instead of causing headlong collisions between local majorities and obtuse governors (leading to petitions, recriminations, and delegations to London), the matter could be carried quickly to London for speedy and satisfactory settlement. While the importance of the governor and his veto declined as a device of imperial control, the home government still possessed, in disallowance, a means by which its interests could ultimately be asserted without paralysing the operation of constitutional government in the colony by poisoning the relations of the governor with his ministers.

At Confederation the power of disallowance of Dominion legislation was retained, section 56 of the British North America Act providing for the disallowance of Dominion legislation within a period of two years after its enactment. As far as the Dominion is concerned this power may be said to have fallen into disuse after 1878.

By section 90 of the B.N.A. Act it was provided that acts of the provincial legislatures could be disallowed by the governor general within a period of one year after enactment. From the beginning the practice was for him to exercise this power, not in his discretion as an imperial officer, but on the advice of his Canadian ministers. At one point this practice was disputed by the imperial authorities when Lord Kimberley, in a despatch to Lord Lisgar in 1873, laid down that in dealing with the disallowance of an amendment to the New Brunswick School Act of 1871 he should act on his own discretion. Edward Blake, who felt that this despatch threatened the operation of ministerial responsibility, gave notice of motion in the House of Commons in 1875 asserting that disallowance ought to be on ministerial advice and responsibility. This view was supported on both sides of the House; Sir John A. Macdonald remarked that the despatch had "rather surprised him" and added, "I say at once that I think the Minister made a grave error in constitutional law."[1] From that time the power of disallowance has been a device by which the Dominion executive has had the power to veto provincial legislation.

In order to understand the uses to which the disallowance power was put it is necessary to refer to statements of policy and the actual disallowances of federal ministers of justice and to indicate the kind of needs which brought the disallowance power into play.

For all the apparatus of federalism in the constitution, Canada, in fact, was given many of the characteristics of a unitary state. Professor Scott has quite properly reminded us that the subordinate position of the lieutenant-governor and the federal power of disallowance detract considerably from the supposedly federal character of the constitution described in the preamble of the British North America Act.[2]

In addition to these constitutional anomalies there is another sense in which the Canadian system departs from the truly federal. Legal and political abstractions tend to ignore the realities of economics and geography and thus in a federal system there is assumed an equality of influence and treatment of the various individual units. In Canada the facts are, and always have been, very different. Not only are the provinces different in size and economic importance and thus able to benefit in varying degrees from national policy, but this difference was so marked for a large part of our history that it was recognized in the constitution, when the federal government retained and administered, for the purposes of the Dominion, the public lands of the western provinces. The western provinces were thus for a time actually in a subordinate position; they were provinces not in the same sense as were Ontario and Quebec, but in the Roman sense.

[1]*Canada, House of Commons Debates*, 1875, March 31, pp. 1006–8.
[2]F. R. Scott, "The Special Nature of Canadian Federalism," *Canadian Journal of Economics and Political Science*, XIII (1947), p. 13.

This flowed directly from the nature of the economy of British North America. As Professor Creighton has observed:

> It was the western trade . . . which largely determined the style of Canadian politics. Transcontinentalism, the westward drive of corporations encouraged and followed by the super-corporation of the state, is the major theme in Canadian political life; and it was stated, in its first simplicity, by the fur trade. The fur trade enforced commitments and determined policies. . . . Until 1663 Canada was governed by a series of trading corporations; then it became a commercial and military state. Colonial government derived its strength from taxes paid directly or indirectly by the western trade. . . . From the first the government was committed to the programme of western exploitation of the river system. The St. Lawrence was an expensive monopoly; and its imperious demands could be met—and even then inadequately—only by the corporate effort of the northern society. . . . Inevitably the instinct of both politicians and business men was toward unity and centralization, both for the management and the support of this monstrous western machine.[3]

There seems to have been a certain historic inevitability about the way in which the political system of Canada has developed around the economic needs of a commercial system centring on the St. Lawrence. The need to organize a high-cost, high-overhead economy compelled economic and political centralization, though this centralization has been offset periodically both by the divergent needs of scattered and culturally different groups which resisted such amalgamation stubbornly and by the narrow margin of safety on which the economy operated as a result of its massive overheads and the highly variable nature of its returns.

At the time of Confederation, this imperious economic destiny was demanding new and bold measures in political and economic organization. Confederation happened at the zenith of expanding capitalism. It was the rich promise of developing half a continent which dazzled the Fathers. The end of the Civil War in the United States had unleashed a tremendous movement of westward expansion, and speedy development was essential if the empty western land was not to be sucked into the continental economic system which was growing up around the marching steel of the American railroads. Such rapid development under Canadian auspices involved a tremendous capital expenditure, and this was only possible if the resources of the London money market could be tapped.

[3]D. G. Creighton, *The Commercial Empire of the St. Lawrence* (Toronto, 1937), pp. 16–17.

The prime conditions imposed by the need for rapid capital accumulation had a marked effect on the political structure of the new Dominion. The immense resources of the London money market could only be made available in Canada if the capital came in uncontrolled, unrestrained, and at its own price. This price was not so much a high money price, as the abortive Canadian loan of 1866 had shown.[4] To the investor a high return is less important than the security of his principal. The unfortunate experience of the British investor in American railroads had made the security of his investment the paramount consideration, at least as far as North America was concerned. Hence Confederation came in Canada at the time and in the manner it did. The federal power over provincial legislation by way of reservation and disallowance, together with the clear assertion that economic matters were the concern of the Dominion, assured uniformity of treatment and security of investment. There was much meaning in Galt's blunt observation that trade and commerce was a subject "in reference to which no local interest could exist."[5]

The Fathers of Confederation, who as federal cabinet ministers and leaders of provincial politics were to be instrumental in carrying out the scheme which they had planned, were fortunate in having a few years of prosperity in which to consolidate the union and to launch the great project of expansion. This breathing space was followed by a major crisis which was to test the adequacy of the machine for the purposes for which it had been built.

The general belief in a harmony of interests, which was an essential part of the *laissez-faire* philosophy dominant in the nineteenth century, is in essence a product of boom conditions. In periods of depression it tends to be contradicted by hard facts. The bitter years between 1873 and 1896 broke down the belief of a general harmony of either political or economic interests. Hard times imposed a severe

[4]"In 1866, with a debt of $77,020,082 the government [of Canada] was 'unable to raise more than half of a moderate loan even when offering eight per cent interest' as a result of 'the disastrous effect on Canadian credit of the experience of British investors.' . . .

"The new Dominion served as a credit structure by which capital became available with government support, and transportation facilities were extended. The St. Lawrence route, with its dependence on extensive governmental intervention in the reduction of transportation charges, and its inability to compete with American roads for through traffic, was forced to rely on fresh government support for the development of new sources of traffic. The political structure was adapted to these demands." H. A. Innis, *Political Economy in the Modern State* (Toronto, 1946), pp. 190–1.

[5]Quoted in D. G. Creighton, *British North America at Confederation* (Ottawa, 1937), p. 52.

strain both on national sentiment and on national policy, which is the cement of common national feeling. The adoption of the National Policy in 1879 as a means of stimulating home production was symptomatic of the difficulty but it, like all policies of protection, tended to distribute the burdens more unevenly than ever. Under the stress of failure of the National Policy, the provinces were forced to take the initiative and pursue developmental policies of their own, or else try to modify federal policies so as to retain a larger share of regional income. Against both of these courses disallowance was a means of reasserting federal dominance.

The pattern for the use of the disallowance power had been set by Sir John Macdonald himself, who was Minister of Justice for the whole of his first ministry, from July 1, 1867, until November 6, 1873. His views on the use of disallowance are well known and the policy which he laid down was in fact followed by his successors until the end of the century. The variations in the number of disallowances were quite marked at different periods but this was caused more by differences in the strength of the federal government and the legislative programmes of the provinces than by any fundamental modification of policy on the part of the ministers of justice.

Macdonald laid down four grounds on which provincial legislation ought to be disallowed. They were: (1) where the legislation was wholly illegal or unconstitutional; (2) where it was illegal or unconstitutional in part; (3) where it clashed with federal legislation in fields of concurrent jurisdiction; and (4) where it affected the interests of the Dominion as a whole.[6] It was evident from the way in which he applied the term that he attached different meanings to "illegal" and "unconstitutional." "Illegal" meant what we would now call *ultra vires*, that is legislation which is clearly beyond the powers assigned to the provinces under the constitution. It has been suggested by Dr. Forsey that Macdonald used the term "unconstitutional" in the British sense of a violation of the traditional rights of British subjects.[7] In the context of the time, that meant the kind of "unsound" or "unreasonable" legislation which affected the rights of contract or vested rights generally, and in fact the circumstances in which disallowance was used support this interpretation. The disallowances between 1876 and 1890 were in most cases attempts to safeguard

[6]"Disallowance: Report of Sir John Macdonald (Minister of Justice)", *Canada, Sessional Paper*, 1869, no. 18.

[7]E. A. Forsey, "Disallowance of Provincial Acts, Reservation of Provincial Bills, and Refusal of Assent by Lieutenant-Governors since 1867," *Canadian Journal of Economics and Political Science*, IV (1938), p. 47.

a conception of property and contract which the federal government considered vital to the success of its national policies.

One of the most important political issues which confronted the Dominion government in those years was the persistent attempt of the province of Manitoba to break the transportation monopoly of the Canadian Pacific and achieve lower freight rates by admitting competing American lines into the province. The Dominion government was drawn as a principal into the conflict because of clause 15 of the Canadian Pacific Railway charter which guaranteed to the railroad a monopoly of traffic between western and eastern Canada in exchange for the railway's undertaking to construct the costly and uneconomic link to Winnipeg north of Lake Superior—a step which was essential in order to provide an all-Canadian route. The monopoly clause was designed to protect the C.P.R.'s investment in the line north of Lake Superior, to protect the West as the Canadian "empire,"[8] and probably to attract English capital.[9]

While the transcontinental line was under construction the Dominion government continued, in spite of rising protest in Manitoba, to protect the monopoly position of the C.P.R. in western traffic. The ultimate weapon in the hands of the railroad and the government was the power to disallow provincial legislation which chartered competing lines.[10] The government believed, however,

[8]In granting a monopoly to the Canadian Pacific "the government was actuated by the desire to build up Canadian trade east and west—thus fostering the growth of such eastern centres as Toronto, Montreal, Quebec, St. John and Halifax—and to prevent the United States western roads from building feeders into Canada and drawing traffic into the United States." W. T. Jackman, *The Economics of Transportation* (Toronto, 1926), p. 21.

[9]"English investors, who . . . hated monopoly at home as they hated the devil but looked with favour born of experience of the working of competitive railways, on monopoly abroad" were influential in protecting the road from competition. O. D. Skelton, *The Life and Letters of Sir Wilfrid Laurier* (London, 1921), vol. I, p. 254.

"I say that the interests of this country demand that the Canadian Pacific Railway should be made a success, and the man who does any act by which that success is imperilled takes a course which is hostile to the interests of Canada. But somebody may ask what about the interests of Manitoba? Are the interests of Manitoba and the North-West to be sacrificed to the policy of Canada? I say, if it is necessary,—yes." *Canada, House of Commons Debates,* 1883, May 4, p. 971.

[10]There is a full discussion of the issue in James A. Jackson, "The Disallowance of Manitoba Railway Legislation in the Eighteen-Eighties—Railway Policy as a Factor in the Relations of Manitoba and the Dominion, 1878–1888" (unpublished M.A. thesis, University of Manitoba, August, 1945, University of Manitoba Library). Mr. Jackson concludes: "Not only did Manitoba's railway problems provide much fuel for the political fires of the country but they also contributed greatly to an alteration in the policy of disallowance of provincial legislation. The

that once the line was in operation and traffic had begun to flow, it would not "be incumbent upon them to preserve the position they have hitherto felt bound to preserve, that of refusing to consent to the construction of lines within the Province of Manitoba, connecting it with the American Railways to the South."[11] It is difficult to say whether this belief of the government was shared by the officials of the railway. As events developed, they, not unnaturally, tried to protect their monopoly position as long as possible, and only yielded it up under strong pressure from the government.

The completion of the transcontinental line in November, 1885, led to expectation in the West that obstruction to the chartering of branch lines to the border would cease, and agitation against the hated monopoly clause mounted. The railway countered with the threat to build no further branch lines in Manitoba. Meanwhile, in 1887 the pressure of the agitation led the Manitoba government to let contracts for the construction of the Red River Valley Line. At a great ceremony on July 2 Premier Norquay himself turned the first sod.

The Dominion government responded promptly to this gesture of defiance by disallowing both the Red River Valley Railway Act and an amendment to the Public Works Act which would have enabled the province to build railways as public works of the province. From this point the battle was joined, the provincial government attempting by a variety of expedients to continue the construction of the railway, the C.P.R. opposing it by obstructive tactics and court actions. The most powerful weapon in the hands of the opponents of the province was, however, financial. When the provincial government sought, in the financial centres of the United States and in the London money market, to raise capital to finance its railway building it found that everywhere the capital markets were closed against it.

The failure of the Norquay government—a Conservative administration—to complete the Red River Valley Line led to its downfall. The consequence of Macdonald's support of the C.P.R. was to drive his own party out of power in the province for twelve years. Growing economic difficulties had led to the capture of most provincial legislatures by Liberal administrations, and the Dominion government was becoming disposed, on this and other issues, to temporize.

---

successful resistance of Manitoba in the case of railway legislation caused the abandonment of disallowance as a means of carrying out the policies of the Dominion." This conclusion, it will be suggested below, is too sweeping.

[11]*Canada, House of Commons Debates*, 1884, Feb. 5, p. 109.

Meanwhile the C.P.R. was in serious financial difficulties. Additional funds were needed to keep it in operation until its traffic and revenues could be built up and in 1888 it advised the government that it would require a further $15,000,000 to save it from bankruptcy.[12] In the circumstances the company was prepared to sacrifice the protection of the monopoly clause in exchange for this financial aid from the government. On this basis the issue was finally settled. Macdonald, in a personal letter to Greenway, the Liberal Premier of Manitoba, promised the removal of obstacles to provincial railway construction. Disallowance, he explained, had been merely a temporary measure to cover the development of the traffic resources of the West. The large harvest of 1887 and the emerging prosperity of the region required an increase in rail facilities, and therefore "the administration will not advise the disallowance of a bill similar in principle to the Act for the Construction of the Red River Valley Railway."[13]

Thus ended the first attempt by a western province to modify a fundamental national policy in its own interest. The issue, which centred on the monopoly power of the Canadian Pacific and the use of the power of disallowance by the Dominion government, was basically economic. For the railway it was a struggle to maintain earnings at an adequate level by high rates made possible by the exclusion of competing lines. This in turn was dictated by the necessity of meeting the high overheads entailed by paying the carrying charges on capital borrowings. In addition, the maintenance of the monopoly was probably a necessary condition for raising additional capital.

For the farmers likewise, the problem was one of cost. Bulk staples sell in the world market on slender margins between cost and final selling price. Thus the farmer, unable to control the world market in which he sells, must exercise constant downward pressure on his costs. Where his costs are held rigid by government action it is only logical for him to exert political pressure in return. Politically the farmers were completely successful in breaking the monopoly of the C.P.R.[14]

[12]G. P. de T. Glazebrook, *A History of Transportation* (Toronto, 1938), p. 308.

[13]*Canada, House of Commons Journals, Sessional Paper*, 1888, no. 4, p. 15.

[14]They failed, however, to attain their economic objectives. The apparent conditions of competition achieved through linkage with American lines failed to reduce freight rates. The Canadian Pacific had reached an agreement with the Northern Pacific to share traffic and rates remained much as before. The western farmers thus learned early in their experience to have little faith in competition as a solution to their economic difficulties. Cf. Glazebrook, *A History of Transportation*, p. 309.

The struggle over Manitoba railway legislation gives by far the clearest illustration of the economic implications of the national policy of prosperity through the development of the West. Not again until the phase of contraction was reached in the struggle between Alberta and the Dominion in the nineteen-thirties were the lines so clearly drawn and the short-run interests of the creditor group so sharply at variance with the urgent needs of a debtor economy.

While the disallowance of railway charters is the clearest instance of the role of disallowance in policing the national economic policy, other disallowances in this period round out the definition of the area in which its use was considered appropriate. The famous Ontario Rivers and Streams Act of 1881, which was re-enacted three times in the teeth of disallowance, was overthrown on the ground that, in granting to all persons rights to use improvements for the purpose of floating down logs on the payment of a reasonable toll, it "seemed to take away the use of the owner's property and give it to another," and that it not only interfered with private right but sought to override a court decision as to what the law in the matter was.[15] A New Brunswick Act of 1888 gave to a new company rights which were inconsistent with those of an existing company incorporated under Dominion law. It was disallowed because it interfered with and restricted a Dominion Act and diminished the value of franchises already granted.[16] This is an example of Macdonald's rule that the power should be used to assert Dominion paramountcy in concurrent jurisdictions. Sir John Thompson, then Minister of Justice, read a stern lecture in commercial morality to the New Brunswick legislature in 1889 in connection with an Act which annulled certain mining leases. This Act, he observed, seemed "to be at variance with the principles of justice and to invade the rights of property, which it is so important to preserve for the credit of the whole country and for the safety of private persons. If it is desirable that a province should resume any part of its patrimony, the methods adopted should be those which recognize and provide for the rights which have accrued under the sanction of the Crown."[17] With one or two slight exceptions the disallowance power was used to protect a conception of contractual rights which was consonant with the federal government's role as broker for the rapid accumulation of capital.

It has been customary to connect the rise to power of the Laurier

[15]E. Hodgins, *Provincial Legislation* (Ottawa, 1896), pp. 177–8.
[16]*Ibid.*, p. 349.
[17]*Ibid.*, p. 750.

Liberals in 1896 with a fairly abrupt change in the Dominion policy with regard to disallowance. The late Professor Berriedale Keith was stating the accepted view among Canadian constitutional historians as well as his own considered opinion when he wrote many years ago: ". . . it is in the administration of Sir John Macdonald that we find the clearest examples of interference by the Dominion with Provincial Acts simply because they transgressed Dominion policy; with the advent of the ministry of Sir Wilfrid Laurier . . . the practice of disallowing Acts on other than legal or constitutional grounds, or on grounds of wide public and Imperial Policy, may be said to have come almost to a stop."[18] Professor Clokie, in a recent work, links the decline in disallowance directly to party policy: "A general diminution of interference began in 1896, when the Liberals, the chief supporters of provincial rights, came to power under Laurier."[19]

The clearest statement of policy with regard to disallowance during the Laurier régime is in a report which was made in 1908 by Sir Allen Aylesworth: "It is not intended by the British North America Act that the power of disallowance shall be exercised for the purpose of annulling provincial legislation, even though your excellency's ministers consider the legislation unjust or oppressive, or in conflict with recognized legal principles, so long as such legislation is within the power of the provincial legislature to enact it."[20] This statement is the basis for the belief that the Liberals abandoned disallowance out of respect for provincial rights. Actually, however, the significant modification of disallowance under the Liberal régime was on another point.

By the end of the nineteenth century there was a much wider acceptance of the implications of democracy than there had been in 1867. Sir John Macdonald was a product of an age in which it was still fashionable to distrust popular bodies, and the scheme of government erected by the British North America Act shows clearly the influence of a distrust of the popularly elected bodies in the United States. Sir John's cynical disregard of provincial legislatures, which is illustrated in his letter to Sir John Rose during the Manitoba railway dispute,[21] and in his use of the disallowance power, was now

[18]A. Berriedale Keith, *Responsible Government in the Dominions* (London, 1912), vol. II, p. 737.

[19]H. McD. Clokie, *Canadian Government and Politics* (Toronto, 1944), p. 209.

[20]Hodgins, *Provincial Legislation,* vol. II, pp. 80–3.

[21]"*Private* OTTAWA, 25th June, 1887.

"MY DEAR ROSE:

"I cabled to you yesterday that the Government of Manitoba was destroying

out of fashion. By the end of the nineteenth century liberal democracy had ceased to be a heresy and had in fact become respectable. The burden of many of the reports of ministers of justice in this period was that it was better for the people of a province to suffer under unjust legislation and to redress their grievances at the ballot box. In that way they were more likely to have good government. The disallowance power, if used to correct such abuses, was an interference with the popular will, which had much better be left to its own devices.

When the Conservatives came into power in 1911 they seem to have followed the same pattern, though they were careful to make it clear that they had not completely abandoned Macdonald's position. Regarding legislation which involved only local hardship, where the Liberals were evidently prepared to leave the remedy to the electorate, the Conservatives might be prepared to intervene. C. J. Doherty, when disallowing an Act in 1918, made it clear that he felt that disallowance was quite proper where hardship, inequality, injustice, or interference with vested rights or contracts were involved. Though such cases should be redressed by the local legislature, there are "principles governing the exercise of legislative power other than the mere respect and deference due to the expression of the will of the local constituent assembly, which must be considered in the exercise of the prerogative of disallowance."[22] However, the very sparing use of the power by the Conservatives made the distance between the two positions slight in actual practice.

The Liberals, on their part, were careful not to deny the possibility

---

the credit of the province . . . [here follows an account of how, if the province's credit is damaged, so is that of the Dominion].

"The present government of Manitoba are altogether careless of the prestige or prosperity of their province. The members of that Government are all impecunious, and think only of a continuation in office. When you reflect on a legislature of 35 members, with a population of some 110,000, coolly devoting a million of dollars to build a railway from Winnipeg to the frontier, between two lines owned by the C.P.R. running in the same direction, one on the east and the other on the west side of the Red River, when there is not business enough for one of the two existing lines, you can understand the recklessness of that body.

"All of this is of course confidential, but you will do good service both to Canada and Manitoba by discouraging on 'Change' the floating of this indebtedness. In all probability the Provincial Act authorizing the construction of the railway . . . for which the million dollar loan is wanted, will be disallowed." (Sir J. Pope, *Correspondence of Sir John A. Macdonald* (Toronto, 1921), pp. 403–4.)

[22]P.C. 1334 of May 30, 1918. See also *Wilson* v. *E. & N. Railway*, [1922] 1 A.C. 202.

that the disallowance power might have to be used against any piece of provincial legislation which threatened the basic assumptions of the national policy at any important point. Yet the power was not used to any extent. This is in sharp contrast to its almost general use throughout most of the Macdonald régime—up, in fact, until about 1888. Macdonald was not a man to use his powers lightly. The fond nickname "Old Tomorrow" symbolized his chronic unwillingness to cross bridges prematurely. He often found, as did the ablest of his successors, that he did not have to cross them at all if he waited long enough. Why then was he forced into action so often? The answer lies in the conditions of the time.

In the seventies and eighties the policy of development in the West had not yet begun to pay off, and a great deal more backing was needed before it would. The appallingly low level of operating revenues of the Canadian Pacific up to 1887 showed that the pump required quite a bit more priming before it would start to draw. And then the tide turned; the great gamble was coming off at last. The Liberals came into power at the beginning of the great wheat boom. Twenty-five years of comparative failure were rewarded by an era of spectacular success. While the Dominion assumed the leadership, there was little need to reassert the old superiority over the provinces. The protest and resentment of the preceding decade were silenced in common participation in the development of the West and in a common pride in national achievement.

Economic factors were all favourable to development. The selling prices of farm products were rising while costs were either falling or rising less rapidly; and there was an extraordinary decline in ocean freight rates. The combination of these circumstances opened the prairies to profitable exploitation. The only problem was to attract the men and the capital to man and equip this vast territory, and to this the Dominion addressed itself.

In 1896, with the termination of the railway land grant policy, Dominion land policy was based on the free homestead. With free land the flow of settlement was enormous and indiscriminate. It was the era when the agents of Clifford Sifton dragged the continent of Europe to find immigrants to fill the new territory. At the same time occurred the greatest population shift in Canadian history. People moved out of the Maritimes and the stagnant areas of rural Ontario to populate the prairies and to turn the towns of the St. Lawrence region into the first great urban areas in the Dominion.

The huge investment of capital required to maintain this extremely rapid pace of economic development was also readily available. British investment overseas increased greatly after the turn of the century and much of it found its way to Canada. Whereas borrowing conditions during the seventies had been stringent and interest rates high, lenders in the nineties were eager and rates were low. It is estimated that between $4,500 and $5,000 million were invested in capital goods during the years 1900–14. The result was widespread prosperity.

Inevitably this was a period of growing national consciousness and national unity. The federal government took the lead by creating opportunities rather than by imposing restrictions, for which, after all, there was no need. Regional incomes were high, provincial revenues buoyant, and provinces, local authorities, and Canadians generally were eager borrowers rather than reluctant debtors. There was no revival of the centralizing tendencies which had marked the leadership of the federal government in the past. The great development had been got under way and required less aggressive protection, while the need for national legislation in the field of business-cycle control or social welfare had not yet emerged.

Between 1867 and 1920 the Dominion power of disallowance had been used ninety-six times. While the rules of policy governing its employment could be comprehended in Macdonald's memorandum of 1869, the grounds could more clearly be stated as follows: (1) where provincial legislation ran counter to some broad imperial interest such as the treaty obligations of the British Empire as a whole; (2) where provincial legislation threatened the success of some major national policy or interest; (3) where provincial legislation was *ultra vires*, without necessarily raising either of the first two grounds; and (4) where provincial legislation was *intra vires* but was contrary to the principles of sound legislation.

Until it was rendered obsolete by the Statute of Westminster the first remained an important ground for disallowance. For example, between 1896 and 1913, out of a total of twenty-nine disallowances no less than nineteen were applied to British Columbia legislation which discriminated against orientals. While a good many of these statutes were *ultra vires* and all of them were manifestly unjust, the reason for disallowance in most cases was that they were in conflict with the Anglo-Japanese Treaty. But even by 1913 disallowance was unlikely on the mere ground that some imperial interest was involved, unless some specific treaty had been violated, and the growth of Canadian autonomy was soon to make it wholly obsolete.

The second ground was more contentious. It was widely believed in the twenties that it had also become obsolete by convention.[23] However the evidence adduced above establishes that all Dominion ministers of justice were careful to make it clear that the power still existed. That it had not been used was owing not so much to a difference in party doctrine about its use as to the fact that no occasion arose which brought it into play.

About the third ground there was more legitimate reason for doubt. The clashes of jurisdiction in the Canadian federal system came more and more to be settled by the process of judicial review instead of by disallowance. The process, though slower and more costly, is a superior technique in a federal system because it removes the dispute from the tangle of political pressures and the fears of political consequences which attend the exercise of executive power. Though the final decision on legislation may not be either more just or more wise it is better that such a decision be made by an impartial body created for that purpose and untainted by the suspicion of political motives. However, it was not until the Alberta cases that the exact status of this ground was clarified.

It was the fourth ground that suffered the most marked modification between 1867 and the inter-war period. By the end of the nineteenth century the general attitude towards the popular will had progressed from a distrust of popular feeling to a position which is summed up in Sir Henry Campbell-Bannerman's dictum that good government is no substitute for self-government. Consequently Dominion ministers of justice became increasingly reluctant to rectify local grievances by the use of disallowance. The Liberals seem to have held the view that such a step was in almost all circumstances unjustifiable, though they did not categorically deny the possibility that it might sometimes be taken. While the Conservative administration of Sir Robert Borden seems to have been more aware that dis-

[23]Cf. Maurice Ollivier: "Does the convention of the constitution in respect to disallowance and reservation of federal legislation affect the disallowance and reservation of provincial legislation? In other words, does the fact that federal legislation cannot be disallowed mean that provincial legislation cannot be disallowed either? The defenders of provincial rights argue that in their own field the legislatures are just as sovereign as the federal house, that section 90 refers to powers that have ceased to exist and that there is a constitutional convention which has arisen from the fact that for many years past the power has not been exercised. . . . although the power of disallowance has not been exercised for a few years, it still subsists and has never been renounced. This opinion has been confirmed by the Supreme Court." *Problems of Canadian Sovereignty* (Toronto, 1945), pp. 47–8.

allowance might be needed to protect interests which lacked the power to protect themselves within the provincial sphere, it was nevertheless extremely reluctant to intervene. Before 1924 the trend was to make this ground more and more unfashionable but there was no evidence to suggest that it was obsolete. It was a Liberal Minister of Justice who, in that year, made it clear that hardship and injustice might in themselves be sufficient grounds for disallowance.

The occasion was the Alberta Mineral Taxation Act, 1923, which was disallowed by Order-in-Council P.C. 702 of April 29, 1924. Among the petitioners for disallowance were the Canadian Pacific Railway, the Hudson's Bay Company, and certain land companies. The C.P.R. requested disallowance not only on the ground that the Act violated the statutory exemption of its western lands which the company enjoyed, but also because the Act interfered with "the rights of mortgagees, bondholders and others who have in good faith invested capital in the province and whose security is jeopardized." Similar reasons were advanced by the Hudson's Bay Company and in addition it was pointed out that the Act discriminated in favour of small owners and their heirs and interfered with the trade and business of the company. The land companies argued that it was unjust, and prejudicial to projects of settlement and the introduction of capital, and that mortgages were not protected, since their security could be taken over by the province without either notice or compensation. Evidence was also presented by officials of the Department of the Interior that the Act would conflict with the rights of the Dominion covering the legal remedy of distress on mining equipment and buildings.

The report of the Minister of Justice, Ernest Lapointe, dealt directly with the application of the fourth ground for disallowance:

> While the discretion thus belonging to Your Excellency in Council ought of course to be wisely exercised upon sound principles of public policy and having due regard to local powers of self-government, there are cases in which disallowance affords a constitutional remedy, and it is implicit that the exercise of the power ought not to be withheld when the public interest requires that it should become effective. . . . There are reasons which influenced the undersigned to submit his recommendation . . . which are not influenced by the mere grounds of injustice or hardship which are urged by the petitioners. . . . There are paramount considerations affecting the government of Canada and the general public interest which demand attention.

Some parts of the Act were, in the opinion of the Department, *ultra vires*. As for the rest, not only does the statute profess to bring about a condition of title which is contrary to express provisions of the Dominion grant, but it is also designed to operate so as to substitute public ownership of Dominion leaseholds for the private or individual ownership which is sanctioned by the Dominion. . . . These provisions . . . are . . . so embarrassing and essentially at variance with the policy of Your Excellency's Government as, apart from all other grounds, to justify and require the exercise of the power of disallowance.

While this Act was disallowed on a mixture of grounds two, three, and four, the report of the Minister makes it clear that even a Liberal administration would, given sufficient provocation, be prepared to upset provincial statutes on the grounds of hardship and injustice. The nature of the pressure for disallowance and the kind of circumstances which led to the statute in the first place are very similar to those which surrounded the Alberta legislation of the Social Credit period.

CHAPTER THREE

# The Distribution of Legislative Power

THE DOMINANT PURPOSES of Confederation emerge clearly in the assignment of legislative powers to the federal and provincial governments. The division of powers in sections 91 to 95 of the British North America Act gave the federal government control of the great apparatus of development—the massive capital equipment which formed the bones of the economy, from canals and railroads to lighthouses and harbours. With it went the two sovereign functions of government—defence and the currency. Thus the full armed power of the state was centralized (with the obvious lesson of the American Civil War in mind) and, what is more important in peacetime, the control of banking, credit, currency, and bankruptcy, in fact of the whole range of relationships essential to the formation of capital was given to the Dominion. The rigid exclusion of the provinces from this field and the use of the power of disallowance to protect the sanctity of contract in the years before 1890 show how important this step was. Its effect was to exclude the provinces from interfering with the direction, control, and operation of the economy.

It is worth remembering that this division was one of principle. The Fathers of Confederation thought that they were giving to the Dominion control over the entire field of economic development, leaving to the provinces only such functions as were exclusively of local concern. The need for precision in statutory draftsmanship meant that they had to state in particular terms what they thought the division of powers was, and inevitably their specific definition reflected the understanding of the business of government in a mid-nineteenth-century state which was largely agrarian, staple-producing, and non-urban on the eve of a period when the functions of government were beginning to grow rapidly and to assume a variety of novel forms. It was just as inevitable, therefore, in view of the method of statutory interpretation which the courts were to apply to the British North America Act, that those actual enumerated functions should survive the division in principle.

By the middle of the eighteen-eighties the particular terms of sections 91 and 92 were being subjected to judicial interpretation, and gradually there grew up beside the written letter of the constitution an increasing body of case law which not only amplified its meaning in applying it to particular situations, but developed a trend and an interpretation which were not immediately obvious from a reading of the Act itself. In general the effect was to confine the legislative powers of the Dominion rather strictly to the enumerated heads of section 91, and to confer on the provinces unexpectedly wide powers by a very broad interpretation of section 92, particularly as a result of the weight given to subsection 13 which assigned to the provinces jurisdiction over "property and civil rights in the province." As a result, the opening phrases of section 91—"It shall be lawful for the Queen, by and with the Advice and Consent of the Senate and House of Commons, to make Laws for the Peace, Order, and good Government of Canada, in relation to all matters not coming within the Classes of Subjects by this Act assigned exclusively to the Legislatures of the Provinces"—were deprived of almost any effect whatever, unless reinforced by particular heads of that section.

Litigation over the terms of sections 91 and 92 of the Act arose as an incident to the resort by private persons to the courts to assert their rights under ordinary statute and common law. Lord Dunedin, in discussing an early case on the constitution, pointed this out when he said: "The case of the *Citizens Insurance Company* v. *Parsons* was not fought directly between the Dominion and the Provinces either as parties or interveners. It was an action by a private individual to recover money under an insurance contract for a loss by fire."[1] It was from these bits and pieces of particular litigation that the larger mass of constitutional principle was erected.

The first important case marked an auspicious beginning for the Dominion. It arose out of a characteristic phenomenon of the times. Habits of intemperance had been characteristic of the hardy but socially inadequate life of the frontier since the days of the fur trade. The necessity of curbing antisocial exuberance and of imposing social sanctions more appropriate to the life of a settled community led to enactments prohibiting the sale of intoxicants even before Confederation. These Acts were normally of a local option type, that is, they imposed restrictions on the sale of beverages in areas which elected by plebiscite to adopt them. Such an enactment was the Canada Temperance Act. It prohibited, under pain of fine or imprisonment, the sale of intoxicants in areas which exercised its "local option" provisions.

[1] *In Re the Insurance Act of Canada*, [1932] A.C. 41.

The case arose out of the prosecution of a certain Russell who had, in defiance of the law, sold intoxicants within the city of Fredericton.[2] Russell had sought to evade the penalties imposed by pleading that the Canada Temperance Act was beyond the powers of the Parliament of Canada, since it dealt with the subject of property and civil rights which had been allotted exclusively to the provincial legislatures by the British North America Act. In this case the Judicial Committee of the Privy Council upheld the Supreme Court of New Brunswick in rejecting Russell's contention and sustaining the power of Parliament to pass the Act. In the course of his judgment Sir Montague Smith said:

Their Lordships cannot think that the Temperance Act in question properly belongs to the class of subjects, "Property and Civil Rights." It has in its legal aspect an obvious and close similarity to laws which place restrictions on the sale or custody of poisonous drugs, or of dangerously explosive substances. These things, as well as intoxicating liquors, can, of course, be held as property, but a law placing restrictions on their sale, custody, or removal, on the ground that the free sale or use of them is dangerous to public safety, and making it a criminal offence punishable by fine or imprisonment to violate these restrictions, cannot properly be deemed a law in relation to property in the sense in which those words are used in the 92nd section. What Parliament is dealing with in legislation of this kind is not a matter in relation to property and its rights, but one relating to public order and safety.[3]

The decision clearly implied that the general power of the Dominion over "peace, order and good government" was paramount over the heads of section 92, even in cases where the subject-matter, in its local aspects, lay within the purview of the provincial legislature. This case, however, was to stand almost alone for over sixty years. Though it is not strictly true to say that it was overruled by later decisions, the courts were from then on extremely reluctant to uphold any such claim to paramount legislative power. Later judges were frequently driven to somewhat extravagant hypotheses to explain away a decision which stuck out with stark inconsistency against the orderly rank of contrary precedents. Thus Lord Haldane observed:

Their Lordships think that the decision in *Russell* v. *the Queen* can only be supported today, not on the footing of having laid down an interpretation, such as has sometimes been invoked of the general words at the beginning of s. 91, but on the assumption of the Board, apparently made at the time of deciding the case of *Russell* v. *the Queen*, that the evil of intemperance at that time amounted in Canada to one so great and so

[2]*Russell* v. *the Queen*, (1882) 7 App. Cas. 830.
[3]*Ibid.*, pp. 838–9.

general that at least for the period it was a menace to the national life of Canada so serious and pressing that the National Parliament was called on to intervene to protect the nation from disaster. An epidemic of pestilence might conceivably have been regarded as analagous.[4]

For their Lordships soon repented of the version of the nature of Confederation implied in *Russell* v. *the Queen.* In *Hodge* v. *the Queen* they denied by implication that the provincial legislatures were no more than the glorified municipal institutions which Macdonald had intended. Within the ambit of section 92 "the local legislature is supreme and has the same authority as the Imperial Parliament or the Parliament of the Dominion, would have under like circumstances" to confer powers on bodies of its own creation.[5]

In 1892, in *Liquidators of the Maritime Bank* v. *Receiver-General of New Brunswick*, the status of the provinces was further clarified by a decision which held that the provincial executive possessed the prerogatives of the Crown, and thus the lieutenant-governor, though he might be a Dominion officer, was nevertheless "as much the representative of Her Majesty for all purposes of provincial government as the Governor-General himself is for all purposes of Dominion government."[6]

The most important case to be decided in these years, and one of the most important in Canadian constitutional history, was *Attorney-General of Ontario* v. *Attorney General of Canada*, generally known as the *Local Prohibition* case. This case, like those of Hodge and Russell, involved the validity of a scheme of regulation of the liquor traffic for Ontario similar in its operation to the Canada Temperance Act. In upholding the validity of this Act Lord Watson, who delivered the judgment of the Privy Council, made it clear that while Parliament could, under the enumerated heads of section 91, enact legislaion which affected subjects enumerated in section 92, it could not, relying merely on the general wording of "peace, order and good government," encroach upon any of the subjects listed in section 92.

To attach any other construction to the general power which, in supplement to its enumerated powers, is conferred upon the Parliament of Canada by s. 91, would, in their Lordships' opinion, not only be contrary to the intendment of the Act, but would practically destroy the autonomy of the provinces. If it were once conceded that the Parliament of Canada has authority to make laws applicable to the whole Dominion, in relation

[4]*Toronto Electric Commissioners* v. *Snider*, [1925] A.C. 396.

[5](1883) App. Cas. 132. Hodge, like Russell, was trying to evade the consequences of legislation designed to curb the sale of liquor.

[6](1892) App. Cas. 443.

to matters which in each province are substantially of local or private interest, upon the assumption that these matters also concern the peace, order and good government of the Dominion, there is hardly a subject enumerated in s. 92 upon which it might not legislate, to the exclusion of the provincial legislatures.[7]

Thus the decline in the leadership of the Dominion under the impact of the depression of the eighties, which many observers inferred from the relaxing of the use of disallowance, was intensified by an erosion of the legislative powers of Parliament by the courts and a concurrent aggrandizement of the provincial legislatures. This judicial interpreting away of the federal power continued steadily and reached its peak in a sharp curtailment of Dominion legislation which had attempted to deal with the complex economic and social problems created by World War I and by the depression of the thirties. At the end of the first seventy years after Confederation the courts had accomplished a major shift in the balance of power between the Dominion and the provinces.

The tendency of the courts to interpret away the paramount power of the Dominion has emerged as one of the most awkward facts in Canadian history. The achievement of a distinct Canadian nation was a triumphant avoidance of a dilemma, one horn of which was continued subservience to imperial control from London and the other the persistent threat of absorption into the United States. The judicial interpretation of the constitution created a third threat to national development, disintegration into a league of loosely affiliated states. It is not surprising, therefore, that the judicial interpretation of the British North America Act has received so much attention from Canadian scholars.

In general, the historians, the political scientists, and the lawyers have, with few exceptions, expressed the opinion that the courts took a mistaken view of the purposes and nature of Canadian federalism, and that they played a major part in altering fundamentally the federation which the Fathers of Confederation intended. In the process they deprived the Parliament and government of Canada of the powers necessary to discharge the responsibilities which an independent state in the twentieth century owes its citizens. There have been, however, wide differences of opinion as to how this came about.

The most satisfactory account of the effect of judicial interpretation on the constitution has been given by the Royal Commission on

[7][1896] A.C. 361–2.

Dominion-Provincial Relations.[8] In the view of the Commissioners, the impact of the courts on our federal constitution was not an isolated phenomenon but an integral part of Canadian history, a consequence of a complex of historical forces at work in Canadian life.

In all western countries there has been one major force at work since about the year 1867. Everywhere, under the impact of industrialization, governments have been driven more and more into collectivist measures to protect their people from a growing number of the vicissitudes of life. This tendency has seemed, to many contemporary observers, the most important phenomenon of their times. Thus A. V. Dicey, one of the greatest of modern English legal scholars, wrote in 1914: "What are the hopes which a reasonable man may cherish with regard to the progress of collectivism in England? Unless he be a person of astoundingly sanguine temperament it would be difficult for him not to perceive that the combination of socialistic and democratic legislation threatens the gravest danger to the country."[9] As Dicey perceived, the general attitude towards the functions of the state had changed profoundly between the middle and the end of the nineteenth century.[10]

Dicey's attitude towards the legislation of his day may be taken as typical of the legal profession. Because of their origins, identical with the commercial middle class, and their training, deeply imbued with the doctrines of *laissez-faire*, judges were gravely disturbed by the legislative trends of this period. The result was that judicial hostility to the implications of much of the legislation from about 1870 on was an important counter-current (which Dicey oddly enough does not

[8]Royal Commission on Dominion-Provincial Relations, *Report* (Ottawa, 1940), Book I.

[9]*Law and Opinion in England* (London, 1914), p. xc (Introduction to the second edition).

[10]"English statesmanship was at the middle of the Victorian era, in short, grounded on the *laissez-faire* of common sense. From this principle were drawn several obvious inferences which to enlightened English politicians seemed practically all but axiomatic. The State, it was thought, ought not as a matter of prudence to undertake any duties which were, or which could be performed by individuals free from state control. . . . Contrast now with the dominant legislative opinion of 1859 the dominant legislative opinion of 1900. . . . The current of opinion had for between thirty and forty years been gradually running with more and more force in the direction of collectivism, with the natural consequence that by 1900 the doctrine of *laissez-faire*, in spite of the large element of truth which it contains, had more or less lost its hold upon the English people." *Ibid.*, pp. xxix–xxxi. The kind of "collectivism" which so worried Dicey may be gathered from the following sentence which begins: "The laws affecting education, the Workmen's Compensation Act of 1897, the Agricultural Holdings Acts. . . ."

mention), slowing down the pace of change in the law which would otherwise have resulted from changes in the state of public opinion.

New legislation contained limitations on the use of property, limitations on the freedom of contract, limitations on the power of disposing of property, limitations on the rights of creditors, the revival of the idea of liability without fault, and generally a notion that the protection of the rights of the individual, far from being the main purpose of the law, might in many cases be contrary to the public interest.[11] Such enactments attacked both the rules and the assumptions on which the common law of the nineteenth century was based, and account for the lack of sympathy with the purpose of legislation which led many judges to interpret it in such a way as to give it as little effect as possible. As Dicey himself had observed, "If a statute . . . is apt to reproduce the public opinion not so much of today as of yesterday, judge-made law occasionally represents the opinion of the day before yesterday."[12]

The cause of the new legislation lay in a change in the economic structure of the community. The introduction of new economic techniques is likely to alter the location of economic and political power. Those groups who own or work with the new productive processes are able to use their strategic position to bend the policy of the state to suit their own needs.

Between 1867 and our own time Canada has undergone an economic revolution as profound as that which took place in England between 1776 and 1900. At Confederation Canada was a predominantly rural, staple-producing community. By the end of World War I her economy had already become more complex. Mechanical techniques and capitalist methods had invaded even agriculture, and the interests and rights which governments were prepared to support and defend differed considerably from those of 1867.

While the Canadian state was essentially Hamiltonian in conception, and the problems of overhead cost had forced a high degree

[11]Cf. Roscoe Pound, *The Spirit of the Common Law* (Boston, 1921), pp. 185 ff. And the following: "Lay bad-men interpretations are superficial. The fundamental difference between the law of the nineteenth century and the law of the period of legal development on which we have entered is not in the least due to the dominance of sinister interests over courts or lawyers or jurists. It is not due, the legal muckrakers notwithstanding, to bad men in judicial office or to intentional enemies to society in high places at the bar. It is a conflict of ideas, not of men; a clash between conceptions that have come down to us and entered into the very flesh and blood of our institutions and modern juristic conceptions born of a new movement in all the social sciences." *Ibid.*, p. 191.

[12]Dicey, *Law and Opinion in England*, p. 269.

of centralization and state initiative from the days of the fur trade, there was at the same time a clash between common and statute law, beween *laissez-faire* and collectivism, very similar to that which was occurring in Great Britain and the United States. The principles of law in Canada derive from the common law, and the Canadian lawyers and judges who applied them were often trained under its influence in England or the United States. The shift in the emphasis in production, from trade and agriculture to manufacturing, was a Canadian as well as an American and British development, which had as its consequence a shift in political power in which the farmer and the merchant had to give ground to the more collectivist aims of an urban proletariat. The statute books reveal that in Canada, as well as in Great Britain and the United States, legislatures were faced from about 1867 onwards with powerful demands to limit complete freedom of contract in order that the self-adjusting mechanism of the economy should not always operate at the apparent expense of the weak.[13]

These changes in the law weakened both the free market itself and those groups whose bargaining position was such that in the absence of economic regulation they could shift the burden of unfavourable market conditions on to less sheltered groups. Naturally, there was resistance to such changes. In a federal country, those resisting were able to cloak their economic motives in a concern for the public interest by raising doubts as to the powers of the legislature to enact laws to which they objected. This course was most effective where the legislature whose jurisdiction they were defending was the least favourable to economic regulation or the least able to make its regulation effective. It is quite clear that in a large number of the cases in this branch of Canadian constitutional law one of the litigants was trying to avoid either the inconvenience of obeying the rules propounded by the legislature or the penalty for having transgressed those rules. Even in cases where a statute had been referred to the courts for an opinion on its validity there is reason to believe that objection often existed more to its purpose than to its source.

In one of the earliest of such cases, a party to a contract of insurance attempted to avoid certain statutory conditions by pleading that the legislature in question lacked the power to enact them.[14] In another, the Brewers and Maltsters Association of Ontario was

[13]Some idea of the extent of this growth of legislation may be gained from Professor J. A. Corry's admirable study *The Growth of Government Activity since Confederation*, Royal Commission on Dominion-Provincial Relations, *Report*, Appendix (mimeo., Ottawa, 1940).

[14]*Citizens Insurance Co.* v. *Parsons*, (1881) 7 App. Cas. 96.

strongly moved by the wanton invasion of the powers of the Parliament of Canada by the legislature of Ontario, when the latter proceeded to licence the necessary but humble trade in which the appellants were engaged.[15] The Union Colliery appeared as the opponent of British Columbia legislation which restricted the freedom of employment of orientals.[16] The Grand Trunk Railway upheld the widest jurisdiction of provincial legislatures over property and civil rights when it was confronted with federal regulations designed to prevent railway companies from contracting out of their liability in damages.[17]

Thus, even before the turn of the century a steady litigious pressure against regulatory legislation had developed in Canada. Moreover, the opening of the West and the growing complexity of society in eastern Canada were creating new problems which increased the responsibilities of governments. The growth in the range of interest of Canadian governments was most marked on the provincial plane. But as their activities grew, the provinces found increasing difficulty in financing their operations.

The financial agreements at Confederation had left the provinces with small and inelastic revenues appropriate to their lowly place in Macdonald's scheme of national government. Two things happened to make the structure of provincial public finance unworkable. One was the impact of the bad years which threw great strains on local welfare services and forced the provinces into public works and other developmental activities. The eastern provinces were drawn into policies of agricultural development and immigration, and several provinces incurred heavy expenditures for railway development. Meanwhile judicial interpretation, by enlarging the stature of provincial legislatures, increased their responsibilities and their burdens of administration. These two factors combined to make the need for ampler and more elastic provincial revenues acute. Beginning with the Nova Scotian demand for better terms in 1868 all provinces tried to increase their share of the revenues of the Dominion. In addition all the provinces were driven by the need for more money into attempts to exploit new fields of taxation.

Here again the dialectic between the ideas of *laissez-faire* and collectivism emerges clearly. The nineteenth-century radicals had marched under the banner of peace, retrenchment, and reform. "Thus

[15] *Brewers and Maltsters Association* v. *Attorney-General of Ontario*, [1897] A.C. 391.
[16] *Union Colliery* v. *Bryden*, [1899] A.C. 880.
[17] *Grand Trunk Railway* v. *Attorney-General of Canada*, [1907] A.C. 65.

the burden of taxes," wrote Dicey, "is gradually forming an immense restriction upon individual freedom, for it must always be remembered that a tax, whatever its form, is always levied upon definite assignable persons with whose means of free action it interferes."[18] The prevalence of a judicial hostility to the tax-collector has produced a well-defined trend to give the taxpayer rather more than the benefit of the doubt in revenue cases, and has been the principal cause of the maddening complexity of taxation law.

In Canada there is no bill of rights to protect the citizen from the tax-collector. But the British North America Act has done almost as well.[19] Since the provinces had been given in the British North America Act a limited taxing power, a taxpayer might avoid liability by pleading lack of jurisdiction. At least there was a sporting chance of success. A significant number of cases even before 1914 turn upon such matters as the definition of a direct tax or the location of an estate for the purpose of levying succession duties. At the same time provincial legislatures were arming themselves with new powers of inspection and regulation over many kinds of business activity. The recipients of these legislative attentions did not rest passively, but fought each extension of provincial activity in the courts.

It becomes plain that the judicial interpretation of the constitution before 1914 was resulting in something much more complex than merely a whittling away of the powers of the Dominion. While the provinces were actively exploring new fields of legislative activity the Parliament of Canada was fully occupied with the task of carrying out the great national policy of expansion and development. Parliament in the Laurier era displayed little interest in novel legislative experiments in the realm of economic affairs. These it was content to leave to the provinces. The result was a somewhat looser federalism than that of Macdonald's day, but it was not inconsistent with fairly strong federal leadership. The national policy was going well and on it the energies of Canadians were concentrated and united. The provinces were given a wider sphere of initiative but they were not able, nor did they wish, to challenge any fundamental aspect of national policy.

It is evident that there was a growing demand for the new type of welfare and regulatory service. This was a minor legislative field and the Dominion does not seem to have displayed much interest

[18]Dicey, *Law and Opinion in England*, p. lxxxii.

[19]Cf. John Willis, "Administrative Law and the British North America Act," *Harvard Law Review* (Dec., 1939), p. 281.

in it. It was on the provinces and more particularly on the local authorities that these new demands fell. When they were met they encountered resistance in the courts, not from the Dominion government, but from interests adversely affected by them. The champions of Dominion power were mainly concerned in upholding a power which was not being exercised.

Already in some provinces there was a beginning of welfare legislation and the gas-and-water socialism which had developed in England. The first two decades of the twentieth century were to see in Ontario a model system of workmen's compensation and the heroic labours of Sir Adam Beck on behalf of the public development of hydro-electric power.[20] The western provinces, partly influenced by English immigrants, were taking kindly to municipal ownership and initiative. The continuous litigation over provincial legislative jurisdiction was symptomatic of growing pressure on the provinces to expand their functions.

More direct evidence is available from the statistics of provincial public finance. Even by 1896, though provincial expenditures in per capita terms had only risen to $2.20 from $1.69 in 1874, there had occurred an important change in the composition of provincial outlay. A substantial fall in the amount spent on transportation with the completion of local railway programmes was more than offset by increases in other items. Justice, legislation, and general government rose from $2,564,000 for all provinces in 1874 to $4,274,000 in 1896. Even more pronounced increases were recorded in public welfare, which rose from $657,000 to $1,472,000.[21] Most provinces showed a great increase in the net debt charges as a result of heavy developmental expenditure. Ontario, which was already supplied with a mature railway system and highly developed municipal institutions able to handle the cost of roads and local works, showed the greatest increase in welfare and educational expenditures. It was the added burden of the latter services which drove the province to resort to direct taxation. Thus the Succession Duty Act of 1892 recited in its preamble the need for welfare services as the justification for the new tax.[22]

The period from 1896 to 1913 reveals even more striking increases in provincial expenditure. In part they were a result of heavy ex-

[20]See A. Brady, "Democracy in the Overeas Dominions," in Chester Martin, ed., *Canada in Peace and War* (Toronto, 1941).

[21]Royal Commission on Dominion-Provincial Relations, *Report*, Book I, p. 63.

[22]*Statutes of Ontario*, 1892, c. 6.

penditures in the West, where municipal institutions in the new provinces were not able to assume very many of the burdens. This accounts in part for the great increase in the cost of general government–from $4,000,000 in 1896 to $15,000,000 in 1913. Part of it is also attributable to the higher cost of regulation in a more complex economy. The rise in education costs from $2,000,000 to $9,500,000 reflects both the much larger area served and some improvement in quality. While expenditures on public welfare tripled there was not so much an increase in the quantity of service as an improvement in the quality for a still very limited class of persons.[23]

The rise in expenditures and the search for new revenues indicate that the provinces had turned out to be much more important agencies of government than the confederation settlement had contemplated. This was partly a result of the slow growth of municipal institutions in some provinces and of developmental policies prompted by the faltering of the national projects in the seventies and eighties; but in the main it was the consequence of the emergence of new functions of government in the fields of welfare and public service, functions for which, at least in the conditions of the time, the provinces were clearly the appropriate agencies. While some of the aggrandizement of the provinces may be attributed to the tenor of judicial interpretation, much of the increase in the stature of the provinces was a *fait accompli*. As the evidence makes clear, the courts were not prepared to accept all of the claims which the provinces felt obliged to assert in order to meet these new needs.

As the developed part of the country increased in area the limited decentralization of the more primitive and much smaller Dominion of the seventies proved insufficient to provide the collective services that were required. The degree of centralization which had been possible under Sir John Macdonald was impossible in the face of the needs of government thirty years later. Techniques of centralized control through rapid communication and the elaborate organization of the administrative process had not developed to a point where effective centralized administration would have been possible over such a large area. Hence the emergence of the provinces as important agencies of government was not so much the result of the perversity of the courts as of administrative necessity. It was not Lord Watson who created the busy provincial governments of his day. He was confronted with them, and fitted them as best he could into the

[23]Royal Commission on Dominion-Provincial Relations, *Report*, Book I, pp. 82–6.

constitution which he and his fellow judges were called upon to interpret.

The contrast between the tight federal rein of the seventies and eighties and the looser partnership of the Laurier era is accounted for by two factors. One was the state of the great national projects and the relationship between Canada and the source of the vital fluid capital which was keeping the economy going; the other was that Laurier, unlike Macdonald, was blessed with a boom. Macdonald had to exercise all his skill and all his powers to reassure a jittery and somewhat reluctant capital market. By comparison things were much easier for the Dominion at the turn of the century. Money was cheap and easy to borrow and the attention of the Canadian public was diverted from internal conflicts by a pervasive boom. Even more than in Macdonald's day the leadership of the Dominion was unchallenged in the field of national economic policy.

The division of legislative power between the Dominion and the provinces was not shaped by the courts in a judicial vacuum. The forces at work upon it in the formative years were moulded by the general winds of doctrine in the legal system itself. In the nineteenth century the old order of *laissez-faire* was gradually yielding to collectivist pressure which was generated by the rise of popular democracy within all the western world.

For such a world the Canadian federal system had not been designed, but under the pressure of events both Parliament and the provinces took on new functions of government so that gradually the whole weight of the constitution was shifted. Against the rise of new government functions there developed a steady litigious pressure which sought to exploit the federal division of legislative power in the constitution as a means of minimizing the change which was taking place in the statute law.

Thus the courts, whose traditional function in English and Canadian law had been the narrow interpretation of statutes and the application of the rules of the common law affecting private right, came to be charged with the shaping of the constitution of a federal state. It is not surprising that they were on the whole unable to bring to this task the political experience, the statecraft, and the sense of history which the task required. From such responsibilities it has been the firm determination of English lawyers since the days of Coke and Bacon to retreat.

During these early years the main lines of the Canadian constitution were blocked out. Because the federal division of powers in the nineteen-thirties was so obviously frustrating and inappropriate, it is too easy to project one's irritation backwards in time. All the harsh words that were written about Lord Watson and the misdirected intentions of the Privy Council were written thirty or forty years after the *Local Prohibition* case. The truth of the matter is that the division of legislative power between the Dominion and the provinces pretty well reflected the inclinations of Canadians in the pre-1914 world. In those days welfare and social policy were not matters of major national concern, and there was no serious conflict of purpose between the Dominion and the provinces.

The world changed between 1914 and 1924 and in the inter-war years the posture of the Canadian constitution was both rigid and inappropriate. Those twenty years are unlikely to be affectionately remembered by many of the world's inhabitants. In the history of the Canadian constitution they are a sort of twenty years' crisis.

CHAPTER FOUR

# The Federal System between the Wars

THE FIRST WORLD WAR had a twofold effect on the Canadian economy. Temporarily it strengthened the economy by providing a steady market and high prices for the great western wheat crop, upon which the complex structure of tariffs and railways which made up the National Policy depended for its success. The health of the Canadian economy was directly linked to the wheat which was produced for the world market. As the annual wheat crop moved from the western farm to the loading ports in the East it served to justify an expensive system of transcontinental railroads, while the proceeds of its sale enabled the farmer in the West both to buy eastern manufacturers, which in turn became the westbound traffic on the railroads, and to pay for the financial services offered him by banks, grain traders, and mortgage companies. Almost the whole Canadian economy was vitally affected by, and organized around, the movement of the annual grain crop into world markets. But in the end the war destroyed the kind of world in which this trade policy could safely operate. The world economy with its international division of labour and its freely convertible currencies tied automatically to the gold standard had died—killed by the war. Periodic reports of its resurrection lacked substantiation.

Moreover, the old *laissez-faire* world of the nineteenth century was contracting its margins steadily before the advance of collectivist ideas and policies. In Canada the retreat from *laissez-faire* was hastened by a change in the nature of the economy and a substantial modification in economic ideas, both popular and—ultimately—academic. These two developments in conjunction brought on a crisis in Canadian national life in the period between the two great wars.

In the first twenty years of the present century the economy of Canada changed almost beyond recognition. Canada came to be a predominantly capitalist and industrialized society, where before it had been neither. Banking, commerce, finance, trade, and manufacturing—all were in greater or less degree composed of a handful of solitary giants, warily preserving the ritual of competition, but betraying a mysterious unison in many of their movements. If the scene had changed, so also had the characters altered. The construction of the railroads and the indiscriminate immigration had brought in waves of settlers often of alien language, alien race, and alien standard of living. They became, in the cities and towns and on the farms, a new proletariat, half-literate and unskilled. Many of the immigrants of those years brought with them little save their clothing and their native stock of ideas. Thus entered the stream of Canadian life the class-conscious agrarianism of the American plains, European social democracy, and the aggressive and individualistic socialist faith of the nascent British labour movement. What was to be the effect of these new attitudes on Canadian politics?

The national political parties which Macdonald and Laurier had led had been built around the acceptance of common policies for the general welfare. The conception of national policy for which they had stood was one of development of the country through accelerated capital formation. The challenge to the old parties in Canadian politics was based in large measure on a loss of faith in the validity of the assumptions upon which their policies had been based. The rise of the Progressives and other new parties in the West, and the growth in the strength of organized farmers and organized labour, stemmed from the belief that the old parties were themselves attached to a class interest which was prejudicial to the general welfare. The old national parties had tried to unite elements from both races and all regions around a particular interpretation of the national interest. The new movements raised doubts whether such a particular conception of a national interest was valid. These movements started from the assumption that group interests in the community were contradictory and that federal politics was the arena in which these antagonistic interests were engaged in a struggle for power. This belief was intensified by the rising prices of the war years, the inflation, and the ostentatious maldistribution of the national income which they created.

The rise of organized pressure groups was by no means confined to farmers and labour. Employers, manufacturers, and capitalists generally, organized to defend their interests against counter-pressures. It seemed that in these years every important group in the community was busily organizing for the protection of its members against the possibility of state action hostile to their interests. This activity was symptomatic of a retreat from the old free market and suggested the emerging outlines of a new kind of economy. The traditional role of the state in *laissez-faire* days had been to preserve the conditions of free bargaining, but by the twenties all groups were organizing on the assumption that the state was not a neutral external force. They had learned that the fruit of political power had been the ability to alter the conditions of sale so that monopolistic situations could be bolstered by political arrangements with sheltered groups.[1]

As the outlying bastions of the free market fell to one kind of organized pressure or another, statements of official policy came implicitly or explicity to reject many of the old assumptions. Thus a Canadian economist remarked plaintively, "Is it symptomatic of a return to some of the doctrines of scholastic theology that we find the idea of a price fixed by competition being replaced by the idea of a 'just price'?"[2] But by the nineteen-thirties such a complaint was singular. Already as a result of the works of Chamberlin, Mrs. Robinson, and others, monopoly was no longer an academic special case, and the emphasis in economic analysis had shifted from long-run equilibrium to the problems of imperfect competition. Meanwhile the Keynesians were opening up new avenues of public policy in the field of business cycle control.

Thus a change in the structure of economic theory—from whose assumptions policy is derived—accompanied by a drastic change both in economic behaviour and in the nature of the economy, had combined to cut the ground almost completely from under the Canadian federal system. This in essence was the crisis in Canadian federalism in the period between the two world wars. Canadians were forced to find new ends in common, and, having found them, to adapt the means—the political constitution—so that those ends could be served.

In the past unity and diversity had been reconciled through a

[1]"The U.F.O. victory was easily explained as a result of dissatisfaction with the Hearst government, a protest vote, the prohibition issue, and other purely local questions. Few realized that the rising tide of agrarian revolt was not confined to the prairie provinces, but swept wherever the new commercialized agriculture had developed. The gathering revolt in the West was too easily dismissed as the result of frontier or sectional grievances. The farmers' victory in Ontario revealed that Progressivism was far more than an expression of sectionalism, frontier ignorance, or the discontent raised by imported Populists or Socialists. The farmers themselves were hardly aware of the underlying causes for the widespread revolt. Even today analyses of the agrarian outbreak often ignore the new agriculture and the demands it made for economic controls by governments sympathetic to the farmers' new role in society. The farmers expressed their reactions to these fundamental changes in the striking phrase, 'go into politics, or go out of farming.'" Paul F. Sharp, *The Agrarian Revolt in Western Canada* (Minneapolis, 1948), p. 138.

[2]H. R. Kemp, reviewing the *Report of the Royal Commission on the Textile Industry* in the *Canadian Journal of Economics and Political Science*, V (1939), p. 77.

common policy of economic expansion. But the old National Policy, around which the political parties of Macdonald and Laurier had been able to rally strength from the whole country, had accomplished its mission and was no longer able to offer common benefits as the reward of unity. The sublimation of local and particular interests which had been achieved before and during the war became impossible. The two-party system, in its old form, seemed to have lost its appropriateness and appeared to be degenerating into a system of numerous parties based on class and region. Neither the Liberals nor the Conservatives could muster a national following. Both had been dislodged from the West by the Progressives. The stalemate in the party contest was partly broken by Mr. King's skilful exploitation of Lord Byng's action in 1926; this palpable red herring enabled Mr. King to emerge with a clear majority and to restore at least the appearance of the old party system.

But, apart from the constitutional issue which Mr. King had created, there was little in the form of positive domestic policy for which he and his party stood. The truth of the matter was that there was nothing for the federal government to do—or rather nothing that a majority of Canadians wanted it to do. As Professor Fowke has put it: "Since the federal government was so largely created as an agency for the colonization of the West it follows that the Dominion government would grow strong throughout the years during which it performed this function and would weaken once this was accomplished—unless in the meantime the central government should discover new and vital purposes."[3]

The country was divided on the issue of a common economic policy. The result was the lack of any strong party with a clear majority and a clear mandate to do anything—except perhaps to put Lord Byng in his place. The federal government was weak in this period because its powers were not pushed aggressively. The lack of clarity in working out a new policy was accompanied by a pronounced timidity in accepting new commitments because of the large public debt which the war had bequeathed to the Dominion.

This trend was reinforced by a shift in the centre of gravity within the structure of the political party. In the railway era the great public works had been fostered by the Dominion. It was to the leaders of the national party, therefore, that seekers after jobs and contracts had turned. The Minister of Railways, at the heart of government spending, and with the thousands of employees of the Intercolonial

[3]V. C. Fowke, *Canadian Agricultural Policy* (Toronto, 1947), p. 141.

Railway in his direct employ, had been the most powerful dispenser of patronage in the country, and an extremely influential member of the cabinet. As long as this was the case the party was subject to central leadership and direction. The leaders of the national party were in control of the war chest and the patronage. They could deal directly with local factions and local interest-groups and bargain directly for local support.

But even in the twenties, while the federal pork-barrel still existed and harbour-works, post-offices, and tariff concessions were politically important, a significant change in party organization was taking place. This was the beginning of the era of the horseless carriage, and the picayune patronage of the local road supervisor was soon to be superseded by the large-scale activities of provincial departments of public works engaged in letting contracts for widening, straightening, paving, and re-paving highways suitable for heavy through traffic. A new system of first-class transportation, under provincial jurisdiction, had emerged which rivalled the railroads. At the same time the provision of electric power became an economic activity of major importance, and it also fell under provincial jurisdiction and in many cases provincial operation. The provinces regulated public carriers on the highways through franchises and were able to license and control a variety of public utilities. Thus the provincial governments entered into direct and important relationships with a great variety of businesses to whom their policies now became a matter of paramount importance. Money contributions went to provincial party officials, and the dominant power in Canadian party organization passed into the hands of those who controlled the provincial party machines. Federal party organizations became pensioners of provincial organizations. This change in the internal structure of the party machine is one of the most important causes of the shift in the centre of power in the federal system away from the Dominion and towards ever increasing provincial autonomy.

This centrifugal tendency was strengthened by the fact that many important new industries, base-metal mining, pulp and paper, and the like, depended primarily on provincial government activities. Such provincial projects as electric power and highways were vital to them, while the mass of public activities of the Dominion, from the tariff to the transcontinental railways, were to them burdens rather than vital interests. They received little benefit from the national railway system. They sold directly into the American market, and therefore did not depend on the complex and roundabout system of foreign trade which in the past had been necessary to offset Canada's adverse trading balance with the United States. There is doubtless more than accidental significance in the increasing clamour for railway rationalization which coincided in time with the rising importance of these new industries.

Under all these influences the decentralization of the Canadian state continued apace. The initiative in public policy passed rapidly to the provinces. The new areas of economic activity lay within the spheres which could be developed under provincial initiative and the provinces took the lead in public works, developmental projects, economic regulation, and welfare in the years before 1930. This loose federalism might have persisted indefinitely if the great depression had not thrown into sharp focus the inadequacy of the provinces as agencies of collective action and forced the federal government and the Canadian people into a searching re-examination of national purpose.

The heavy borrowing and large expenditures associated with development and with provincial welfare services were bound seriously to affect the operation of any national fiscal or monetary policy. The abandonment of the gold standard by most countries in the nineteen-thirties and the general increases in public indebtedness greatly increased the effect of governmental fiscal and monetary policies on the course of the business cycle. At the same time it became widely realized that taxation and public borrowing could be employed as deliberate instruments of policy to influence the level of employment and income. Taxation and borrowing are not, however, instruments of policy which are capable of efficient use by provincial governments. In the first place developmental expenditure and monetary policy require careful integration to be effective. In the second place such operations are costly and the burden tends to be in inverse proportion to the level of national income. In bad times the need for public works to sustain employment and income is greatest while the visible returns from such undertakings are bound to be at their lowest.

Provincial revenues were not only inelastic but they tended to fluctuate in direct ratio to changes in the level of income of the community. Consequently, when the need was greatest provincial revenues were least buoyant and least able to bear the burden.

Not only were the provinces able to bear their burdens in inverse proportion to the need, but there were great differences in ability as between province and province. The concentration of both wealth and income in a few favoured areas meant a wide range in the productivity of provincial taxes and a great difference in provincial ability to assume responsibility for welfare and developmental services. In addition, all provinces had been borrowing heavily throughout the nineteen-twenties so that when the depression of the thirties came along further heavy expenditures were highly imprudent.[4]

The depression was a direct challenge to the conception of Canadian federalism which had developed up to 1930. It raised two problems which the existing division of functions between the provinces and the Dominion was quite incapable of solving. One was the emergency of depression. That emergency was met after a fashion by large transfers of income, engineered by the fiscal powers of the Dominion, and administered by the provinces. But such a solution left many possible avenues of government attack on the depression still closed and proved both costly and inefficient.

The second problem was that nothing had been devised to take the place of the old national policy which had served its purpose and come to an end. It was necessary to work out afresh the constitutional relationships of the Dominion and the provinces so that the central government would have scope to carry out the economic policies appropriate to it, without impairing the decentralization required to meet differing regional needs in economic and social policy. It seemed in the nineteen-thirties that the existing division of

[4]"The municipalities in the drought area which had lost the whole of their income could not maintain existing essential services, much less pay out large sums to meet the operating costs of the farms. Real estate values in many urban centres would have collapsed completely under the taxation and debts necessary to take care of the local concentration of unemployed. However, even if the relief burden had been uniformly distributed over all the municipalities of the country it would have been necessary to increase tax collections from real estate by 50 per cent. This was quite impossible.

"The relief costs could only be met with the wider revenues and credit resources of the senior governments. The resources of the provincial governments, however, were not by themselves sufficient. Over the whole period 1931–37 the relief expenditures amounted to more than 25 per cent of the total municipal-provincial revenues. In nearly every province during the early thirties these revenues fell short of the requirements for ordinary purposes. There were distressing deficits even before anything had been provided for relief. In not one province in any year following 1930 did the municipal-provincial revenues left over after provision for ordinary services meet the total cost of relief. The amount of borrowings necessary to pay for the whole of the remaining requirements would have bankrupted most of the provinces and municipalities in the country.

"The magnitude of relief costs hopelessly exceeded the financial capacities of the provinces and the municipalities. During the eight-year period their combined revenues fell short of total relief and current expenditures by over $750 million. The assistance of the Dominion with its powers of taxation and borrowing was essential." Royal Commission on Dominion-Provincial Relations, *Report*, Book I, pp. 162–3.

legislative power in the constitution between the Dominion and the provinces was an insuperable barrier to an efficient distribution of the responsibilities of government.

In the encircling gloom of the depression many Canadians hoped for a solution either by constitutional amendment or by forcing the courts to adopt a fresh approach to the problem of the constitution. But neither of these methods was likely to provide the answer. The experience of all federal systems is that it is extremely difficult to alter a constitution by amendment. It may be possible to achieve some changes in detail but any major change must overcome both general lethargy and the passionate resistance which comes from the holders of vested rights and interests.

The other solution is equally difficult. Hope in such a solution stems from the belief that constitutional deadlock can be resolved by some change in the structure of the courts or in their personnel. What is at fault, however, is not the decisions of the courts, for they may be overridden. The difficulty lies rather with the assumptions underlying the body of law and with the method of interpretation which judges have developed in the light of those assumptions. Under the pressure of events the assumptions may be modified, but the patience of the general public may be severely tried by the cautious and slow process by which judges adapt the law to meet new conditions.

Federal systems are characterized by complex amending procedures. They are prone, therefore, to constitutional change by judicial action rather than by formal amendment. This may mean such delay in necessary changes that federal constitutions seem periodically to be in grave danger of succumbing to their own inflexibility. Nevertheless, the slowness of federal constitutions to respond to environmental challenge has the great advantage that it permits public opinion to crystallize, so that the adaptation of the constitution by the courts comes as a triumphant conclusion to a time of confusion and lack of direction. The new constitutional equilibrium is achieved and new life is breathed into the old institutions without impairing the sanctity of their form. The courts, because their independent and neutral role is accepted in constitutional states, are uniquely fitted to perform this ritual.[5]

[5]"Dicey adds that the distribution of the different powers of government between the central body and the member states, which federalism necessitates, requires courts to possess authority to act as interpreters of the Constitution. *Federalism substitutes litigation for legislation.* Hence it can flourish only among communities imbued with the legal spirit and a reverence for law." (My italics.) Zechariah Chaffee, Jr., "International Utopias," American Academy of Arts and Science, *Proceedings*, LXXV (no. 1, Oct., 1942), 39–53.

The severe strains created by the period between the two wars caused a painful readjustment in the political structure of Canada which was reflected in the course which was taken by judicial interpretation of the constitution. The unsettlement of international events, the uncertainty involved in a fundamental shift in the social philosophies of the democracies, and the intractable economic problems bemused both governments and courts. The result, in all of the western democracies, was a dangerous rift between the will of the state and what the courts, as interpreters and guardians of the constitution, were willing to concede. Struggling in the midst of the competing claims of vested interests, the courts found grave difficulty in discovering in this babel the legitimate course of the public interest. The old legal saying is that hard cases make bad law. The cases which confronted the courts were indeed hard and the law in a good many instances was indubitably bad.

It was in this period that Canadian legislatures began to make the first serious inroads upon the free market. The primary cause of this trend was the war. When the war came to an end many of the problems of economic dislocation continued. As a consequence the controls over the allocation of supplies and over excessive prices which had been instituted during the war were by Act of Parliament conferred in 1919 on the ill-fated Board of Commerce. It was in connection with this board that the courts, perhaps for the first time, were confronted with the problem of fitting the positive state into the federal categories of the Canadian constitution.

The Supreme Court of Canada had been asked, in the form of a reference, to pass on the constitutional validity of the powers of the Board of Commerce. To the questions referred to it, the Supreme Court was unable to give an effective answer. Three judges concluded that Parliament possessed the power, while the three remaining judges were equally insistent that the wide powers of economic regulation conferred on the Board invaded a field of legislation reserved by the constitution to the provincial legislatures. It was a case which, in the last analysis, could only be settled in terms of economic theory.

Lord Haldane, who delivered the opinion of the Privy Council, evidently thought that the powers conferred on the Board were of an exceptional and extraordinary character—though it would now be difficult to share such a view—for he said in the course of his judgment:

> It may well be that the subjects of undue combination and hoarding are matters in which the Dominion has a great practical interest. *In special*

*circumstances, such as those of a great war*, such an interest might conceivably become of such paramount and over-riding importance as to amount to what lies outside the heads in s. 92, and is not covered by them.[6]

And again:

Legislation setting up a Board of Commerce with such powers appears to their Lordships to be beyond the powers conferred by s. 91. They find confirmation in this view in s. 41 of the Board of Commerce Act, which enables the Dominion Executive to review and alter the decisions of the Board. It has already been observed that circumstances are conceivable, such as those of war or famine, when the peace, order, and good government of the Dominion might be imperilled under conditions so exceptional that they require legislation of a character in reality beyond anything provided for by the heads of s. 92 or s. 91 itself.[7]

This is indeed a long way from *Russell* v. *the Queen*. What is the explanation of this decision and the trend of interpretation which it represents? Lord Haldane's reasoning, although elaborate, is not always easy to follow.[8] An important element in the arguments appears to be the repeated view that the Act in question represented something altogether abnormal, and outside the range and scope of the functions of government as properly conceived. There are two aspects of the judgment which support this explanation.

The first arises from the nature of the agency itself, as is evident from the above quotation. The board, which is an agency enjoying rather wide discretionary powers and considerable independence of Parliament, is a very common device in Canada, particularly for dealing with problems of administration where the matter is technical in character, or where political pressure in the execution of policy is unlikely to serve any useful purpose. The independent administrative agency has been unpopular in England because it has tended to

[6]*In re Board of Commerce*, [1922] A.C. 198. My italics. [7]*Ibid.*, p. 199.

[8]"It was said of Gladstone that when it suited his purpose no one could wander more widely from his subject. It may be said of Mr. Haldane that no one can invest a subject in a more lucid fog. A lucid fog, I know, seems like a contradiction in terms; but no one who has heard Mr. Haldane speak for, say, three hours will deny that there is such a thing. The lucidity of his mind is as conclusive as the fog in yours. The clearer he becomes to himself, the more hopeless is your bewilderment. If only one could feel that he himself was getting a little lost in this amazing labyrinth of locution, one would feel less humiliated. But it is obvious that the less you understand him the more he understands himself. He smiles urbanely upon you, and points the fat didactic finger at you with pleasant intimacy. He does you the honour of pretending that you follow him, and self-respect compels you to accept the delicate tribute to your penetration. It is a comedy which saves him a lot of trouble." A. G. Gardiner, *Prophets, Priests, and Kings* (London, 1914), p. 283.

usurp functions of both Parliament and the judiciary. At no time was it in greater disrepute in legal circles than in the period which followed the dismantling of much of the war-created machinery of government in the early twenties. The fact that the decisions of the Board of Commerce were subject to review and alteration by the executive, rather than by Parliament, created in the English mind the illusion of concentrated state power of an emergency character. Thus the independent board, controlled only by the executive, appeared in the light of contemporary anxiety to transcend the words of sections 91 and 92 altogether.

The second explanation of Lord Haldane's judgment reinforces the first. Throughout the judgment there is the clear assumption that the eradication of hoarding and undue combination was scarcely an activity which should commend itself to the sense of propriety of a national parliament. Such matters, indeed, might be causes of local annoyance, and perhaps occasionally might be dealt with by local governments, but to pretend in ordinary times that hoarding and market-rigging were the proper subject for the attention of a national government suggested that they must be a cloak for some unwarranted extension of the proper sphere of the state.

Lord Haldane's decision in the *Snider Case* is of the same order.[9] There he took the almost incredible step of finding that a statute, which had been in force for nineteen years without serious question, was *ultra vires* the Parliament of Canada. In fact, his judgments follow a consistent pattern of nineteenth-century liberalism. This is, admittedly, not easy to explain since his philosophical outlook was scarcely Benthamite and his political sympathies were openly with the British Labour party. But the judgments, with their painstaking inability to be sympathetic to the intention of the legislature and their disastrous effect on novel functions and novel methods of government, remain.

The process of litigious attrition against section 91 of the British North America Act appeared to be arrested in two well-known cases which arose in the early thirties. In the first case the Supreme Court was sufficiently intimidated by the extremely narrow interpretation of section 91, which Lord Haldane had enunciated, to hold that jurisdiction over the subject of aeronautics was beyond the powers of the Parliament of Canada. The decision was reversed in a famous judgment of Lord Sankey's which seemed at the time to give a more liberal interpretation of section 91. His decision was reinforced by another

[9]*Toronto Electric Commissioners* v. *Snider*, [1925] A.C. 396.

in the same year which gave to the Dominion jurisdiction over radio communcation.[10]

When Mr. Mackenzie King returned to office in 1935 he referred a number of statutes which had been passed in the dying months of the Bennett régime to the Supreme Court for an advisory opinion on their validity. Under such circumstances it is unlikely that the Court would be led to believe that the government was strongly attached to the legislation. In any event, whether the hint was intended or taken, the Supreme Court was able to find only two of the enactments, and a part of a third, valid. In this opinion it was largely sustained by the Privy Council.

Some evidence of the attitude of Mr. King's government to the Bennett "New Deal" may be gained from the line of criticism adopted by the Liberals when they were in opposition. Apart from criticisms in detail there seem to have been two main arguments advanced from the Liberal side of the House. These emerged clearly in the debates on the Natural Products Marketing Bill. One point on which great stress was laid was that wide and arbitrary powers were to be given to a body which was independent of Parliament.[11] In the course of the debate Mr. King quoted several passages from Lord Hewart's *New Despotism* warning of the dangers of delegated legislation and of the usurping of legislative and judicial powers by administrative agencies.[12]

The second line of argument was that the bill went beyond the powers of Parliament and invaded the sphere of legislation reserved to the provinces.[13] Not much was made of the argument but, since

[10]*In re Aeronautics*, [1932] A.C. 54; *In re Regulation and Control of Radio Communication*, [1932] A.C. 304. It was in the latter case that Lord Dunedin remarked drily, "Although the question had obviously to be decided on the terms of the statute, it is a matter of congratulation that the result arrived at seems consonant with common sense."

[11]"This measure imposes upon a competitive capitalistic economy such as we have in this country a bureaucratic interference from above through a series of marketing boards." Mr. J. L. Ilsley, *Canada, House of Commons Debates*, 1934, vol. II, p. 2211. "As one reads the provisions of the bill he discovers that its primary purpose is that of limiting production, restricting trade and creating monopolies in the production and sale of natural products. . . . I submit, Mr. Speaker, that legislation of this kind violates the fundamental principles of British liberty, violates our constitutional system of government, violates every tradition on which our parliamentary system rests." Mr. Mackenzie King, *ibid.*, vol. III, p. 2343.

[12]*Ibid.*

[13]"I believe that when this measure is properly studied it will be found that some of its provisions are also contrary to the provisions of the British North America Act." Mr. Mackenzie King, *ibid.*, vol. III, p. 2349. "But I do believe it

Mr. King himself used it, it may be taken as a hint of his attitude after he achieved office. In this debate the Liberals employed the whole range of outraged constitutionalism which has come to be the stock argument of those whose quarrel with modern administrative techniques is at bottom concerned more with the ends to be served than with the means of achieving them. The visions of Star Chamber which danced in their heads may have been inspired by the purest of motives but in the debate they were clearly more disturbed over what the government proposed to do than over the method which it had adopted of doing it.

The result of the destruction by the courts of these statutes was practically to paralyse the Dominion as an agency for regulating economic activity. Specifically it had not the power to legislate regarding hours and conditions of labour (except in certain narrowly defined national undertakings such as railroads) even if such legislation was necessary to ratify obligations which had been entered into by the government; it lacked the power to set up a scheme of social insurance; it could not provide for the marketing of natural products; in short, the Dominion had practically no jurisdiction over labour, prices, production, and marketing except in wartime. All that survived the slaughter were an amendment of the Criminal Code in connection with combines and an extension of a form of bankruptcy procedure to farmers under the Farmers' Creditors Arrangement Act.[14]

The courts had reasoned themselves into a blind alley. As a result of the narrow construction which had been placed on section 91 they had lost sight completely of the conception which had been advanced by Lord Fitzgerald in *Hodge* v. *the Queen* when he said: "The principle which [*Russell* v. *the Queen*] and the case of *The Citizens Insurance Company* illustrate is, that subjects which in one aspect

will be found that when it comes to be interpreted this measure will meet with much the same reception by the Courts as did the Combines and Fair Prices Act and the Board of Commerce Act of 1919." Mr. King, *ibid.*, p. 2350.

[14]The legislative competence of the Dominion was upheld in *Attorney-General of British Columbia* v. *Attorney-General of Canada* (s. 498a of the Criminal Code), [1937] A.C. 368, and *Attorney-General of British Columbia* v. *Attorney-General of Canada* (Farmers' Creditors Arrangement Act), *ibid.*, 391. The Dominion power was repelled in *Attorney-General of Canada* v. *Attorney-General of Ontario, ibid.*, 326, *Attorney-General of Canada* v. *Attorney-General of Ontario, ibid.*, 355, *Attorney-General of British Columbia* v. *Attorney-General of Canada, ibid.*, 377. In *Attorney-General of Ontario* v. *Attorney-General of Canada, ibid.*, 405, the powers granted to a Dominion Trade and Industry Commission were upheld in part.

and for one purpose fall within sec. 92, may in another aspect and for another purpose fall within sec. 91."[15] The courts had by this time made it next to impossible for any category of legislation which had been interpreted as falling within section 92 to assume such proportions that legislation covering it could validly be passed by the Parliament of Canada. It did not seem to matter whether the Dominion was trying to do something which was not administratively feasible at the provincial level, as the following quotation from Lord Atkin makes clear:

> The Board was given to understand that some of the Provinces attach much importance to the existence of marketing schemes such as might be set up under this legislation: and their attention was called to the existence of Provincial legislation setting up Provincial marketing schemes for various Provincial products. It was said that as the Provinces and the Dominion between them possess a totality of complete legislative authority, each within its own sphere could in co-operation with the other achieve the complete power of regulation which is desired. Their Lordships appreciate the importance of the desired aim. Unless and until a change is made in the respective legislative functions of Dominion and Province it may well be that satisfactory results for both can only be obtained by co-operation. But the legislation will have to be carefully framed, and will not be achieved by either party leaving its own sphere and encroaching upon that of the other.[16]

The result of these decisions was extremely serious from the point of view of national policy. While it was theoretically true that the provinces could enact legislation to deal with new matters which lay outside the legislative sphere of the Dominion, many of the measures which were required were of a type which could only be effective on a national scale. An obvious example is unemployment insurance. Some provinces have a large concentration of unsheltered industries, such as lumbering and shipbuilding, which are highly susceptible to industrial fluctuations. For such provinces to maintain a scheme of unemployment insurance which is actuarily sound would impose an impossible burden of contributions on the industries covered in those regions. The difficulty is partly that new measures of social policy lie beyond the financial resources of most provinces, but partly it is that the problems to be dealt with spill untidily over provincial boundaries and can be dealt with effectively only by the Parliament of Canada.

The barrier imposed by the constitution against federal action sometimes seemed to apply also to the provinces. A British Columbia

[15](1883) 9 App. Cas. 130.

[16]*Attorney-General of British Columbia* v. *Attorney-General of Canada*, [1937] A.C. 377.

marketing scheme was held by the Supreme Court to be *ultra vires* on the ground that it interfered with interprovincial trade.[17] The trouble is that often it is difficult to ascertain the destination of a particular natural product, say a potato, at the point of grading; at that point an interprovincial potato in quite indistinguishable from one destined to be consumed within the province. These and similar difficulties created by judicial criteria are nearly insuperable. The result is that the whole purpose of regulation is defeated because no system of regulation is possible which will observe the abstract criteria imposed by the constitution. Professor F. R. Scott sums up the situation in this way:

> The Natural Products Marketing Act was declared *ultra vires* by the unanimous judgment of the Supreme Court and by the Privy Council. Both courts admitted that the Dominion had jurisdiction over international and interprovincial trade, but this legislation was considered to interfere in a "sweeping fashion" with individual trades within provinces. Such interference with local trade, instead of being looked at as ancillary to the whole Dominion scheme, was considered sufficient to destroy the entire Act. Thus we have now in Canada two examples of marketing legislation; the first a provincial Act in British Columbia which the Supreme Court threw out because it interfered with interprovincial trade, and this Act which was thrown out because it interfered with local trade. The courts, in other words, have created a no man's land in the constitution and are able to invalidate any marketing legislation they do not like.[18]

A large part of the shaping of the powers of the Dominion and the provinces has been the result of conflicts of economic as well as of constitutional doctrine. In this conflict the sympathies of the courts have been, in terms of economic doctrine, on the side of the conservatives.[19] The emergence of legislation of a collectivist type,

[17]*Lawson* v. *the Interior Fruit and Vegetable Committee*, [1931] S.C.R. 357.

[18]F. R. Scott, "The Privy Council and Mr. Bennett's 'New Deal' Legislation," *Canadian Journal of Economics and Political Science*, III (1937), p. 240.

[19]Cf. J. M. Keynes: "The ideas of economists and political philosophers, both when they are right and when they are wrong, are more powerful than is generally understood. Indeed the world is ruled by little else. Practical men, who believe themselves to be quite exempt from any intellectual influences, are usually the slaves of some defunct economist. Madmen in authority, who hear voices in the air, are distilling their frenzy from some academic scribbler of a few years back. I am sure that the power of vested interests is vastly exaggerated compared with the gradual encroachment of ideas. Not, indeed, immediately, but after a certain interval; for in the field of economic and political philosophy there are not many who are influenced by new theories after they are twenty-five or thirty years of age, so that the ideas which civil servants and politicians and even agitators apply to current events are not likely to be the newest. But, soon or late, it is ideas, not vested interests, which are dangerous for good or evil.'" *The General Theory of Employment, Interest and Money* (London, 1936), pp. 383–4.

whether enacted by the Dominion or by the provinces, has been retarded by the almost unconscious desire of the courts to discover some way of exorcising this undesirable phenomenon.

The plea of *ultra vires* has become the automatic litigious response to attempts by governments to regulate economic life, just as the due process clause was employed for a similar purpose in the United States. The success of *ultra vires* as a device for evading undesired regulation has been astonishing. In something like one-half of the leading cases of this sort, attempts by the Dominion and the provinces to regulate economic activity have been frustrated. On balance provincial legislation seems to have come off worse, for the courts were by no means prepared to accept as valid all of the activities which aroused the interest of provincial legislatures. To the extent that the Dominion was relatively timid in pushing its powers after 1920 those powers remained undefined.

This is not to say that the Dominion did not suffer a loss of power as a result. There was a real loss over matters which were of common national concern and where no legitimate local interest existed. This loss of power was partly to the provinces and partly to a no man's land where neither the Dominion nor the provinces could exercise effective jurisdiction. But the cause was not so much a desire on the part of the courts to build up the provinces at the expense of the Dominion, as it was a dislike of the kind of programme which was beginning to be enacted by Parliament. It was easy to rationalize this dislike by developing a conscientious passion for literal meanings in sections 91 and 92 of the British North America Act.

The same trend is unmistakable in the taxation cases. Over the whole period from Confederation to 1939 there were thirty-one leading cases of major importance involving the taxing power. Twenty-eight concerned the right of a province to levy various taxes in various situations. In fourteen of them this right was upheld, in thirteen the provincial legislation was found to be *ultra vires*, and in one a restricted interpretation was applied to a succession duty imposed by the province of Quebec.[20] Of the three other cases included in the list, all were attempts to evade taxation by the Dominion—a difficult feat in the light of the wording of section 91, subsection 3, which empowers the Dominion to raise money by "any mode or means of taxation." In the first of these three, *Attorney-General of British Columbia* v. *Attorney-General of Canada*,[21] it was unsuccessfully contended that the Dominion could not levy customs duties on liquor imported

[20] *Lambe* v. *Manual*, [1903] A.C. 68.
[21] [1924] A.C. 223.

by a department of a provincial government. In the second, in the same year, it was established that a provincial minister of the Crown was liable for income tax,[22] and in the third that the profits of illicit trade in liquor were taxable income.[23]

Increasingly, constitutional case-law had become a reflection of conflict over the major issues of economic and social policy. If they are looked at in this way, one-half of the important leading cases in Canadian constitutional law involved an attempt by the state to interfere with the free disposal by individuals of their property.[24] The results of this constant litigious pressure against limitation of the freedom of action of the individual are imposing. In one-half of the cases the plea of *ultra vires* was successful in defeating the intention of the legislature. It is impossible to avoid the conclusion that the resulting spheres of authority of the Dominion and the provinces are the incidental outcome of a clash between individualism and collectivism.

Thus, only on the surface has this struggle been a conflict between two conceptions of federalism. Basically it has been a dialectic of two sets of ideas. These ideas in turn, as we have seen, have been set in conflict by two forces. One force has been the current of world opinion over the last half century. The other has been the change in the nature of the Canadian economy. The assumptions of *laissez-faire* and individual self-help fitted the facts of frontier life. With greater diversification, a growth of scale in enterprise, an increase in urbanization, and an increase in economic interdependence which was accompanied by a growth of group consciousness, collective wants became more important and individual freedom of action so limited as to destroy the validity of the old individualistic assumptions.

The extension of the franchise, the granting of provincial stature to the prairies, and the opening up of new areas and new kinds of economic activity gave a measure of political power to groups which did not benefit directly from the old national policy. The clash in interest and in ideas took place through the party system in elections and in the legislatures, and resulted in legislation which was a concession to the newly emerged interests. The struggle was continued in the courts

[22] *Caron* v. *the King*, [1924] A.C. 999.

[23] *Minister of Finance* v. *Smith*, [1927] A.C. 194.

[24] One hundred and forty-four cases were considered, that is to say, all of those reported in E. R. Cameron, *The Canadian Constitution and the Judicial Committee*, vol. I (Winnipeg, 1915), vol. II (Toronto, 1930); C. P. Claxton, *Canadian Constitutional Decisions of the Judicial Committee of the Privy Council 1930–1939* (Ottawa, 1939). The number of cases involving, as of major concern to at least one of the parties, the issue of economic regulation or the taxing power was seventy-three out of one hundred and forty-four.

where the interests which felt themselves inconvienced by these restrictions on their freedom of action were able to enlist the aid of a judicial theory of interpretation and legislative propriety which found ways of nullifying the effect of undesirable legislation.

The paralysing effects of judicial interpretation on the Canadian constitution in the years between the wars was a reflection of the collective indecision of the Canadian people. For much as an increase in the activity of the state was demanded by a large section of the population, this same increase was bitterly contested by other groups who stood to gain more by the old equilibrium than by the new. Thus every halting step in the direction of satisfying collective wants was transformed into a debate on constitutional first principles. The courts were dragged in because of this uncertainty and, whether composed of Canadian judges or the learned lords of the Privy Council, were torn by the same uncertainties. Their method of reasoning and the whole spirit of the common law itself contributed to the resulting stalemate, but the courts were not more confused than the people for whose constitution they acted as custodians.

The judges could not separate themselves completely from their own personalities. As men they were parts of two great communities engaged in the anxious re-examination of the principles for which they were organized. While thesis and antithesis appeared before them stubbornly irreconcilable, the very principles of the law of which they were the guardians were shifting into a new balance.

Behind the array of legal conflict sectional interests awaited the persuasion of events to re-discover the common ground on which they stood. Three factors were already discernible which produced the overwhelming common interest which would re-create national policy in concrete terms. The depression itself imposed the discipline of common co-operative measures to avoid not only the bankruptcy of governments, but the bankruptcy of an idea. And already in the same period other countries caught in the same conflict were being driven into irrevocable choices which were to bring them again into war. The common excitement and the common peril of war were bound to catalyse internal conflicts of interest. At the same time wartime needs necessarily increased the degree of collective activity and of centralization, and some at least of the sectional eggs were certain to be scrambled. Lastly, there might come a new synthesis of legal principles, so that judges might approach the new needs of the state with a philosophy of law which had accommodated itself to the new ends which the state sought to serve.

CHAPTER FIVE

# The Attempt to Establish Social Credit

THE SOCIAL CREDIT MOVEMENT arose, as every political movement in the West before it had arisen, at a time when the long-run advantages of the national economy were more than offset by its costs. Like the Manitoba movement in the eighteen-eighties, the Alberta movement was essentially an attempt to use political power to redress the balance of forces in the market. In a federal state the natural way to make that attempt was through the capture of a provincial government and the formulation of a provincial policy opposed both to the national economic interest and to the national government. The formation of a Social Credit government under the premiership of William Aberhart in 1935 symbolized a rejection of the National Policy and of the subordinate role which the West played in that policy.

The origins of the Social Credit party and the channelling of western revolt through the Progressive movement have been told elsewhere.[1] "The rise of the Social Credit movement and of the Co-operative Commonwealth Federation," writes Professor W. L. Morton, "marked the beginning of a new phase of Canadian political development, a phase of class rather than sectional politics, of urban rather than rural dominance."[2] While it is true that the Dominion-provincial struggle over Alberta after 1935 was part of a new phase in Canadian politics the change was at first more of degree than of kind. The near disintegration of the Canadian federation under the impact of the depression, coupled with the failure of the Social Credit forces to make any substantial gains elsewhere, led to an attempt to attain the objectives of the movement by exploiting the power and position of the provincial legislature rather than by modifying national policy through securing legislative change in Ottawa.

Since Confederation the Canadian government had embarked on policies designed to increase the flow of investment and to influence

[1]In W. L. Morton, *The Progressive Party in Canada*, (Toronto, 1950), and in the forthcoming study, also in this series, by J. A. Irving.

[2]*The Progressive Party in Canada*, p. 287.

the actions of the money markets of the world to the advantage of the Canadian economy. Indeed, Confederation itself, as well as the achievement of responsible government, were all part of the interaction of the Canadian economy and the money market. "The demand for new staples adapted to the industrial needs of Great Britain under free trade," wrote Professor Innis, "compelled the development of responsible government in the staple-producing regions to create devices for borrowing capital for the construction of canals and railways."[3] As far as the external capital market was concerned, the Dominion was driven from the beginning to the use of its power and influence to police Canadian borrowers in order to preserve the goodwill of the financial interests which controlled the flow of funds. Thus we find Sir John A. Macdonald intervening through the London banker Sir John Rose in order to prevent the government of Manitoba from raising funds to build a railway which seemed to threaten the security of the capital invested in the Canadian Pacific. In 1888 the threat of disallowance was used to prevent the province of Quebec from converting part of its public debt at a lower rate of interest. In the early years of the National Policy disallowance was repeatedly used to protect the interests of creditors against hostile action by provincial legislatures. Back of this action lay the necessity of preserving among investors a feeling of security which was a prior condition not only to low interest rates but also to a ready flow of investment funds.

The prairie provinces were the focus of the National Policy and the area most affected by it. The National Policy had brought them into being as part of Canada and to it they owed their existence. Yet each of the three great props of national expansion had been resisted bitterly in the West. Manitoba had fought for a decade against the all-Canadian rail route, while the tariff and the more elusive issues of monetary policy have been persistent factors in the politics of the Canadian West.

The reason for this resistance lay in the nature of the western economy. The wheat economy was a prime example of the international division of labour. But this unsheltered over-specialization was highly dangerous, for, "with the decline, and in some cases complete breakdown, of the international trading system which made such specialization possible, the Prairies threatened to become an equally classic example of an area doomed to chronic depression."[4]

[3]Introduction to K. E. Knorr, *British Colonial Theories* (Toronto, 1944), p. xii.
[4]Royal Commission on Dominion-Provincial Relations, *Report*, Book I, p. 197.

The almost complete specialization in a single commodity, combined with the high fixed costs which had resulted from accelerated development, made the West highly vulnerable to downward changes in the world price of wheat. Whenever this happened, the Dominion, committed to protect the interests which had served the National Policy, found itself confronted with strong pressure from the West to modify its traditional attitude.

In this respect the western provinces were in an exceptionally weak bargaining position. The things that concerned them most—immigration, agricultural policy, and transportation—were either fields exclusively federal under the constitution or concurrent fields in which the Dominion possessed a dominant initiative. Inevitably there emerged a struggle between the federal government and the provinces.

In the past this struggle had meant the gradual capture of a series of provincial governments by parties opposed to important aspects of national policy. Thus Canadian federalism produced at times an odd modification of parliamentary government in which the main focus and strength of the opposition to the government of the day was not in the parliamentary opposition but in the provincial governments. In 1896 Laurier had been able to pull the scattered groups of provincial Liberals together into a strong majority government at Ottawa. The fact that he was able at the same time to carry on the National Policy of his predecessor was due to the buoyant conditions of the time. After the end of the First World War it became more difficult to emulate Laurier. The end of the boom phase of national development fostered regional discontent and the growth of parties opposed to the national leadership of the Dominion. Because of the increased importance of group interests it became more difficult to unify the nation around any single set of policies. The disintegration of the Progressive movement into a series of sectional parties was the result of this failure of the common will. The depression repeated the process by throwing up a fresh set of groups in certain provinces whose *raison d'être* was a fixed opposition to Ottawa.

The genesis of this opposition lay in the fact that the full force of the great depression was felt on the prairie economy. In 1929 the total value of wheat grown in Alberta was $103,067,000 and the price per bushel was $1.14. In 1935 the total value had sunk to $60,000,000 and the price had fallen to $0.61 per bushel. The acreage under the plough in the two years was approximately the same. In the intervening years the price per bushel had actually fallen to $0.32 and the total value of the crop in 1934 had been little more than $46,000,000.[5] The shutting down of the world markets had reduced the purchasing power of the farmer to incredibly low levels. In addition drought conditions had brought whole areas of the West to complete destitution.

This great decline in purchasing power had come to an economy with very high fixed costs, many of which were in the form of debt charges. The rapid opening up of the West in the thirty years before 1935 had been based in the main on public and private borrowing. The community services had sprung into being very rapidly and they had been financed by provincial and municipal borrowing, usually launched in periods of abnormally high income and on the expectation that that income would continue.[6] "The combination of falling prices, drought and rigid costs was disastrous to agriculture in the Prairie Provinces. . . . During 1931, 1932 and 1933 there was virtually nothing with which to meet living expenses and the net cash income was not sufficient to meet depreciation of buildings and machinery."[7] The prairie economy was therefore in the position of a community forced to live on its capital, but to a considerable extent that capital was owned elsewhere. Hence the dominant political issue was the clash of interest between a class of debtors who lived in the midst of economic ruin and a class of creditors most of whom did not.

Public debt was by no means the only problem of the prairies. Both the purchase and the improvement of land had been based largely on farm credit. It has been estimated that mortgage debt on farms in Alberta amounted in 1931 to $162,000,000. When debts under agreement for sale, implement debts, bank indebtedness, and other debts are added in, the total for that year was $317,800,000. In 1936 the total had become $395,000,000.[8] The fixed charges alone on this amount of debt, which ranged from 7 to 10 per cent on mortgages and agreements for sale, were almost impossible to meet in a community where income had fallen so drastically and where most costs,

[5]*The Case for Alberta* (Edmonton, 1938), p. 16. The government of Alberta refused to appear before the Royal Commission on Dominion-Provincial Relations and addressed its case instead to "The Sovereign People of Canada." *Ibid.*, Foreword.

[6]A. F. McGoun, "Alberta Legislation (1935)," *Canadian Journal of Economics and Political Science*, I (1935), p. 599.

[7]W. A. Mackintosh, *The Economic Background of Dominion-Provincial Relations*, Royal Commission on Dominion-Provincial Relations, *Report*, Appendix 3 (Ottawa, 1939), p. 67.

[8]*The Case for Alberta*, p. 118.

other than debt charges, had fallen much less sharply than agricultural prices.

In the state of near desperation which had been engendered by the depression it was natural to turn to governments and political parties for a solution to an overwhelming political problem. The year 1935 saw landslide elections all over Canada and in almost every case the government in power was swept away by the blind anger of simple people who wanted something done and at once. For Alberta any programme which combined an approach to the problem of income with a fresh attack on the debt question was certain of enthusiastic support. The social credit doctrine combined those two in a heady mixture. Social credit was not a new thing in Alberta in 1935. Major Douglas had been brought out to Canada in 1923. The United Farmers of Alberta had from its beginnings a number of members actively interested in social credit. But this group did not achieve a position of influence until the nineteen-thirties. In the conditions of that decade lies in large part the explanation of the election of the Social Credit party in Alberta.

If any kind of attack was to be made on national monetary policy by the province of Alberta there was a serious obstacle in the way of its fulfilment. Monetary control was one of the exclusive powers of the Dominion and over the years successive governments had shown great zeal in protecting their monopoly of this field. The result was bound to be a clash between the two levels of government. Bound up to some extent with the constitutional issue was the further question of whether, in fact, social credit measures could be applied effectively within the restricted area of a single province.

With regard to these questions there was marked disagreement among the advocates of social credit. Mr. Aberhart, who had done much of the work of popularizing social credit ideas in Alberta, believed that the system could be put into action and that it would solve the problems which beset the Alberta economy. In appearing before the Agricultural Committee of the Alberta legislature in 1934 he said:

> The problem of the education of the people in the social credit idea is so much greater in the whole of Canada than in the province of Alberta alone. I am satisfied that this Legislature will agree that no public law or system can be well introduced until public opinion is solidly behind it. The Dominion of Canada is too large a field to get the people all to understand it. . . . Thus we would have a better chance of putting it in the province than in the Dominion.

The second point is the constitutional one. Ten legislatures, nine provinces and the Dominion would have to agree. Two minds with but a single thought may be possible, but the functioning of ten legislatures in harmony taxes the most hopeful imagination. I can imagine the differences of opinion that might arise if all the provinces were asked to agree to one thing. . . .

The problem of federal debt would prove a barrier. There is a possibility of the province liquidating its debt, but it would be impossible for the Dominion to do so without breaking the banks. Our provincial debt is something over $144,000,000. I have been told that the savings deposits in the banks of Alberta amount to $218,000,000. If we can sell bonds to our citizens, we can liquidate our external debts. The sale of the bonds would be purely optional and this transaction would transfer our external debt to an internal matter to be handled by social credit. This can be done by the provinces with greater ease than in the Dominion.

If the system were introduced into Canada, the provinces would have to look after their own affairs in any case. Since it is not interfering in any way with the carrying on of Dominion business, why need we wait? Why could not the Domnion say, "Go ahead, Alberta, and try it out."[9]

He reinforced his argument for provincial social credit by a homely image which revealed his skill at popular advocacy: "The farmer usually summer fallows one field at a time—never the whole at once."

But the orthodox social crediters disagreed. They insisted that Aberhart had failed completely to understand Major Douglas's doctrines and that in fact there were both practical and constitutional difficulties in the way of introducing social credit into Alberta. This disagreement was brought out in the examination of Mr. Larkham Collins, one of the representatives of the Douglas Social Credit League:

Q. Mr. Brownlee: I suppose, Mr. Collins, that I may say that I quite agree with you in what you have just said and in any correspondence with the Douglas Social Credit League it has been directed absolutely to find out whether or not in their opinion the scheme is applicable to the province and your opinion is really the opinion expressed to me in a letter by the

[9]*The Douglas System of Social Credit: Evidence taken by the Agricultural Committee of the Alberta Legislature, Session 1934* (Edmonton, 1934), p. 19. Earlier in his evidence he employed a favourite figure of speech: "Just as the blood flows out from the heart, feeds, clothes and shelters every cell of the body, picks up the impurities of the body and returns to the heart after purification in the lungs, so the credit dividends should flow from the state credit house to every consumer on to the retailer, to the wholesaler and to the producer and then back to the credit house to start over again. If you let anything interfere with the blood stream you will cause disorder and sickness. If you let anything interfere with the flow of credit, the state will be weakened thereby. Our province is sick today, and I believe the cause is the interference with the flow." *Ibid.*, p. 17.

secretary of the League in Canada, who says, "I would not like to say it is not possible of application to the province, but difficulties of provincial action are immeasurably greater than federal action."

A. Yes, I believe that to be true.[10]

Major Douglas himself, who later appeared before the committee, agreed that the introduction of his policies in Alberta would be seriously hampered by the limited powers of the province under the constitution. He said:

> So far as Alberta is concerned, I take it from the information that has been given me, that all power over finance and banking as such has been skilfully removed from the power of this house. You have, if I may sting you into annoyance in this matter, been reduced to the status of a parish council in regard to the most important matter which affects you in Alberta. That is only a part of the general policy which is being pursued with great skill on the part of the advisors of the financial system to make every question larger and larger and larger, so that you have to get a bigger and bigger conference before you get anything done, eventually leaving everything a world question, so that nothing can be done in regard to it unless you have a world conference, and we all know what comes out of world conferences.[11]

He then proceeded to advocate the tactics which the Aberhart government was led, eventually, to adopt. He suggested that the province should exploit its constitutional powers to the limit by taxing and restricting the activities of financial institutions in order to coerce them into co-operation with the government.

> The first thing to do [he said] is to concentrate on the financial institutions and employ whatever powers you have got left, not to put too fine a point upon it, to penalize these institutions. You have got to get a sanction in

[10]Mr. Collins also quoted Major Douglas as saying: "It is not an insoluble problem, but a difficult one and I should not like to give an offhand opinion as to what extent a unit the size of Alberta could act alone." In the letter from which the above quotation was drawn Major Douglas had also said: "In regard to the question as to the possibility or otherwise of instituting a Social Credit regime in Alberta, I think the shortest practical answer that I can give you is the one which I give to such questions everywhere, and that is, that the inauguration of a Social Credit system anywhere is really neither a theoretical nor an economic problem, but in the last resort, is a military problem. The present financial monopoly has devoted at least 100 years, if not more, to obtaining control of the ultimate sanctions of civilization, such as the police and military forces, and so long as this control is maintained, the question as to whether it is legal to take certain steps for the breaking of the monopoly of credit is quite academic, since if it *did* happen to be legal, the law would unquestionably be altered to make it illegal. In the words of Pooh Bah in 'The Mikado' 'Such is the law; it is, I made it so.' The real task of the Social Credit army is not, I need hardly say, to raise a new military army, but to detach the existing forces from the possibility of use in such a situation."

[11]*The Douglas System of Social Credit*, p. 96.

the political field to bring to bear on this situation to get something done. It is not the slightest use as far as I can see going to the financial people and saying: "This has to be done because of the state of the world, because the people are starving in the midst of plenty." Whether because whom the gods destroy they first send mad, or for what reason, they seem impervious to any argument of that kind. They are simply pursuing a perfectly standardized scheme and nothing seems capable of deflecting them from it, so that you have to get some power of bringing these people to reason. The question is what power can you bring to bear in Alberta? Can you tax them heavily? Can you place restrictions on the carrying on of that business? Those are questions not for me but for you. How can you go up to a bank manager or a bank director and say, "Look here, if you do not do certain things, if you won't listen to what we have to say about this sort of thing, we are going to make you feel it. We don't care how we make you feel it, but we are going to make you feel it. It is not personal; the questions at stake are much too great for anything of that kind, but we are going to locate you in the eyes of the public as being the people who are causing this trouble, and in every possible way which is still left to us by our legislative powers, we are going to put up something to bargain with. We are going to impose on you these things and we will take them off when you will do such and such, according to what we are advised by our expert advisers, but we have got you on the spot."[12]

Thus he laid down what was in the end very much like the strategy of the Aberhart government in implementing its policy of income expansion. The concrete proposals which he made were in fact followed in detail in the legislation of 1937. He was also able to foresee the kind of opposition which such a policy would arouse:

If it so happens that you put up a scheme such as my own or any other which traversed the existing financial system and it happened to be legal . . . it would be made illegal within six months. . . . If the law is not sufficient to permit you to put a good scheme for the benefit and protection of the public, then the law should be changed so that you can do it. So you have to see what you can do to fight back and, as I say, I think that a question for you in this house with your knowledge of the laws of this country rather than for me.

Given the power, either I or dozens of other people could provide you in three months with a scheme which would work perfectly and put Alberta, or Canada, depending on the extent to which it is applied, forever outside the range of poverty. But you cannot do it because you won't be allowed and it is your problem to find out how to get the power to put into operation a technically sound scheme.[13]

In the session of 1935 the legislature returned to the problem of the constitutional feasibility of social credit. By this time Mr. Aberhart had placed before the public a programme which contained two main items. The first was the provision of additional purchasing

[12]*Ibid.*, pp. 96–7.

[13]*Ibid.*, p. 97. See note 10 above for an elaboration of this theme.

power by the issue by the province of credit certificates and the second was the establishment of a system of "just" prices. The Agricultural Committee of the legislature was at pains to extract evidence which stressed the difficulty which would confront a provincial government attempting to carry out such proposals. The committee was told by the Dean of the Faculty of Law of the University of Alberta that the issue of credit certificates and the use of the taxing power in the "just price" scheme would be beyond the power of the legislature of a province.[14]

While the hearings of 1934 and 1935 emphasized the obstacles which would confront a provincial government attempting a social credit programme they helped to shape the issues in the coming election campaign. The 1935 hearings showed how far the U.F.A. government had lost the initiative, for they were clearly designed to demonstrate the constitutional difficulties which would make the Aberhart proposals impossible of achievement. Meanwhile events had moved rapidly.

On the eve of the election year the United Farmers of Alberta were deprived of the experienced leadership of Mr. J. E. Brownlee. The almost universal appeal of social credit forced his successor, Mr. R. G. Reid, into a gamble to steal the thunder of the advocates of social credit. As a result of a rapid interchange of cablegrams the government was able to engage Major Douglas himself as Chief Reconstruction Adviser.[15] Douglas duly arrived in Edmonton in May of 1935 and provided the government with a set of interim proposals which included the establishment of credit institutions and the setting up of an information service including radio broadcasting facilities to counteract unfavourable propaganda from hostile financial interests.[16] His proposal for the creation of credit institutions was that they be

[14]*The Constitutionality and Economic Aspects of Social Credit: Evidence . . . before the Agricultural Committee of the Alberta Legislature, Session 1935* (Edmonton, 1935), pp. 8–9.

[15]Major Douglas's communications succeeded in creating an atmosphere of intrigue and melodrama. Cf. the following: "Please send earliest available legal opinion on currency position. Also limitation of general provincial sovereignty. Cannot reach Alberta before middle May. Obstruct hasty changes B.N.A." Text published in Edmonton *Bulletin*, March 27, 1936.

[16]"In Great Britain the position [of the social credit movement] is probably even more important, though less apparent to casual observation, in view of the closely-knit Press organization and the monopoly of broadcasting, which is intimately associated with the Bank of England." Everywhere he saw the sinister hand of the central banks against him. *First Interim Report on the Possibilities of the Application of Social Credit Principles to the Province of Alberta: Submitted to His Majesty's Premier and Legislative Council of Alberta, at Edmonton, Alberta, May 23rd, 1935 by Major C. H. Douglas* (Edmonton, 1935), pp. 6–8.

set up either under the provisions of the Bank Act (there is nothing to prevent a province from subscribing the necessary capital and applying for a charter to operate a bank) or outside its provisions. In his covering letter he suggested four ultimate objectives of policy to the provincial Government for which they should seek a mandate. These were (1) a drastic reduction of taxation, particularly upon real property, (2) a maintenance dividend as of right, possibly small at first, and graded so as to be at a maximum after middle age, (3) measures designed to produce a low price level within the province, with adequate remuneration to the producer and trader, and (4) development of internal resources based rather upon physical capacity than upon financial considerations. These objectives, he added, could only be attained by access to local credit.[17] There the matter rested, for action was of course deferred by the general election in August.

Thus even before the election the province was won over by social credit. In a sense it can be said that social credit was not an issue in the election; it was the context in which the election was fought. No campaigner dared attack the central doctrine of social credit from the platform, for no audience would listen to such an attack. To the problems of debt and purchasing power which dominated the election social credit seemed to offer—though no one was quite clear how—an answer and a remedy. The United Farmers of Alberta had been in power for too long. Not only did they have to face the hostility which all governments in that year had to face from a bewildered electorate, they had endured several awkward scandals which deprived them of strong leadership and weakened their appeal to the voters. They had, in addition, no convincing answer to social credit. They, and the other parties, could do little with it except try to make some capital out of its obvious appeal—for by this time the province was mesmerized by the prospect of endless purchasing power at the stroke of a pen. When election day came the voters naturally turned to the party which actually bore the name of the new promise and swept it into office.

The victory of the Social Credit party meant that the Alberta electorate had endorsed a programme of alleviating the depression by increasing purchasing power. The means by which this could be accomplished by a provincial government were strictly limited by the constitution. Section 138 of the Bank Act of 1934 seemed to stand in the way of the issue of social credit dividends, while any attempt

[17]*Ibid.*, p. 10.

to lower prices along the lines of Mr. Aberhart's "just price" mechanism would be an interference with interprovincial trade as well as the regulation of trade and commerce.[18]

But were these barriers insuperable? No such programme had ever been tried and it was conceivable, in an era when the powers of the Dominion were at their lowest ebb, that it might in fact survive the scrutiny of the courts. Mr. W. S. Gray of the Attorney-General's Department, who was later to draft the Aberhart programme in legislative form, had already provided the government with a legal opinion in which he had suggested that valid legislation could be brought within the all-embracing arms of the Property and Civil Rights clause of section 92.[19]

This was not to be an immediate issue. In the first few months of office the attention of the government was necessarily taken up with mastering the details of departmental administration and with negotiations over a possible refunding of the provincial debt. It was one thing to expound the principles of social credit from the platform and quite another for cabinet ministers, new to administration and lacking in expert advice, to translate them into legislation. However, it was necessary to produce something.

Thus it was that, while the first session of the legislature in 1936 dealt largely with the two problems of relief and revenue deficiency, it contained one enactment of a social credit nature. This was a rather general statute, the Social Credit Measures Act (c. 5, first session, 1936), which stated the intention to "bring about the equation of consumption to production, and to afford each person a fair share in the cultural heritage of the people of the Province." A more drastic measure was the Provincial Loans Refunding Act (c. 6, first session), which compulsorily reduced the interest payable on the bonded indebtedness of the province. It was only a part of a complex process of legislation and negotiation over the burden of the public debt, which we shall consider separately in chapter VII.

In the same session was passed a highly controversial piece of legislation which was to have a brief life and an interesting sequel. This measure, described as the first recall bill ever to be passed in the British Empire, had been part of the platform of the Social Credit party in the general election. The bill seems, nevertheless, to have

[18]*The Constitutionality and Economic Aspects of Social Credit: Evidence . . . before the Agricultural Committee of the Alberta Legislature, Session 1935*, pp. 2–3, evidence of Dean Weir.

[19]*First Interim Report . . . by Major C. H. Douglas*, pp. 8–9.

been brought down with some reluctance. It provided that a member of the legislature must vacate his seat on the presentation of a recall petition bearing 66⅔ per cent of the names on the voters' list in his constituency. In recall measures in force in the United States the customary percentage is from 10 to 30. In fixing such a high proportion the Alberta government, as the debate made clear, was under the impression that it would be difficult, if not impossible, to invoke the Act to secure the recall of a member. This, as Mr. Aberhart was soon to discover, was not the case.

The mere enactment of the Social Credit Measures Act was insufficient to satisfy many of the supporters of the government. To them the pace of the revolution for which they had voted was maddeningly slow. They felt that the failure to grapple with the key problem of purchasing power was to put the cart before the horse, and that, if the government could be persuaded to carry out its social credit measures, the other problems which so consumed its energies would be exorcized at the same time.

Their disappointment was made more poignant by a growing suspicion of the government's good intentions. One of Mr. Aberhart's first acts, on assuming office, had been to appoint an actuarial expert, Mr. R. J. Magor of Montreal, as financial adviser to the government. Mr. Magor had recently served in a similar capacity in Newfoundland, and his appointment aroused a considerable amount of speculation and some criticism within the party. Major Douglas, who had been appointed adviser by the Reid administration, and was still under contract to the government, immediately took umbrage at this step and proceeded to belabour the Premier with letters and cables of protest. He accused Mr. Aberhart of falling in line with the wishes of the financial interests and accepting the advice of a man who was, in his words, an agent of the bankers. To this Mr. Aberhart replied by denying that the bankers had anything to do with either Mr. Magor's appointment or his advice and appealing rather plaintively to Major Douglas to supply the government with detailed advice on a Social Credit plan.[20]

Restiveness within the Social Credit movement was particularly marked among the "orthodox" or Douglas social crediters, as distinct from the followers of Mr. Aberhart. This group made public a letter from the official party in England which purported to show that Major Douglas had repudiated the social credit ideas of the Premier, and pointed to one serious difficulty which the government had en-

[20]*Canadian Annual Review*, 1937–8, p. 337.

countered—the complete lack of co-operation between Mr. Aberhart and Major Douglas. In spite of the vociferous demands of its supporters the government had been unable to bring the founder of social credit to Edmonton to continue his function as adviser to the province, a post to which he had been appointed by the Reid administration. The letter, which was strongly critical of the government ran as follows:

> He [Aberhart] is doing nothing contrary to orthodox finance, with the possible exception of the repudiation of the Loan Council agreement, which was entirely due to the fact that Douglas himself, through the press, warned the people of Alberta of the possible consequences. . . . Refunding of interest rates is a well-known method employed by the orthodox financial system and has been going on ever since the depression started. . . . To say that Douglas would not come on invitation from the Alberta government is incorrect. The cables and letters exchanged clearly show that no direct invitation was ever issued until the last week in December, and that only after Douglas, by cable, had asked that his resignation be announced. The reason for the request to be relieved of his contract is quite obviously due to the fact that the Government was prepared to accept financial advice from their own appointee [Mr. Magor] . . . without reference to their chief reconstruction adviser, Major Douglas himself.[21]

The growing dissatisfaction with the government among its supporters was only partly allayed by the legislation passed in the second session of the legislature, which met, commencing on August 25, for six days. The first important piece of legislation was the Alberta Credit House Act. This Act, which set up a branch of the government for the purpose of issuing credit, validated a previous registration of citizens which had been carried out to determine those eligible for the benefits of the social credit programme. Under the Act the persons who had registered were to be eligible for "interest free" loans, that is, loans on which the interest was not to exceed 2 per cent, for the purpose of either home building or the starting of a business. They had covenanted to co-operate with the government, not to claim payment of Alberta Credit in Canadian currency, nor to tender Alberta Credit in payment of taxes. In addition retailers promised to give a preference to Alberta-made goods, and to accept payment wherever possible in Alberta Credit. Other classes in the community were also expected to accept a part of their incomes in Alberta Credit. The covenants exhorted the payment of a just rate of wages by employers and the observance of reasonable hours of labour. Those registering were also to be eligible for the promised

[21]Toronto *Globe*, July 24, 1936. The Loan Council negotiations are dealt with in chapter VII below.

monthly dividend which would be paid in Alberta Credit. It might be noted in passing that the theory behind the Alberta Credit scheme was at this stage more mercantilist than social credit, aiming as it did at a high level of domestic, that is Alberta, production of goods and services by an intensified campaign to buy at home and thus economize on "foreign exchange," in this case Canadian currency.

The Credit House was to have its headquarters in Edmonton and branches throughout the province. It was to be operated by a board of five, and its principal function was, in the words of the Act (s. 18) "to furnish to persons entitled to Alberta Credit facilities for the exchange of goods and services in the Province in order to effect equation between the purchasing power of such persons within the Province and production within the Province." The Credit House was empowered to accept deposits, and, with its ability to make loans and payments, was evidently intended to perform many of the functions of a bank, though the draftsmen were careful to avoid verbal conflict with either the Bank Act or section 91 of the British North America Act. The emphasis on activities "within the province" was strongly to suggest that the scheme fell within the scope of section 92.

The characteristic of the Act which most alarmed the watchful *Winnipeg Free Press* was the extent of delegated legislation which it permitted. "A startling departure from the custom of parliamentary government, or rule by the legislature," it noted solemnly, "is contained in one of the final sections of the Act (Sec. 31) which empowers the government, by order-in-council to vary, add to or supplement with new provisions, any of the provisions of this Act.' "[22] The tendency to delegate legislative powers to the executive, which is an essential part of the elaboration of the control of the economy by the state, was a characteristic of much Alberta legislation of this period, and is thought to have increased the hostility of the courts to Alberta enactments.

The government had embarked on a régime of social credit. It had legislated. But as yet the revolution had not come. Outside Alberta there was little excitement over this part of the Aberhart programme. The federal government for the moment seemed prepared to await more positive results, as the following news report suggests:

> Close watch is being kept on the deliberations of the Alberta legislature and the various devices being set up for giving effect to the Albertan system of Social Credit.

[22] *Winnipeg Free Press*, Sept. 1, 1936.

The suggestion is rather recurrent that much of what is being done is really an infringement upon the federal authority. But it is abundantly plain that there will be no interference here. Alberta gave its prophetic premier a mandate of the widest scope.

Ottawa indicates no intention of allowing it to be said they frustrated his purpose to deliver the goods—or at least something on account on his extensive undertakings.[23]

Meanwhile the 1936 legislative programme had appeared to many of the more extreme social crediters as palliative half-measures, and by the end of the year there were again restive stirrings among the back-benchers. This revolt seems to have been precipitated by the arrival in Edmonton, towards the end of the year, of John Hargrave, an active member of the English social credit group. Urged on by Hargrave, a number of members began to press for a full-scale social credit programme to be enacted at the coming session of the legislature.

At a divisional conference of the party in Edmonton on December 29 several speakers referred to the drastic legislation being prepared for presentation to the party caucus which was to meet on January 12. One speaker, Mr. Kuhl, member of the legislature for Jasper-Edson, told the delegates that Alberta should establish legal tender money and "make every other money in the province illegal tender."[24] While this declaration may be dismissed as the irresponsible ebullience of a back-bencher, the rebels were clearly in a determined mood and it was reported that as a gesture of conciliation the Premier had appointed a committee of five members with Hargrave as its technical adviser to draft a programme.[25] This step led to rumours in the press of a split in the cabinet over the issue and there were repeated reports that the resignation of the Provincial Treasurer, Mr. Cockcroft, was imminent.[26] When he did in fact resign at the end of January, 1937, his resignation was attributed in part to differences within the cabinet over the new programme.[27]

However, this outbreak seems to have been smothered for the time. At the caucus the proposals for a social credit programme were adopted with some amendments and the rebels waited impatiently for the legislation to be revealed in the coming session. There must have been considerable compromise between the two wings of the party at this stage, for Hargrave suddenly left Edmonton with the

[23]*Ottawa Journal*, Aug. 29, 1936.
[24]*Edmonton Journal*, Dec. 31, 1936.
[25]*Ibid.*
[26]*Ibid.*, Jan. 13, 1937.
[27]*Ibid.*, Jan. 29, 1937.

terse announcement: "I regretfully find myself unable to co-operate further with Mr. Aberhart and his cabinet."[28]

The session began quietly and, to the annoyance of the rebels, no drastic legislative programme made its appearance. One of the rebels criticized the budget sharply on the ground that it was "orthodox," and it was urged that consideration of the budget be set aside until the question of social credit measures could be dealt with. There were rumours that the members would hold up the budget unless the Premier agreed to the introduction of the Social Credit Bill, a document of some 600 sections which had been prepared by the extremists.[29] At the same time critics of the government from the Social Credit side were demanding that the services of Major Douglas or some other technical adviser be obtained without further delay.[30]

In spite of the announced determination of the insurgents to hold up supply, both the Premier and the new Provincial Treasurer, Mr. Solon Low, announced that the budget would not be withdrawn and that the government would stick to its guns.[31] Finally stalemate was averted in party caucus, with the rebels consenting to the passage of an interim supply bill in return for renewed assurances that the programme would be speeded up.[32] Another important part of the bargain was contained in an amendment to the Social Credit Measures Act which provided for its administration by a board of five. The five members who were appointed to the Social Credit Board were outside the circle of the government, although none of them had been openly identified with the insurgents. Thus this non-ministerial body, which the press was to dub "the little cabinet," was entrusted with the task of giving concrete form to the aspirations of the Social Credit movement.

One of the Board's first moves was to re-open negotiations with Major Douglas. Douglas himself refused to return to Alberta, but he sent two of his associates, L. D. Byrne and George Frederick Powell, as "investigating and advisory envoys" to the Alberta capital. There the two envoys shortly became attached to the Social Credit Board as "technicians."[33] The Board conceived its task to be the framing of legislation to be laid before the Legislative Assembly, which the gov-

[28]*Calgary Herald*, Jan. 25, 1937.
[29]Calgary *Western Farm Leader*, March 19, 1937.
[30]*Edmonton Journal*, March 4, 1937.
[31]*Ibid.*, March 29, 1937.
[32]*Edmonton Journal*, March 31, 1937.
[33]*Ibid.*, July 8, 1937.

ernment, its interim supply exhausted, would be forced to meet in the summer.

In August the House met in a momentous four-day session. The first bill to be approved was the Credit of Alberta Regulation Act (1937, c. 1, second session) which would have enabled the province to regulate the credit policy of the chartered banks operating in Alberta. To the social crediters the control of bank credit was essential to their scheme of economic recovery, and they did not underestimate its importance, as the following statement reveals:

> It is questionable whether any single piece of legislation had commanded such universal attention. Alarm was evident in the banking centres of London and New York. The financial press of the world hurled abuse at the Government which had dared to challenge the sovereignty of finance. The disallowance of this legislation was demanded.
>
> And all this excitement was caused by the simple act that merely required the banks operating within the Province of Alberta to order their administration of the financial system so as to give the people of the Province access to their own resources within their own boundaries. This legislation did not interfere with the banks, banking, coin, currency, or any administrative matter coming under the federal jurisdiction. It only provided that the banks operating within the Province could not continue violating the property and civil rights of the people by so manipulating the operation of the monetary system as to deny the people access to their abundant resources.
>
> It was an act establishing the basic democratic right of the people to determine the results which should accrue to them from the administration of their affairs by the responsible authorities.[34]

This Act was rounded out and reinforced by two others designed to aid in its enforcement, the Bank Employees Civil Rights Act (c. 2) and the Judicature Act Amendment Act (c. 5). The essence of the former was that it denied access to the courts by unlicensed bank employees, while the latter prohibited attack on the validity of provincial statutes in the courts.

This was certainly legislation which not only pressed the theory of provincial rights to its utmost extremity but was in effect a challenge to the Dominion to interfere with the programme of a provincial government aggressively pursuing its radical mandate. By it the government stood committed to a rejection of the financial system of Canada and of the basic assumptions of national unity in matters of national scope.

[34]*Annual Report of the Social Credit Board to the Legislative Assembly of the Province of Alberta at the 1939 Session* (mimeo.), p. 2. Copy in the Legislative Library, Edmonton.

Before the legislation could take effect, the assent of the Lieutenant-Governor was necessary, and there were rumours in the press that he would reserve the three bills. The government also seems to have had doubts as to whether assent would be forthcoming, and as to the advice the Attorney-General, Mr. John Hugill, would give the Lieutenant-Governor. Mr. Hugill's position was a difficult one. The original Aberhart cabinet had included at least three members who were "moderates" and whose adherence to social credit doctrine was questionable. They were Mr. C. C. Cross, the Minister of Lands and Mines, Mr. Charles Cockcroft, the Provincial Treasurer, and Mr. John Hugill, the Attorney-General. Differences with Mr. Aberhart had led to the resignation of Mr. Cross in December, 1936, and of Mr. Cockcroft in the following month. Mr. Hugill remained. One can imagine the discomfort of an experienced barrister, the product of an English public school and a university in the Maritime Provinces, moderate in his political views and absorbed principally in his departmental duties, confronted by a cabinet of hot gospellers, presided over by the messianic Mr. Aberhart.

Mr. Hugill had already been asked in the House by a member of the opposition whether the government possessed the power to legislate upon the subjects of banks and banking. To this Mr. Hugill had replied that no complete answer was possible to an academic question, but referred the House to the terms of section 91 of the British North America Act.

This reply somewhat disconcerted the government's supporters, and an attempt was made to extract a favourable opinion from him in party caucus in the course of that brief and stormy August session. The Premier himself inquired. "So that we may be certain of our Bills receiving the assent of the Lieutenant Governor, we suggest, that the Attorney-General assures us that he feels in a position on every count to recommend that the Lieutenant-Governor gives his assent to every Social Credit Measure."[35]

This assurance Mr. Hugill, who had not seen the legislation before its introduction, was unable to give. On the last day of the session, shortly before the prorogation of the House, he accompanied the Premier to an interview with the Lieutenant-Governor. The Lieutenant-Governor asked his Attorney-General whether the bills which

[35]*Constitutional Principle (No. 1): In re the office of His Majesty's Attorney-General (Speech of John W. Hugill, K.C., M.L.A., Delivered in the Legislative Assembly at Edmonton, Alberta, on Tuesday, February 28th, 1939)*, (Calgary, n. d.), p. 11.

had been passed by the legislature were within its constitutional competence.

As the Attorney-General [said Mr. Hugill afterwards] I gave the only advice possible, viz., *that the proposed enactments were not within our legislative competence.* . . . Having had the temerity to disagree, Sir, with the opinion of the Honourable Premier as expressed during the audience alluded to, my resignation, as requested, was of course, as promptly tendered immediately after the Assembly had risen and I could address myself to it.

The acceptance of such a formula would be and the acquiescence in the enactment of such legislation, is tantamount to shaking the very foundation of our constitution and national unity.[36]

Nevertheless the Lieutenant-Governor, Mr. J. C. Bowen, bowed to the wishes of his cabinet and assented to the legislation. He was new to office, his predecessor having died in the spring of 1937. He seems to have been uncertain at the time what course to pursue, and his assent came as somewhat of a surprise.[37]

The resignation of Mr. Hugill was under the circumstances inevitable. He justified his advice to reserve assent on the ground that the Attorney-General was the official legal adviser of the Lieutenant-Governor and if his duty as legal adviser conflicted with the principle of cabinet solidarity he must choose to uphold the law as he understood it and risk severing his connection with the cabinet. He also argued that his professional oath as a barrister made it necessary for him to uphold the law and prevented him from giving advice contrary to what was to him the plain letter of the law.[38]

Though his course in leaving the cabinet was correct throughout there must be some doubt about the wisdom of his advice to the Lieutenant-Governor. While the Lieutenant-Governor possesses all the normal reserve powers, there is an element of incongruity in his exercising them on ministerial advice. The rules governing the use of the reserve powers were laid down, on the initiative of Sir John A. Macdonald, in a Minute of Council of 1882:

The Lieutenant-Governor is not warranted in reserving any measure for the assent of the Governor-General on the advice of his ministers. He should do so in his capacity of a Dominion officer only, and on instructions from

[36]*Ibid.*, p. 12.

[37]Cf. Toronto *Globe and Mail*, Aug. 7, 1937. "Formal assent to the Social Credit legislation was given by the Lieutenant-Governor, removing all doubt of his reservation of signing the bills pending appeal to constitutional authorities in Ottawa."

[38]Hugill, *Constitutional Principle*, p. 6.

the Governor-General. It is only in a case of extreme necessity that a Lieutenant-Governor should without such instructions exercise his discretion as a Dominion officer in reserving a bill. In fact, with the facility of communication between the Dominion and provincial governments, such necessity can seldom if ever arise.[39]

If, as seems probable, neither Mr. Hugill nor Mr. Bowen understood this, then someone in Ottawa ought to have done something to see that they did. The press at the time was full of rumours of what was in the wind, and official Ottawa can hardly have been unaware of what was taking place. But, as we shall see, several months were to elapse before the question of the governor's reserve powers was to come again to public notice.

The resignation of Mr. Hugill marked a turning point in the history of the Social Credit régime. He was the last of the moderates in the cabinet and with his departure the policy of the administration headed into a direct challenge to Dominion authority. Forces leading to such a challenge were present from the beginning, but the groping steps of the first year of power seemed to indicate that the government hoped at first to achieve its ends without drastic legislation. The reluctance with which they yielded to the extremists was probably due more to misgivings as to the success of such tactics than to a desire to cooperate with the Dominion. Mr. Aberhart's behaviour over the Loan Council negotiations suggests that this was the case.[40] In any event the very strength of the opposition which the three Acts provoked prevented the Alberta government from turning back.

The sweeping character of the legislation passed on August 6 was too much for the banks, and, indeed, for the federal government. While the banks must have made immediate representations to the Department of Justice, the Minister acted without waiting for them to present the customary petition. Within ten days, most of which must have been required for true copies of the legislation to reach Ottawa, the federal government had acted. By P.C. 1985, dated August 17, 1937, the Credit of Alberta Regulation Act, the Bank Employees Civil Rights Act, and the Judicature Act Amendment Act were disallowed.

The Aberhart government was momentarily stunned into silence by the revival of a power which they, and a good many other people, had thought obsolete. It had come to be generally believed that the federal government would not use its overriding powers to thwart the will of

[39]E. Hodgins, *The Dominion and Provincial Legislation*, p. 78.
[40]See below, chapter VII.

a popularly elected government carrying out its mandate. But, apart from the fact that the three Acts fell clearly into that class of legislation against which the use of the power of disallowance was considered proper, two influences determined the revival of disallowance in this case. One was the alarmed insistence of the chartered banks that the legislation was intolerable; the other was the noticeable fact that the more radical the Alberta legislation was, the greater Aberhart's political strength became. Up to this time the view in Ottawa had been that it would be far better for the Aberhart régime to suffer for its own excess of zeal than for the Liberals to incur political odium by interfering, a position, needless to say, perfectly in accord with Mr. King's traditional caution. Far from becoming unpopular as a result of its radical legislation, however, the Aberhart government seemed to be more popular than ever. From the final session of the 1937 legislature there begins a period of open conflict with the Dominion which was to continue for nearly five years.

The legislature was summoned in September for the third session in that turbulent year to consider a fresh crop of provocative and controversial bills. The first important piece of legislation was an amended and consolidated version of the Credit of Alberta Regulation Act, in which all direct references to banks, bankers, and banking had been replaced by the terms "credit" or "business of dealing in credit." It was thought that by thus avoiding verbal conflict with section 91 of the British North America Act the grounds on which the Act could be attacked would be avoided. In spite of this the bill was, as Mr. Lucien Maynard, a recent addition to the cabinet, assured the house, "in principle just the same" as its predecessor. Mr. Maynard continued: "Any institution that restricts its activities to section 91 will not be affected. We are interested only in the credit of the people, not in the business of banking."[41]

The second was the Accurate News and Information Bill. This bill gave wide powers to the Chairman of the Social Credit Board to force newspapers to publish, under pain of severe penalties, such statements as might be required to correct public misapprehension of the government's policies. A newspaper could thus be called upon to publish statements correcting or amplifying any statement which it had made with regard to any policy or activity of the government. The feature of the bill which most disturbed the press was the requirement which made mandatory the disclosure by a newspaper of its news sources and the names of writers of news stories or articles. It is well known

[41]Toronto *Evening Telegram*, Oct. 5, 1937.

that the only condition under which a newspaper reporter can obtain necessary information is his ability to respect and protect the anonymity of his sources. This professional reticence had caused grave annoyance to the Alberta government when ill-timed or inaccurate leaks of information had been played up in the press. Such action as the bill contemplated was rendered necessary in the government's view by the hostile attitude of the press generally towards the régime: "An act was passed providing that newspapers and other publications within the Province publishing false or misleading statements on matters of public policy should be obliged to publish authoritative corrections to such statements, without in any way interfering with their right to publish anything they wished. This Act was rendered necessary by the organized press campaign of abuse and misrepresentation which was released following the passage of the original Credit of Alberta Regulation Act."[42]

It is quite true that through all this period the Alberta government had, with the solitary exception of the Calgary *Albertan*—in which for a time they had a controlling interest—a thoroughly "bad press." Every action of the government was played up in the western newspapers from a critical point of view and it was seldom indeed that any action of the government came in for praise or even escaped comment. Obsessed with the rightness of their cause and convinced of the wrongheadedness of the opposition, the government could only believe that the newspapers were a party to the international bankers' plot which figured so largely in the social credit theory of causation. They therefore undervalued the enormous amount of publicity which such elaborate press coverage in the national and even world press was giving to them. They also seriously underestimated the extent to which popular distrust of the press was turning this apparently adverse publicity to their advantage. Thus they were led to enact an unwise and humourless piece of legislation which enabled their opponents to accuse them of censorship.

The motives behind the third Act, the Bank Taxation Act, are more complex. In a sense it was a straight piece of punitive legislation, quite in line with the strategy which Major Douglas had outlined as a way of bringing the banks to "see reason." The legislation may therefore have been only a bargaining counter and act of retaliation for the initiative which the banks had taken in the disallowance of the legislation of the second session.

To many social crediters, however, it was a measure of fiscal reform

[42]*Annual Report of the Social Credit Board, 1939*, p. 1.

dictated alike by the considerations of social justice and monetary theory. On the one hand, it sought to shift the burden of taxation from individuals to "institutions," and, on the other, it enabled the treasury to extract its revenue painlessly from the manufacturers of the circulating medium who—in social credit theory—were engaged in an almost costless enterprise.[43]

One other piece of legislation of interest was passed by the legislature at this session. While it is irrelevant to the main issue of social credit, the circumstances surrounding it convey forcibly the atmosphere of that summer. An act was passed repealing the Recall Act of 1936. The unhappy truth was that a petition, which seemed certain to gain the necessary two-thirds signatures, had been launched in Okotoks–High River against the Premier himself. Mr. Aberhart's sense of mission was stronger than his belief in popular sovereignty, and the government hastily introduced the bill which repealed the Recall Act.[44]

[43]The Social Credit Board was later to justify the legislation on both grounds: "In dealing with taxation and in conformity with the same above [the advice of Major Douglas and his technicians in connection with debt adjustment policy] your Board recommended that taxes on individuals be reduced and the burden shifted to the institutions. In carrying out the advice of its technicians your Board recommended the removal of the Ultimate Purchasers Tax and its replacement by a tax on the banks. While the Ultimate Purchasers Tax was suspended the tax upon the banks designed to yield practically the same amount and approved by the Legislature was rendered inoperative [by the reservation of assent by the Lieutenant-Governor].

"A third measure was passed by the Legislature providing for the taxation of banks for revenue purposes, so that the burden of taxation on individuals could be reduced. The justice of this measure lay in the indisputable fact that banks, as the sole manufacturers and issuers of monetary credits, alone paid taxes without any cost to themselves. The following quotations in support of this fact are chosen at random from a mass of evidence on this question.

" 'It is not unnatural to think of the deposits of a bank as being created by the public through the deposits of cash representing either savings or amounts which are not for the time being required for expenditure. But the bulk of deposits arise out of the action of the banks themselves, for by granting loans, allowing money to be drawn on an overdraft or purchasing securities a bank creates a credit in its books, which is the equivalent of a deposit.'—Section 74—Report of the Macmillan Committee of Great Britain on Finance and Industry in 1931.

" 'When a bank lends *it creates money out of nothing*. The borrower becomes indebted to the bank for a sum to be repaid in the future with interest and the bank becomes indebted to the borrower for a sum immediately available.'—R. G. Hawtrey, Assistant Secretary, H. M. Treasury of Great Britain in 'Trade Depression and the Way Out.' "

*Annual Report of the Social Credit Board for 1937–38* (Edmonton, 1938, mimeo), p. 8. Copy in the Legislative Library, Edmonton.

[44]*Globe and Mail*, Sept. 23, 1937.

On October 6 the Lieutenant-Governor, Mr. Bowen, reserved for the consideration of the Governor-General-in-Council the three contentious bills which had been passed by the Legislative Assembly, the Accurate News and Information Bill, the Bank Taxation Bill, and the Bill amending the Credit of Alberta Regulation Act. The action of the Lieutenant-Governor, apparently the first of its kind in the history of the province,[45] caused angry consternation in the ranks of the government and added yet another constitutional problem to those which had already arisen in the course of the year.

It is not entirely clear why the Lieutenant-Governor chose to reserve the three bills. It is possible that he was acting belatedly on the advice which Mr. Hugill had given him in the preceding session of the legislature. If that is the case neither he nor Mr. Hugill seems to have been familiar with the conventions governing the power of reservation, so clearly laid down by the Dominion Government as early as 1882. This is perhaps not altogether surprising, since the occasions on which a lieutenant-governor is called upon to employ his reserve powers are necessarily rare, and do not seem to have arisen before in Alberta. If, as the available evidence suggests, it had not occurred to Mr. Bowen to seek counsel in Ottawa, nor for anyone in Ottawa to acquaint themselves with what was going on in Edmonton, the blame cannot be wholly placed on the Lieutenant-Governor. He ought not to have reserved the bills without instructions, however, and, as far as is known, he neither received instructions nor sought advice from the Dominion government.

This is not to say that his action was unconstitutional, for it was not. But there were other methods of cutting down the legislation which were more in accord with the political assumptions of the twentieth century. The unwillingness of Lieutenant-Governor Bowen to give his assent to the three bills had the effect of needlessly arousing a controversy over the nature of responsible government which had ceased to be an issue in Canadian politics for nearly a century. From his own point of view the action of the Lieutenant-Governor was quixotic and it is likely that he came in time to regret it. If he did not, it is not the fault of the Social Credit party in Alberta. The party was quick to seize on this issue for propaganda purposes, and attempted to show that the Lieutenant-Governor's action, and with it that of the Dominion government, involved a flagrant revival of arbitrary and unconstitutional prerogative powers reminiscent of the early Stuarts.

The clash between the province and the Dominion was now open

[45] *Edmonton Journal*, Oct. 6, 1937.

and bitter. At the points of contact, where individuals were involved, the protagonists became devoid of reason and sense of proportion. Individuals themselves became issues and objectives of policy. Two of the persons caught up in this cold war were Lieutenant-Governor Bowen and George Frederick Powell, one of the "technicians" whom Major Douglas had sent out from England.

Mr. Bowen had left himself exposed and vulnerable by his reservation of the three bills. In the eyes of the government he was simply a creature of a Dominion ministry which was itself at the mercy of the international bankers who sought at every turn to frustrate the legitimate aspirations of the people of Alberta. The 1938 session of the legislature revealed that the people were not prepared to forgive their enemies.

The normal item in the estimates for the expenses of the Lieutenant-Governor was dropped. While the salary of the governor is paid by the Dominion government, all the other expenses of his office including the maintenance of some semblance of royal state are borne by the province. The normal vote for this purpose was $3,500 which was intended for the upkeep of Government House, and for the car, chauffeur, and secretarial services of the governor. No expenditure, it was stated, was to be made on Government House, unless required by "other than the present occupant of the building."[46] This act of vindictive retaliation came almost exactly at the end of Mr. Bowen's first year of office. It was to be the first of a number of reminders that the legislature had not forgotten his exercise of the power of reservation in the previous year.

Another reaction of the Social Credit party to the disallowance of its legislation in the summer of 1937 was a leaflet attacking the banks and their supposed friends among the enemies of the government in Alberta. The publication of this leaflet provided a further cause of bitter acrimony, not only between the government and its critics in Alberta, but also between the Alberta legislature and the federal government.

When the Legislative Assembly reconvened on September 29, 1937, to deal with the problem created by the disallowance of its legislation over banking in August, the leader of the Conservative group, Mr. Duggan, rose on a question of privilege to point out that he had been referred to in a government leaflet as a "bankers' toady."[47] It was shortly disclosed that the persons responsible for the leaflet were J. H.

[46]*Edmonton Journal*, Sept. 26, 1937.
[47]*Edmonton Journal*, Sept. 30, 1937.

Unwin, Government Whip in the legislature, and George Frederick Powell, a member of the staff of the Social Credit Board. Powell and Unwin were arrested and faced with a criminal charge of publishing a defamatory libel.

From the first the case lost all semblance of a simple criminal prosecution and became an issue between the government and its enemies. Those who disliked the government could not be expected to restrain their pleasure at its discomfiture, particularly since Powell, who seems to have regarded those with whom he came in contact as a species of oafish colonial, had made few friends in his brief stay in Edmonton. On the other hand, while there was nothing in the arrest, prosecution, or conviction of the two men that could be described as unfair or illegitimate, the Social Crediters saw in the prosecution of Powell and Unwin nothing but persecution. "On the face of it, whoever is instigating the proceedings is asking for a great deal of trouble, and is likely to get it," was the reaction of Major Douglas, when apprised of the event by an English newspaperman.[48]

Powell and Unwin came up for trial before Mr. Justice Ives, and were convicted of publishing a defamatory libel. Mr. Unwin was sentenced to three months at hard labour at Fort Saskatchewan. Mr. Powell, on whom primary responsibility was fixed, was given a six months' sentence, coupled with a recommendation for deportation. The judge further expressed the view that there was growing turmoil and disrespect for law in Alberta, which might well lead to breaches of the peace. For this, he felt, Powell was partly responsible.[49]

This was by no means the end of the Powell case. It was kept before the public by the government as a means of giving a personal focus to the struggle as long as Powell remained in the country. The Journals of the Legislative Assembly for 1938 show a resolution dated February 11 demanding the release of Powell and Unwin and referring to them as having been "convicted of defamatory libel in respect of the publication of a humorous dodger containing an unfortunate combination of ambiguous words which were never intended to attack the character or reputation of anyone." To the last the Social Crediters insisted on the "humorous" character of this clumsy leaflet with its "unfortunate combination of ambiguous words."

Major Douglas entered the lists with a series of letters to Mr. King on the subject of Powell's detention. In his first letter, dated December 10, 1937, Douglas stated that he had "been requested by the Alberta

[48]Toronto *Star*, Oct. 6, 1937; Nov. 12, 1937.
[49]Toronto *Globe and Mail*, Nov. 16, 1937.

Government to render assistance in presentation to the supreme cou of Canada and in any reference to the privy council of certain aspects of the policy of the province," and asked whether he too would risk detention and deportation if he came to Canada to assist the province. Mr. King replied that Powell had been duly convicted by the courts of an offence under the Criminal Code, and that he assumed that Major Douglas was not contemplating any breach of the law. The seven letters ended with a discussion as to whether there was anything of public interest in the correspondence to warrant their release to the public. Mr. King felt that no public interest was involved, but Major Douglas differed and accordingly released the full texts.[50]

Possibly because the sentences had been rather severe considering the nature of the offence, or perhaps because of the great amount of public discussion which they aroused, both Powell and Unwin were released after serving one-half of their terms. Powell returned to England as soon as he was released. On the morning of the day on which he entrained for the east the government passed an order-in-council authorizing the payment to him of $4,000 "in consideration of his services."[51] Thus rewarded, he left Alberta forever, his principal service to the Alberta government having been that of an embittered and unwilling martyr.

One final incident of the Powell case occurred in the summer of 1938. On August 18 the Edmonton police magistrate, A. H. Gibson, K.C., was dismissed from his post by order-in-council without cause being stated. Mr. Gibson insisted that his dismissal was the direct result of his having committed Powell and Unwin for trial in the preceding year. "I have no hesitation in saying that the reason for my dismissal," he said, "was the government's resentment over my action in the Powell-Unwin case and the fact that they hold me more or less to blame for the fact that the accused men were sent to jail."[52]

It had now become apparent that all of the questions which had arisen would be subject to litigation, and the Dominion government referred the whole question of the reserve powers over provincial legislation to the Supreme Court of Canada. On October 2, 1937, the power of disallowance was referred to the Court, and shortly afterwards reference questions were also submitted on the power of reservation and on the competence of the Alberta legislature to enact the three bills which had been reserved by Lieutenant-Governor Bowen.

[50]*Edmonton Journal*, March 10, 1938.
[51]*Ibid.*, May 23, 1938.
[52]*Ibid.*, Aug. 26, 1938.

The issues of reservation and disallowance were argued together before the Court, while the third question was considered separately.

In the first reference the province was represented before the Court by O. M. Biggar, K.C., and other eminent counsel. The Alberta case was based essentially on the contention that the judicial interpretation of the constitution had given to the provinces a status which they had not been able to assert in Macdonald's day, and that the judicial declaration that the provincial legislatures were sovereign in their own sphere was inconsistent with the exercise of the power of disallowance over provincial legislation which did not invade the express powers of the Parliament of the Dominion.

"One argument advanced," said Sir Lyman Duff in his judgment, "is that the literal construction of section 90 is inconsistent with the reasons for judgment given on behalf of the Judicial Committee by Lord Watson in *Liquidators of the Maritime Bank of Canada* v. *the Receiver-General of New Brunswick* and by Lord Haldane in *In re Initiative and Referendum Act*."[53] But this was not an argument which he was prepared to accept. "There is nothing, however, in all this that is in the least degree incompatible with a Lieutenant-Governor reserving a bill for the signification of the pleasure of the Governor General who is the representative of the Crown or in the disallowance of an Act of the Legislature by the Governor General acting on the advice of his Council, who, as representing the Sovereign, constitute the executive government for Canada."[54] A court of law, he continued, must deal with the meaning of the statute itself, and not with the conventions which had grown up governing the use of these powers under particular circumstances. Accordingly, "It is undisputable that in point of law the authority is unrestricted."[55] Likewise, with regard to reservation: "There is nothing in the *British North America Act* controlling this discretion; nor is there any other statute having any relevancy in the matter."[56]

It is quite possible that the extreme character of the Alberta legislation heightened the awareness of the Court of the function of the dis-

[53]*Reference Re the Power of the Governor General in Council to Disallow Provincial Legislation and the Power of Reservation of a Lieutenant-Governor of a Province*, [1938] S.C.R. 71, *per* Duff C.J., at p. 75.

[54]*Ibid.*, p. 77.

[55]"We are not concerned with constitutional usage. We are concerned with questions of law which, we repeat, must be determined by reference to the enactments of the *British North America Acts* of 1867 to 1930, the *Statute of Westminster*, and, it might be, to relevant statutes of the Parliament of Canada if there were any." *Ibid.*, p. 78.

[56]*Ibid.*, p. 79.

allowance power in the constitution. Thus Mr. Justice Cannon referred to contemporary events in elaborating the connection between a strong central power and the preservation of a unified national interest. He said: "An additional reason for the preservation of this power of disallowance of provincial statutes is its necessity, more than ever evident, in order to safeguard the unity of the nation. It may become essential, for the proper working of the constitution, to use in practice the principle of an absolute central control which seems to have been considered an essential part of the scheme of Confederation; this control is found in the Lieutenant-Governor's power of reservation and in the Governor General in Council's power of disallowance."[57]

The unanimous judgment of the court therefore was that the powers of disallowance and reservation were quite unimpaired by the process of constitutional evolution. Much confusion of thought on this point had been created by the failure of writers on the constitution to make clear the distinction between the effect of constitutional change on the legal position of disallowance and its effect on the policy governing its use by the Department of Justice. By sweeping this confusion aside the Supreme Court was able to dispose of Mr. Biggar's argument and reach a conclusion wholly favourable to the Dominion. The policy principles governing the use of disallowance have nothing to do with its legal scope, but merely lay down the kind of circumstances in which disallowance is considered an appropriate remedy, and the occasions when the Department of Justice should leave matters to the remedial action of either the courts or the electorate. This was made clear in Mr. Lapointe's statement on the Department's position over the Alberta legislation and also in his refusal to disallow the Quebec Padlock Act.

In January, 1938, the essence of the Social Credit programme was tested by the Supreme Court of Canada for its constitutional validity. From the beginning the argument was extended beyond the mere significance of the bills themselves through the attempts by the Dominion and the chartered banks to relate them to the whole programme of the Alberta government which was, in their view, an attack on the main structure of the constitution. The three bills, the Dominion claimed, were "part and parcel of one legislative scheme aimed at acquiring control over policy and institutions which alone possess, in the view of the Social Credit Government, the power to

[57]*Ibid.*, p. 83.

'monetize the credit of the people of Alberta.'" This scheme, however, involved "encroachments on the legislative authority of the Federal Government in relation to banking, incorporation of banks, issue of paper money and regulation of trade and commerce." Against this the Alberta government contended that the general purpose of the present government of Alberta was irrelevant to the question before the Court.[58] In addition to the two governments, argument was heard from the chartered banks on the constitutionality of the Bank Taxation and Credit Regulation Bills, and from the Alberta Daily and Weekly Newspaper Associations on the Press Bill.

The Tax Bill was opposed on three grounds: that it did not seek to impose a direct tax, that it extended beyond the bounds of the province, and that in any event its primary purpose was not taxation but the coercion of the banks. It was claimed that the sheer magnitude of the levy implied that it should be passed from the banks to their customers. The banks submitted that it would compel the eight chartered banks operating in Alberta to pay an annual tax of $2,081,929, and that this would increase their total tax bill in Alberta by 2,883 per cent. Against this the increase in taxation on life insurance companies had been 50 per cent, on finance companies 100 per cent, on power companies 90 per cent, and on other companies only 25 per cent. Since the tax was levied on paid-up capital, reserves, and undivided profits, it bore on the shareholders, many of whom were resident outside the province. Such a steep increase in taxation was clearly discriminatory and in its context surely coercive. "The taxing power," the banks' factum stated, "cannot be invoked except for the bona fide purpose of raising revenue. Any exercise of that power to effect a totally different governmental policy must be invalid." The course of legislation showed, it was suggested, that the real intention of the legislature was to coerce the banks into submitting to provincial control by means of licences and local directors, the majority of whom would have been government appointees. Machinery for this control was provided in the companion bill governing the operation of institutions engaged in the business of dealing in credit. The Tax Bill, the argument continued, "confers on the minister powers, in form unlimited, of demanding information from the banks under heavy penalties all of which is coercive, and intended to force the banks to assist the government in establishing its policy of social credit." The bill would also destroy or nullify the status, capacities, and powers of the banks in Alberta, although the banks were

[58]Toronto *Evening Telegram*, Jan. 6, 1938.

Dominion corporations. If the object of the bill was not to control banking operations it would tend nevertheless to drive the banks out of Alberta and leave the field clear for a provincial banking system. Should all of the provinces adopt similar schemes of taxation it would completely vitiate control of banking by the Dominion, and force the banks into insolvency.

As for the Credit of Alberta Regulation Bill, the chartered banks argued that it was not a *bona fide* licence for revenue purposes but an attempt to gain control of the credit-providing facilities of the banks. While it purported to deal with property and civil rights it in fact dealt with phases of banking which were removed from provincial jurisdiction by the express words of the British North America Act. "Even if the subjects of banking and bills of exchange do not directly include dealing in credit," it was argued, "the power to lend by means of negotiable instruments is such an integral part of banking that it must be regarded as necessarily incidental thereto, making the relevant provision of the bank act paramount over any conflicting provincial legislation." The provision for the appointment of local directorates was void because it was in conflict with the requirements of the Bank Act that directors should be elected by the shareholders. The factum concluded: "Accepting deposits and making loans are such an integral part of a bank's business and so interdependent that provincial control over either cannot be tolerated with safety, nor can such control be validly exercised."[59]

On March 4, 1938, the Supreme Court handed down its judgment. It was unanimously of the opinion that all three bills were *ultra vires* of the province. It went further. The Chief Justice, in the principal judgment, recalled the central scheme of the Alberta Social Credit Act to find that this Act was itself *ultra vires*, and thus the whole legislative edifice of social credit was brought to the ground in a single judgment. "It is not a part of our duty (it is perhaps, needless to say)," said Sir Lyman, "to consider the wisdom of these measures. We have only to ascertain whether or not they come within the ambit of the authority entrusted . . . to the legislature of Alberta."[60]

The Court had found it necessary to go back to the Alberta Social Credit Act itself in order to deal with the intent of the legislation before it. Under the operation of that Act, Alberta Credit was to be made available to individuals by means of a monthly dividend and through a retail discount. The discount rate by which buyers of goods

[59]The banks' factum is quoted in the *Edmonton Journal,* Jan. 7, 1938.
[60][1938] S.C.R. 100, *per* Duff C.J., at pp. 106–7.

and services were to receive a rebate was to be fixed by a commission, and was to depend on the ratio of the money value of the unused productive capacity of Alberta to the total productive capacity. The use of this discount procedure to increase purchasing power would only work where it was possible to pay both the price and the discount in Alberta Credit. "The practicability of this scheme," said Sir Lyman, "postulates therefore, a willingness on the part of sellers of goods and services, in Alberta transactions, to accept Alberta Credit in payment; in other words acceptance generally in Alberta of Alberta Credit as the circulating medium."[61] This was to be accomplished through the Credit House, which was empowered to accept deposits of currency and securities, to transfer credit, and to receive deposits of credit vouchers and transfers of Alberta Credit. "A customer of a Credit House has no right to require payment of legal tender at his discretion, unless his deposit is a currency deposit, and cannot transfer such a right to another, but, he is and must necessarily be, if the system is really to be operative, in relation to his account in the Credit House, in the same position as the customer of a bank."[62]

The Alberta legislation had been based on the assumption that the "business of dealing in credit" was part of the everyday contractual relations which, since the early eighties, had been held by the courts to be essentially matters of property and civil rights and therefore under provincial jurisdiction. Hence the attempt in the amended Credit of Alberta Regulation Act to make a distinction between banking proper and the business of dealing in credit. The Alberta draftsmen were pushing the meaning of property and civil rights rather far, but probably not much farther than it had been pushed in the briefs which had successfully overthrown the Bennett New Deal legislation only the year before.

But in this case the courts were not prepared to allow that elusive concept to swallow up a further segment of Dominion power:

> The general character of the classes of subjects enumerated in section 91, especially of those mentioned above [Trade and Commerce, Currency and Coinage, Banks and Banking, Legal Tender], is important. A comparison of the nature of these subjects with the subjects included in section 92 seems to suggest that credit (including credit in this novel form) as a medium for effecting the exchange of goods and services, and the machinery for issuing and circulating it are among the matters assigned to the Dominion under section 91 and not among those intended to be assigned to the provinces under any of the categories of section 92.[63]

[61] *Ibid.*, p. 113. [62] *Ibid.*, p. 114.
[63] *Ibid.*, p. 115.

Consequently the Chief Justice reached the conclusion:

It is not within the power of the province to establish statutory machinery with the functions for which this machinery is designed and to regulate the operation of it. Weighty reasons could be urged for the conclusion that, as subject matter of legislation, in part at least, it comes within the field designated by "Currency" (no. 14 of section 91). We think the machinery in its essential components and features comes under head no. 15, Banks and Banking, and if the legislation is not strictly within the ambit of no. 14 and no. 15, or partly in one and partly in the other, then we are satisfied that its subject matter is embraced within category no. 2, Trade and Commerce, and that it does not come within section 92.[64]

It was this long and closely reasoned argument which was used in deciding the validity of the legislation before the Court. Since the Social Credit Act was itself *ultra vires*, then the Credit of Alberta Regulation Bill—which was dependent upon and ancillary to it—also fell to the ground. The Bank Taxation Bill was an attempt to infringe upon the Dominion control over banking:

It is not competent to the provinces of Canada, by the exercise of their powers of taxation, to force banks which are carrying on business under the authority of the Bank Act, to discontinue business: and taxation by one province on a scale which, in a practical business sense, is manifestly prohibitive is not a valid exercise of provincial legislative authority under section 92. Such legislation, though in the form of a taxing statute, is "directed to" the frustration of the system of banking established by the Bank Act, and to the controlling of banks in the conduct of their business.[65]

There was general rejoicing among the enemies of the Alberta government when this unexpectedly sweeping victory was gained in the courts. It was generally predicted that the Social Credit Board would cease to function now that its powers had been stripped away. While the government had feared an adverse decision on the three reserved bills, the action of the Supreme Court in destroying the legal basis of the whole social credit programme came as a profound shock.[66]

The 1939 *Annual Report* of the Social Credit Board expressed their resentment at the Supreme Court's action, and stated the grounds on which the Alberta government appealed the decision:

[64]*Ibid.*, p. 116.
[65]*Ibid.*, p. 131–2.
[66]They had expected that the Court would reject the two bank bills and one high government official was quoted as saying, "We really didn't care a rap about the press bill anyway." Toronto *Globe and Mail*, March 5, 1938.

The Supreme Court ruled that the Credit of Alberta Regulation Act, 1937, and the Accurate News and Information Act could not be considered on their own merits. They had to be taken in conjunction with other acts passed by the Legislature. They ruled that the Alberta Social Credit Act, which was not referred to the court, was *ultra vires* of the Provincial Legislature. And because the Chairman of the Social Credit Board, which was set up under the Social Credit Act was mentioned in the Credit of Alberta Regulation Act, 1937, and the Accurate News and Information Act, therefore these bills were *ultra vires* of the Alberta Legislature. This was the main argument upon which their judgment was based.

The Province appealed these judgments as, in the first place, its counsel had not been given any opportunity to submit evidence in rebuttal of the grounds upon which the judgment was based, and, in the second place, the principle of ruling that an enactment which had not been referred to the court was *ultra vires* and therefore two other acts which had no direct connection with it were also *ultra vires* was, on the face of it, not merely novel but fantastic.

Prior to the appeal the legislature repealed the Social Credit Act, replacing it with the Social Credit Realization Act. The purpose of this, in the words of the Social Credit Board, was to remove "the grounds upon which the Supreme Court's judgment was based and [to leave] the way clear for the Privy Council to consider the measures upon their merits. Strangely enough," the *Report* continues, "the Privy Council declined to even consider the appeal—because the Social Credit Act had been repealed."

Since the Alberta government was no longer interested in pushing the Press Bill the only case upon which the Privy Council was called to rule was the Bank Taxation Bill. It found no difficulty in upholding the Supreme Court.[67] According to the Social Credit Board's *Report* the Privy Council had reached its conclusion because "the proposed taxation of the banks was considered onerous . . . in face of the incontrovertible fact that the banking institutions because of their power to create money under the rules of the financial system they operate, alone are in a position to pay taxes without any cost to themselves."

The rejection by the courts of the Social Credit measures had a profound effect on the movement. There was no further serious attempt to achieve social credit by legislation, and its attainment on a provincial scale was practically abandoned. Henceforth the emphasis of the Aberhart policy lay in measures to ease the burden of private and public debt on the province, and in extending the party organization beyond Alberta.

[67]*Reference re the Alberta Bank Taxation Bill*, [1939] A.C. 132.

CHAPTER SIX

# The Conflict over Debt Adjustment

THE SOCIAL CREDIT PROGRAMME of monetary reform, designed to give to the provincial government control of credit policy for the purpose of monetary expansion in accordance with Douglas theory, was not the only means attempted to increase purchasing power in Alberta. A less direct method was the reduction of the farmer's overhead through the amelioration of his debt. Already the needs of western agriculture had forced all prairie governments, and the Dominion itself, to enact some kind of debt adjustment legislation. The Aberhart government, which had already taken some steps in this direction, now flung itself into the programme of debt adjustment with the joy of doing battle against the citadels of finance.

The remedy of debt adjustment itself was not new. Agrarian movements in the past had sought to use political power to re-negotiate the terms on which the agricultural community dealt with the rest of the economy. It is an over-simplification to regard these moves as a deliberate flight from the idea of the free market. Invariably the original tactical mistake of agrarian movements was to believe that they could solve their difficulties by creating a freer market. The attempts to reduce the conditions of monopoly in transportation, first through the granger laws in the United States, and in Canada by efforts to create competitors for the C.P.R., were aimed at lowering the railway rates. The success of agrarian reform movements began with their realization that the free market in which they operated was rigged, and rigged against them.

This is not to say that rigging the market against the farmers was either morally reprehensible or economically unsound. The special needs of any age will pull the legal system into a shape which will favour one kind of economic activity against another. A shift in the balance of power, or an impelling social need, will, in the next age, alter the legal context to emphasize new sets of rights which society is prepared to defend and uphold against all comers. The condition of western Canada in the early thirties presented just such an impelling social need, and the remedy of debt adjustment, at least as imposed in the Alberta legislation, involved a substantial modification of the law.

While the struggle with the creditor interests was carried on by political and constitutional means it was in essence economic. It stemmed from the fact that governments and farms, unlike other undertakings, are not expected to go bankrupt. If the income of a corporate business falls, the claims on that income may be diminished by the reduction or abolition of the dividends which are paid to its nominal proprietors as earnings on their capital. If this adjustment is not sufficient the business can reorganize or even go through bankruptcy proceedings so that the losses are spread chiefly among the nominal owners who have provided the capital. No such short-run adjustment is possible to farmers or to governments. If their economic situation worsens, the best they can do is to carry their capital obligations at lower rates of interest as their old contracts mature. But they are unable in the short run to affect materially the burden of "old" debt. Farmers and governments borrow to finance undertakings just as business firms do, but because of the complex process of institutional development they do not raise their capital by selling rights to participate in future income—what Berle and Means call "splitting the property atom"; rather they secure their capital by a straight debt transaction. They are, as a consequence, peculiarly vulnerable to changes in the price level and in their earning capacity.

Another result of this development is that their obligations tend to be held by a different type of investor and are subject to a different set of rules than are the equities of private companies. Bonds and mortgages, because of their fixed income character, are favoured holdings of trustees as well as of such financial institutions as banks and trust and loan companies. The Canadian banks, because of their high liquidity requirements, were not at that time permitted to hold mortgages, but they were large holders of government bonds. The value of bonds—government and other—held by trust and loan companies in Canada in 1937 amounted to at least $1,000 million.[1] These securities are not regarded as speculative holdings and consequently changes in their capital or income value are resisted by exceptionally strong institutional pressures.

The very large concentration of these debt holdings in the hands of institutional lenders is politically important since such bodies are in

[1]A. F. W. P. Plumptre, *Central Banking in the British Dominions* (Toronto, 1940), p. 133.

a stronger position to bring pressure on governments than are scattered and unorganized creditors. One competent observer wrote in 1936:

> The present conflict between governments and financial institutions is not in practice a simple conflict between debtor and creditor or labour and capital (although it undoubtedly arises from the fixed claims to income associated with certain forms of private property) but a conflict between governments and salaried trustees. These trustees who are officials of insurance companies, trust companies, banks, and investment banking companies constitute a small and powerful financial bureaucracy. It is their business to defend the assets under their administration and they may be expected to resist any downward adjustment of interest charges which is not forced upon them by overwhelming odds.[2]

This financial bureaucracy is in a position to resist any change which will adversely affect the assets entrusted to its care. Like all vested interests in periods of social change it takes a conservative attitude because it is better off under the old rules than it expects to be under the new ones. Its legitimate defence is to glorify the status quo and to take advantage of the conservative character of the machinery of the law. That is why most major economic and social changes take on the character of constitutional struggles. What the economic historians call a revolution is a shift in the relative social importance of certain major economic activities. The legal relationships which upheld the old order have to be modified. The principal beneficiaries of the old order are, in such circumstances, quite properly constitutionalists, identifying—as men will—the loss of their own special position in society with the overturning of the constitution itself. Conversely, those who suffer under the conditions of the old order become the radicals.

In western Canada in the early thirties the whole community was adversely affected by the depression. The whole brunt of the drop in national income seemed to fall on the prairies, where nearly everyone was in some way involved in a network of long-term fixed obligations.[3] In some way the burden of these obligations had to be reduced.

[2]D. C. MacGregor, "The Problem of the Public Debt in Canada," *Canadian Journal of Economics and Political Science*, II (1936), pp. 186–7. Also quoted in Plumptre, *Central Banking in the British Dominions*, p. 169.

[3]"The existence of public debts which have to be serviced out of taxes, and of private debts such as mortgages, personal loans, loans to family businesses and farmers, hire-purchase (time payment) agreements and so forth, puts a very large section of the population in the position of equity owners: shareholders in

When incomes fall drastically [writes Mr. Plumptre], as they did following 1928, the problem is not whether, but how, fixed contracts should be unfixed and adjusted. Much adjustment comes about as a result of voluntary agreements. The letter of the law, the pound of flesh, is not demanded. Some creditors adopt a generous position because of a genuine consideration for the condition of the debtors and because they believe that in the long run virtue receives a tangible reward; others reach agreements in order to make the best of a bad and troublesome job. But whatever the motives of voluntary adjustments, they seldom seem to meet popular demand.[4]

The consequences of liquidating such non-homogeneous, personal, and essentially illiquid assets as farms, homes, and used articles of farm and household equipment were bound to be the generation of a widespread sense of grievance and injustice. In time, the result was political, and in Alberta found expression in a determined use of political power to break the hold of the creditors.

Such a policy was bound to be opposed by the various creditors, organized and unorganized, of the province and its people. These creditors were to a large extent, as we have seen, the great insurance, trust, and mortgage companies, most of whom had head offices in Montreal or Toronto and business in all parts of Canada. A considerable part of the earning assets of these institutions was in the form of provincial government bonds, municipal bonds, and private mortgages. The holdings in western bonds and mortgages amounted to such a large proportion of the assets of some companies that a general default or adjustment of debt might so far impair their capital as to threaten them with insolvency. It was therefore imperative in their view that such devaluation of their assets should not take place and they were prepared to resist it by every means in their power.

Just as the financial institutions were singled out by the Alberta government as the centres of malign power to be crushed, so also the mortgage companies, the banks, and the insurance companies, who stood to lose by a general modification of the law in favour of debtors, identified the government of Alberta as their principal enemy. Piecemeal opposition might be shown to other governments, but bargaining and accommodation were possible. The Social Credit government of Alberta was recognized as an adversary of a different calibre. The struggle took place over the whole arena of politics, and the crucial sectors of the front were legal and constitutional.

---

a nation-wide concern which has issued senior securities having a prior lien on earnings. These shareholders—the farmers, the small home-owners and wage-earners generally—not only share in but bear the brunt of, the fluctuating national income." Plumptre, *Central Banking in the British Dominions*, p. 295.

[4]*Ibid.*, pp. 295–6.

Before 1937 the creditor group had no special grounds for alarm in Alberta. In spite of the much-advertised unorthodoxy of the Aberhart government, its programme was no more menacing than that of any other government in a debt-ridden area. The practical men of Bay Street and St. James Street were not worried by the possibility of the creation of purchasing power by such nebulous means as that advocated by the Social Crediters. Even the economists, to whom they paid little attention in most matters, had assured them with unprecedented unanimity that there was nothing to fear from social credit. What they had to fear was the use of political power to compel a general downward adjustment in the value of their western assets. Moreover, they were in the position of having their liabilities in one jurisdiction and their assets in another. If it happened that the legislative objectives of the two jurisdictions were at odds it would be impossible for them to do business. If the differences were extreme—as between Alberta and the Dominion after 1935—their position might be grave.

The creditor interests insisted that they were not opposed in principle to equitable adjustments; they were not, for example, opposed to adjustments before 1935 which merely postponed without reducing payment of principal and interest. Actual debt reduction was to them another matter. In their view it was an inequitable transfer of income.[5] In short they seem to have adopted the position that it would be better in economic terms for the debtors to adjust themselves to the equilibrium position of the creditors, than for the creditors to write down their assets in line with the equilibrium position of the debtors.[6]

This was not the kind of adjustment of the problem which the

[5]"In the endless discussion concerning the debt problem, many people talk of 'monetary reform' as a way out. Exactly what this means is not clear, nor is there any unanimity of thought among its advocates. If it means getting back to the old-fashioned virtues, living within our means and paying our debts, bankers will be all for it and the situation may yet be saved. But we strongly suspect that most of the 'reformers' have in mind some kind of money manipulation designed to elude the payment of debt. In other words, it is our old acquaintance, repudiation, under a seemingly respectable name. There is, in our judgment, no excuse in this country to avoid the payment of our obligations, and notwithstanding statements made in some prominent quarters I do not believe that our democracy will deliberately choose this method. Repudiation, instead of being a solution, is a step which brings evils exceeding those of the debt problem as it now stands. This of itself should cause Canadians to seek a reasonable and fair remedy." The Bank of Toronto, Eighty-third Annual General Meeting, Jan. 18, 1939, Address of the President, Mr. J. R. Lamb, *Canadian Annual Review*, 1937–8, p. S.86.

[6]Interview with Mr. Jules Fortin, Secretary, Dominion Mortgage and Investments Assn., Toronto, May 27, 1946.

government of Alberta was prepared to tolerate. "The slow working of economic forces might, of course, after a long enough time," says *The Case for Alberta*, "rectify the situation by eliminating those most involved through bankruptcy and foreclosure, but this would require, even under ordinary circumstances, a long period of time and is not the sort of solution which the people of Alberta are willing to accept. Neither is it the kind of solution that is desirable from a national standpoint. No government today would tolerate widespread bankruptcy among any class of its population particularly when the cause of debt accumulation is beyond the control of the debtor class."[7]

It is only fair to say that no government in Canada was prepared to sit by and watch the agricultural industry of western Canada grind slowly to a new long-run equilibrium. But there were three different approaches to the problem of adjusting the burden. The mortgage companies, as we have seen, were prepared to accept a postponement of obligations. They knew that they could not get blood from a stone and realized that it was to their interest to keep the farmer on the land. They preferred, however, to make individual settlements on a basis of relative bargaining strength and an estimate of each debtor's position.

A second, and more sympathetic, approach was to recognize that the combination of drought and low prices had created an emergency situation which had in many cases permanently impaired the ability of western farmers to pay off their debts. The solution would be to provide machinery for mandatory settlements on the basis of what the farmer could within reason pay. In that way the creditor would have to write off some of his assets but he would retain a good chance of recovering the remainder, while the farmer would be able to stay on the land, still in possession of his farm and with the reasonable expectation of sufficient income to live on, over and above his contractual obligations. This was the theory behind the Farmers' Creditors Arrangement Act, which Parliament had enacted in 1934, and of the earlier debt adjustment acts of all of the prairie provinces.[8]

[7]Government of Alberta, *The Case for Alberta* (Edmonton, 1936), pp. 114–15.

[8]This theory was incorporated into the preamble of the federal Act by an amendment inserted in 1943 in the following terms:

"Whereas in view of the depressed state of agriculture in the three prairie provinces during the period immediately following 1929 the present indebtedness of certain farmers in that area is beyond their capacity to pay: and

"Whereas it is in the national interest to retain such farmers on the land as efficient producers and for such purposes it is necessary to provide means whereby

The third approach to the debt problem went further. It recognized the fundamental difficulty that the farmer, who was subject to fixed overheads and whose income frequently fell too sharply to maintain high fixed charges, was the victim of a system which failed to provide him with a source of equity capital. The advocates of this approach to the farm debt problem invariably stressed two points: (1) that the problem was not a single emergency, but a recurring one, and (2) that the law should be altered in such a way that the holders of farm mortgages and other secured debts would be forced to accept such modifications of interest and principal as would distribute the burden of adverse price changes more equitably between the farmer and his creditors. This view was put forward in Parliament by Mr. T. C. Douglas in the following terms:

> Why should not the wages of money come first? Why should not the wages of labour simply be written off? That is what the minister is saying. The minister is saying that the wages of capital are the only wages that are to be sacrosanct, that the only contract is a property contract, and that the money that has already been paid out by the farmer and his family and all the work they have put in on the farm are not to be regarded at all. That is his whole assumption. If the proceeds from the farm amount to $5,000 the creditor should take it all, and the man's family who have already paid in so much and have done so much work on the farm go without anything. What is wrong with that, the minister asks? There is a great deal wrong with it. There is a complete failure to recognize the farmer's equity and the hard work that has been done by the hundreds of farming people all across this country. If the minister is going to argue along that line there is no common ground upon which we can argue, because in his eyes the only sacred thing is the obligation to the people who have invested their money. We are trying to get the minister to recognize that when there is a loss, as there has been a loss in western Canada of millions of dollars because of the depression and the drought, that loss must be shared equally by both sides, and the labour that the farmer has put in and the payments that have already been made by him warrant him in having some return from the proceeds of that farm. He has as much right to it as the creditor.[9]

To translate Mr. Douglas's argument into a principle of public policy would have meant, however, a fundamental alteration in the law governing debts secured against land or goods. While it might

---

compromises or rearrangements may be effected of debts of such farmers, and also to simplify the operation of the Bankruptcy Act with respect to farmers generally."

This preamble "exactly describes the intentions and purposes" of the Act, according to Mr. Ilsley. *Canada, House of Commons Debates*, July 21, 1943 (unrevised), p. 5305.

[9]*Ibid.*, pp. 5299–300.

be both just and economically desirable that the burdens should be shared more equitably the law had developed on different lines. "The principle underlying the lending," said Mr. Ilsley, "is that the lender assumes a fixed monetary obligation that is wholly inconsistent with the principle of partnership. The principle of partnership works sometimes to the advantage of the lender, and sometimes to his disadvantage. The bondholder has certain disadvantages and certain advantages. The shareholder has certain disadvantages, and certain advantages. But the bondholder is not a shareholder, nor is the lender of money on security a partner."[10]

Prior to 1936 there was a long history of legislative intervention between creditors and debtors in Alberta to protect the latter—as indeed there was everywhere. This was not unconnected in the long run with the widening of the franchise and the increased availability of capital which decreased the social necessity for its protection. Even before the creation of the province a territorial ordinance, the Exemptions Act of 1898, protected certain property of an execution debtor against seizure under all writs of execution. Such exemption was customary at the time and for Alberta it was defined as a homestead of not over 160 acres or house actually occupied to the value of $3,000, a certain minimum of tools or productive equipment, and food for a limited time. Later amendments took account of the indispensability of a tractor and a motor car to a western farmer. In 1935, mortgage debt was brought within the exemptions by a provision that a mortgagor, under a chattel mortgage executed after the passing of the Act, could claim any chattels as free from seizure under a writ of execution, even where such chattels were included in the mortgage.

The first direct legislative attack on farm mortgage debt as a special problem occurred in the Drought Area Relief Act of 1922, which provided that persons farming in the designated drought areas in the southern part of the province could retain against all creditors enough of the 1922 crop to enable them to maintain themselves and their families and continue farming operations until the 1923 crop was harvested. The Act was administered by a commissioner empowered to file in court a certificate which stayed all legal proceedings until the certificate was set aside.

In 1923 this Act was replaced by the Debt Adjustment Act, 1923, which made it possible for farmers in the southern and east-central parts of the province to apply to a Debt Adjustment Board for a

[10] *Ibid.*, p. 5289.

certificate which, when granted, would stay all proceedings against the property of the debtor. It may be noted that the onus of action was on the debtor and the purpose of the legislation was merely a postponement of proceedings in approved cases.

The impact of the depression led to several extensions of the scope of this provision after 1930. In 1930 actual residents anywhere in the province who were personally engaged in farming were brought under it. In 1933 protection was extended to resident home-owners and merchants. At the same time there was a significant shift in the onus. Under the 1933 Act it fell to the creditor to obtain a certificate before undertaking proceedings for any debt, the whole of the original consideration of which arose prior to July 1, 1932. Without such a permit no proceedings could be commenced.[11]

Up to 1936, Alberta legislation had contained two elements. One was the general body of law common to all Canadian provinces and copied from English statute law, which segregated out for his own maintenance a certain specified minimum of the assets of the debtor, whether the remainder of his assets were adequate to satisfy the secured creditor or not. Secondly, in common with other agricultural communities in the West, the legislation provided an administrative agency empowered to stay proceedings on secured debts under circumstances defined by the legislatures.

It was on this foundation that the Alberta legislature enacted a series of statutes which constitute its special contribution to the jurisprudence of debt adjustment. To the social crediters, and to many other westerners, one of the prime causes of the debt problem was the excessive interest which had been exacted by lenders. These lenders, it was said, had pressed their loans on the province and should therefore share some of the blame for the debt problem. The argument ran as follows:

> Loan companies in many cases were to blame for the manner in which loans on property were granted. Before loans were made the properties which were to be mortgaged were appraised by agents of the lenders. It must be admitted that lenders often encouraged over-borrowing against inflated values and this has aggravated our debt problem. If they had been able to visualize the future, they would have advanced less and would not have loaned in certain areas. It is only reasonable to conclude that they must, as a matter of equity, accept the responsibility for their own poor judgment and should not now endeavour to throw the whole burden on the borrower.

[11]The main elements in debt legislation in Alberta are outlined in *The Case for Alberta*, pp. 135–8.

Another element in the creation of debt is to be found in the high pressure salesmanship of machine companies and other companies selling merchandise to farmers. Credit was offered freely, and prospective buyers were encouraged to purchase goods on the basis of prospective future revenue which never materialized.

It was seldom that a debt was created which did not carry a high interest rate. A detailed study of private debt in the Province would reveal that in many cases the principal amount has already been paid by way of interest charges and in some instances two and three times over. A high interest rate therefore is one of the main factors in the private debt problem of the west today.[12]

The moral foundation of high interest rates had never been firm in western Canada. To the farmer, and particularly to the farmer who had voted Social Credit, there was an important ethical distinction between the principal of a debt, which was justly owed, and the interest thereon, which was regarded as the usurious exaction of a creditor. This wicked imposition, against which there was ample scriptural denunciation, could not be placed in the same category as honest debt.

The Social Credit debt adjustment legislation of 1936 approached the problem of debt with this underlying ethical distinction implicit in its terms. In part it merely enlarged the scope of previous enactments. But it went further. By a revision of the Debt Adjustment Act in 1936 three important changes were introduced. The Act was made to apply to all debts contracted prior to July 1, 1932. It was also provided that the decisions of the Debt Adjustment Board should be final. The Board was further given the power to declare a moratorium.

The Reduction and Settlement of Land Debts Act, passed in the same session, went for the first time beyond the mere postponement of debt, although it was careful to leave the principal sum undisturbed. It provided that the interest which had accumulated since July 1, 1932, was uncollectable, and such payments as had been made after that date should be considered to have been paid on account of principal. It also provided that interest on other debts should not exceed 5 per cent.

At the same time the government attempted to reduce compulsorily the interest payable on its own indebtedness. An order-in-council of 1936 reduced the interest payable on provincial bonds by 50 per cent. This order-in-council was later given statutory form by the Provincial Securities Interest Act, 1936 (second session, c. 11).

These drastic measures provoked a strong reaction from creditors.

[12]*The Case for Alberta*, p. 126.

The Reduction and Settlement of Land Debts Act was described by the *Financial Post* as "an unprecedented attack upon private capital in Canada." This was not social credit, but "a social and economic revolution commonly known as Communism. Recent debt legislation is akin to confiscation of private property. It strikes at the very roots of commerce, business and finance in a way which characterized the early stages of the Russian Revolution."[13] It was also resisted in the courts. On February 19, 1937, the Act was declared by Mr. Justice Ewing of the Supreme Court of Alberta to be *ultra vires* of the province. An appeal from this decision was rejected by the Appellate Division of the Supreme Court of the province on June 4, 1937.[14] The Provincial Securities Interest Act was also successfully opposed in the Courts. The Independent Order of Foresters, a fraternal benefit organization with large holdings in Alberta securities, brought an action to recover in full the interest on $181,000 of bonds of the Lethbridge Northern Irrigation District. It attacked the constitutionality of the Act, by virtue of whose terms it had been tendered only one-half of the interest due on its bonds. Mr. Justice Ives of the Supreme Court of Alberta dealt in his judgment with the question of jurisdiction in the following passage:

> Here the plaintiff is the owner of "Property and Civil Rights" outside Alberta. This Province has no power to limit those rights or their enforcement. To deny the plaintiff its right to bring an action in our Courts would clearly enable the Province to do indirectly what it cannot do directly, viz., modify the Interest Act.
>
> The Provincial Securities Interest Act clearly has but one purpose and deals with but one matter—the reduction of interest. That is its "pith and substance." It is not severable and it is wholly ultra vires the power of the legislature.[15]

The first round had gone against the province and the area of the legal battle was marked out for future encounters. The two Acts had been attacked successfully in the courts on the ground that they dealt with the subject of interest, which had been assigned exclusively to Parliament under the British North America Act. The courts held that, while a provincial legislature can deal with debts because they are a form of property as well as a kind of civil right, the power to legislate

[13]*Financial Post,* Sept. 19, 1936.

[14]*Canadian Annual Review*, 1937–8, pp. 476–7. The case is *Credit Foncier Franco–Canadian* v. *Ross et al.*, [1937] 2 W.W.R. 353; on appeal *Royal Trust* v. *Attorney-General of Alberta*, [1937] I D.L.R. 709.

[15]*Independent Order of Foresters* v. *Lethbridge Northern Irrigation District*, [1937] 2 D.L.R. 109, *per* Ives J. at p. 111. An appeal was abandoned when the Act was replaced by other Acts in 1937.

over property and civil rights cannot be used in such a way as to alter or frustrate federal law in a legitimate field of federal legislation. Even if the effect of the Reduction and Settlement of Land Debts Act had not been to frustrate the provisions of the Dominion Interest Act it would, the court found, have been unconstitutional on another ground. Section 12 of the Act had provided that the Lieutenant-Governor-in-Council might declare any kind of debt to be a debt to which the Act did not apply. This was a delegation of legislative power to the executive which was beyond the powers of the legislature, and therefore on this ground alone an important part of the Act was unconstitutional.[16]

These two first attempts by the government to reduce the burden of debt on the productive life of the province and on the government itself were thus speedily frustrated in the courts. Clearly the attempt to ease the burden by segregating principal legitimately owed from interest usuriously exacted had not succeeded. While the doctrine appealed strongly to the theology of the Premier and the instincts of his followers, it was not one to which the courts were sympathetic.

Although balked in one means of attaining its objectives, the Alberta government was still determined to explore others. The first session of the legislature in 1937 was occupied with the consideration of proposals to reduce the principal rather than the interest on outstanding debts. Actual proposals were at this stage somewhat nebulous, partly because private negotiations were being carried on with the mortgage companies: it was reported that the Dominion Mortgage and Investments Association and the Mortgage Loans Association of Alberta were endeavouring to reach a compromise solution with the government along the lines of the Saskatchewan Debt Adjustment Act of 1936.[17] Whatever the success of these negotiations, a bill was introduced which would have divided debts into "old" and "new" on the same basis as in the Reduction and Settlement of Land Debts Act of 1936. On "old" debts incurred prior

[16]This point has never been dealt with authoritatively by the courts. There are a few decisions in Canadian constitutional law on the powers of a provincial legislature to delegate its powers to the executive, but they are not consistent and no clear doctrine has ever been enunciated. It has been suggested that a provincial legislature has less power to delegate legislative powers to the executive than has Parliament. Cf. G. S. Rutherford, "Delegation of Legislative Power to the Lieutenant-Governors in Council," *Canadian Bar Review*, XXVI (1938). In fact, in some provinces, e.g. Quebec, the delegation of very wide powers to the Lieutenant-Governor-in-Council has not been successfully challenged in the courts. See also chapter x, pp. 186 ff.

[17]*Edmonton Journal*, Feb. 20, 1937.

to July 1, 1932, the debtor need pay only 50 per cent of the principal.[18] This bill was allowed to stand over and was never passed, but a Postponement of Debts Act which empowered the Lieutenant-Governor to declare a moratorium on debts at any time was passed.

In the same session important amendments were made by the Debt Adjustment Act, 1937 (c. 79). This Act, which came into force on June 17, 1937, authorized the government to set up a Debt Adjustment Board as a body corporate with power to appoint agents and delegate authority. No action at law or other judicial proceedings against residents of Alberta for the recovery of debts generally could be instituted without the consent of the Board. The Act applied to debts incurred prior to July 1, 1936, and contained the saving clause that, while proceedings were prohibited, creditors would not lose their rights through lapse of time under the Statute of Limitations. One characteristic of the Act is worth noting. Like many other Alberta statutes it applied only to residents and provided no protection to non-residents. In its general provisions, however, it was very similar to other moratory statutes administered by non-judicial boards in other prairie provinces, and did not differ in any fundamental respect from the 1936 statute which it replaced.[19]

In attempting to reduce the burden of its own indebtedness the government was more determined. Following the adverse decision with respect to the Alberta Securities Interest Act, the impugned Act was repealed and replaced by three other statutes: the Provincially Guaranteed Securities Act, 1937 (c. 11), which prohibited proceedings in respect of securities guaranteed by the province without the consent of the Lieutenant-Governor-in-Council; the Provincial Guaranteed Securities Interest Act, 1937, (c. 12), which re-enacted the provisions of the old Act regarding the reduction of interest; and the Provincial Securities Interest Act, 1937 (c. 13), which reduced the interest on provincial securities by 50 per cent.

The Independent Order of Foresters forthwith returned to the attack and in an action commenced before Mr. Justice Ewing on October 9, 1937, challenged the first two of these acts. On November 1 the Provincial Guaranteed Securities Interest Act was held *ultra vires,* and its companion Act was held to be invalid in so far as it affected the case in which the judgment was given. A writ of execution was awarded against the Irrigation District for the collection of the

[18]Bill 87, the Debt Reduction Act, 1937.

[19]Report of the Minister of Justice dated June 13, 1938, attached to Order-in-Council P.C. 1367 of June 15, 1938.

claim. On December 10 the government filed notice of appeal. The case eventually wound its way to the Judicial Committee of the Privy Council, where the appeal of the Alberta government was dismissed because the two statutes related, in their Lordships' view, to the subject of interest.[20] Meanwhile the third Act, which sought to reduce the interest due on provincial securities, had also been overturned in the courts.[21]

Again the province had been defeated in the struggle with the creditors. Moreover the rejection by the Supreme Court of the Social Credit Act and the Credit of Alberta Regulation Bill in March, 1938, seriously damaged the prestige of the Social Credit movement. Its speedy collapse was confidently predicted in orthodox political and financial circles. But with the defeat of its social credit measures and the need to retain popular support, the Alberta government showed clearly a change in policy in the legislative session of 1938. Henceforth the main emphasis shifted from the frontal attack on low purchasing power to the programme of debt relief.

There was as well increased attention paid to strengthening the support and organization of the party outside of Alberta. One of the chief agencies in this activity was the Social Credit Board. Until its powers were shorn away by the courts and the Dominion government it had been almost a department of government in itself. It now became the principal propaganda agency of the Social Credit movement, charged under the Social Credit Realization Act of 1938 to "take measures for providing the public with information on policies of the Board and to counteract influences likely to jeopardize the realization of Social Credit aims."[22]

In the 1938 legislative session the government presented an aggressive policy of debt adjustment and increased taxation of "eastern interests" which not only caused more real alarm than the social credit programme itself, but looked like a useful electoral appeal for the party in Saskatchewan. The strength of the campaign in Saskatchewan was apparently impressive. "Political veterans," says a report in the Toronto *Star*, "who are not given to panic, are thoroughly apprehensive the movement may sweep to victory there, to establish in that province and Alberta the foundations of a Social Credit Empire that will eventually reach from the Great Lakes to the Pacific."[23]

[20]*Canadian Annual Review*, 1937–8, p. 477.
[21][1937] 2 D.L.R. 109.
[22]*Canadian Annual Review*, 1937–8, p. 484.
[23]Toronto *Star*, May 16, 1938.

The legislative programme became an important issue in the campaign. In the session which finally closed on April 6, the new taxation policy was prominent. With the announced intention of shifting the burden of taxes "from property to production" the Agricultural Land Relief Act vested 7 per cent of all agricultural produce in the province in the Crown. The primary dealer buying such produce was required to account for the province's share. The Act was not immediately proclaimed, pending its reference to the courts. There was at the same time a new tax on banks and other corporations and a tax on mortgages. This latter provided that 2 per cent of the amount owing of principal of first, second, or third mortgages on land, was to be levied on the persons entitled to receive the principal. The tax on banks was increased by 50 per cent. A Mineral Taxation Act imposed a levy of one-third of a cent an acre on certain lands on which mineral rights had been granted, and the Wild Lands Tax, which had been abandoned in 1936, was revived. These were all aimed at large corporations doing business in the province. There was an upward revision of income taxes levied on corporations, additional taxes on loan and trust companies, and an increase in the surtax on succession duties.

Three new acts dealt with debt adjustment. An amendment to the Limitation of Actions Act prohibited any action to enforce debts created on or before July 1, 1936, between the time the legislation should be proclaimed and March 1, 1939, and provided that certain actions in respect of debts incurred prior to July 1, 1936, must be commenced before July 1, 1940. Such proceedings could not be commenced after the latter date unless the debtor had entered into a new agreement for payment before that date. Under the Home Owner's Security Act foreclosures were prohibited on rural homes under mortgages executed before March 1, 1938, and similarly on urban homes unless the sum of $2,000 had been deposited for the benefit of the urban home-owner. The Debt Proceedings Suspension Act granted a moratorium on private debts between March 1, 1938, and March 1, 1939.

Some of these statutes stretched the constitutional powers of the province rather far and almost all of them were highly annoying to the various corporate and creditor interests in the province. Seven of the acts passed in the 1938 session, and two passed in the third session of 1937, were the subject of petitions for disallowance. But disallowance could not be hoped for with an election pending in Saskatchewan. There was a Liberal government in Ottawa, and the Saskatchewan government which was going to the polls on June 8 was also Liberal. Saskatchewan was in fact the last major Liberal stronghold in western Canada. Whatever the elaborate principles which ministers of justice might construct around the use of the federal veto power, the fact remained that disallowance was the act of the executive branch of a party government. Therefore, nothing was done regarding the Alberta legislation under attack while the provincial election campaign was on. In fact deliberate attempts seem to have been made to suggest that disallowance was improbable, at least in the case of acts which were *intra vires*. This is suggested by the following story in the Toronto *Star*, an eastern Liberal newspaper, during the course of the election campaign:

> The decision may not be made known until June 8, or later. June 8 is the date of a provincial election in Saskatchewan in which the Social Credit party is actively participating and the fate of the Alberta measures may not be announced until the vote is completed.
>
> Two weeks ago government policy was said to be generally opposed to disallowance of any act that was within the legislative competence of a province. Several of the bills presently under consideration are held to be in that category, and until last weekend disallowance, particularly before judgment of the privy council of federal right of disallowance is obtained was improbable.
>
> Today it is declared likely at least three of the measures passed at the last session of the Alberta legislature will be disallowed, but not until after the Saskatchewan vote.[24]

At the time of the Saskatchewan election campaign the Social Credit movement attained its greatest strength as a force threatening the established order. It drew thunderous denunciations from the eastern press, of which the following from the Montreal *Gazette* is typical:

> Unfortunately it [the Alberta Government] has not been content to acknowledge the futility of its main policy and as the only sound alternative to govern the province according to established principles of political economy, justice and good faith, but has now run amok through a field of radical legislation that is without precedent in any country, civilized or savage. It has legalized theft. Having attempted to exploit the banks, to muzzle the press, and to tie the hands of the courts, and having been frustrated in these efforts, it has proceeded to the enactment of laws which are equally if not more vicious. Notably, it has to its discredit the Securities Tax Act, the Home Owners' Security Act, and an amendment to the Limitation of Actions Act, all passed this year.[25]

[24]Toronto *Star*, May 13, 1938.
[25]*Gazette*, May 12, 1938.

The echoes of this historic struggle penetrated even to the imperial fastness of Printing House Square, and *The Times* addressed a leading article in its most statesmanlike manner to the question:

> It seems to be feared that if the Liberal Government at Ottawa were to disallow acts passed in Alberta to relieve farmers from their mortgage obligations the Liberal Party, both Provincial and Federal, would be denounced as agents of the money power, from whose grip the Social Crediters are endeavoring to rescue the unfortunate farmers, and that the effect upon elections might be disastrous.
>
> On the other hand, a bold stand against confiscatory legislation demonstrating that Mr. Aberhart and his lieutenants had no power to carry out their promises might well have precisely the opposite effect.
>
> The average Western farmer has no more desire than any other Canadian to evade his just obligations, so long as he is able to fulfill them, and he is shrewd enough to realize that the ultimate result must be to diminish the value of his land as a financial asset and make it difficult for him to raise money in the future.

It was clear, the editorial went on, that some adjustment was necessary because the burden of debt had become impossible. Unfortunately, "the harassed farmer has been tempted to listen to quack advertisers recommending short cuts out of his difficulties."[26]

Nominally, the election was to decide which political party would be able to form a government in Saskatchewan. The world (or at least Canadian opinion and *The Times*) knew better. The stakes were high and the principals were Mr. King and Mr. Aberhart. Mr. King, with all the skill of a matchless party leader, avoided premature provocative action—such as the disallowance of Alberta legislation—and concentrated his energies on strengthening his party's cause in Saskatchewan. In the 1938 session of Parliament, he had been careful to demonstrate where the Liberal party stood in the battle between the common man and the money power. He had been accused of being the creature of the private banking and financial interests. The Bank of Canada Amendment Act, 1938, was calculated to refute the charge.

The original Bank of Canada Act had constructed the Bank as a sort of sham Bank of England, with its ownership in the hands of private stockholders and its control divided between the stockholders and the government. The only classes of persons denied the right to be stockholders or directors of the Bank were foreigners and bankers. When the Liberals came into power in 1935 they had honoured their pledge to nationalize the Bank by issuing new stock so that the

[26]Quoted in the *Globe and Mail*, May 21, 1938.

government had a bare majority of both stockholders and directors, without disturbing the private proprietors of the Bank. They were thus able to gain political capital on two separate occasions by "nationalizing" the Bank of Canada. In 1938 the private stockholders were bought out and with this step the directors all became nominees of the Crown. This measure was carefully timed to play its part in the Saskatchewan election.[27]

Whether because of the nationalization of the Bank of Canada and other measures designed to strengthen the Liberal cause in Saskatchewan, or because the parched black earth of Saskatchewan proved unfertile ground for the Social Credit message, the Liberals won the Saskatchewan election. Out of 39 official candidates the Social Credit party was able to elect only two, in spite of an elaborate campaign in which Premier Aberhart and most of his cabinet had been active participants. Undaunted by this defeat, Aberhart professed that he was not discouraged and announced "we are already on our way to another salient."[28]

But the Saskatchewan election had been the crucial salient and its loss had been the critical defeat. From this reverse the Social Credit party as a national organization never fully recovered, though as long as Aberhart lived it retained its character as an aggressive protest movement, seeking to widen its base beyond the narrow confines of Alberta and displaying a steady and unceasing hostility to the National Policy of the federal government.

Scarcely had the results of the Saskatchewan election become fully known when the central government moved to disallow the more contentious Alberta legislation. On June 16, 1938, before the Order of the Day had been called, Mr. King rose in the House of Commons and tabled copies of the Order-in-Council which had disallowed two Alberta acts on the preceding day.[29]

In all, nine Alberta acts were the subject of petitions for disallowance by various groups and organizations. The Minister of Justice, Mr. Lapointe, in a memorandum attached to the Order-in-Council, enumerated the following petitioners: the Canadian Life Insurance Officers Association, the Dominion Mortgage and Investments Association, the Investment Dealers' Association of Canada,

[27]"In 1938 a Liberal Government in the Province of Saskatchewan was seeking re-election, the chief opposition coming from Social Credit forces; and the Liberal Government at Ottawa, supporting their provincial associates by introducing a popular measure of monetary reform, once again nationalized the Bank of Canada." Plumptre, *Central Banking in the British Dominions*, p. 149.

[28]*Edmonton Journal*, June 13, 1938.

[29]Order-in-Council P.C. 1367 of June 15, 1938.

the Edmonton Chamber of Commerce, the Canadian Bankers' Association, the Hamilton Chamber of Commerce, the Boards of Trade of Toronto, Winnipeg, Calgary, Lethbridge, Montreal, and Three Hills, the Board of Regents of Victoria University, and the Anglican Diocese of Calgary. Representations had also been received from a great number of individuals and corporations in Canada, the United States, and abroad.

The Minister's memorandum included a detailed analysis of each act in order to establish the general scope and purpose of the Aberhart programme. With regard to the Debt Adjustment Act of 1937 he felt that no useful purpose could be served by disallowance, since the effect would merely be to revive the Debt Adjustment Act of 1936, which was similar in principle, and little different from debt adjustment acts in the other western provinces.

The Minister felt that more legitimate objection might be raised to amendments of 1937 and 1938. He noted that the effect, in part, of the Debt Adjustment Act, 1937, Amendment Act, 1937, was to require a permit from the Debt Adjustment Board for the enforcing of a proposal under the Farmers' Creditors Arrangement Act where the fault of the debtor was due to causes within his control. "This provision," said Mr. Lapointe, "would seem to be in conflict with the terms and intended effect of the Farmers' Creditors Arrangement Act and so *ultra vires.*" By the Debt Adjustment Act, 1937, Amendment Act, 1938, it was further provided that a resident debtor could, on certifying his assets and debts and admitting his inability to pay, require the Board to issue a certificate which would have the effect of staying any proceedings upon debts incurred before July 1, 1936, unless authorized by the Board. Meanwhile no dealings by the debtor with his assets were to have any validity without the consent of the Board and the Board was given wide powers to receive and dispose of crops and livestock and to distribute any surplus (after providing for the debtor and his family) among his creditors in such a manner as the Board "may deem fair and equitable."

> The stay of proceedings thus provided together with the authority vested in the Board to receive assets and distribute the same, in its discretion, [Mr. Lapointe argued] constitutes an effective method of coercing creditors. In pith and substance, this is legislation in relation to bankruptcy and insolvency, a subject assigned by the British North America Act to the Parliament of Canada. Parliament has enacted the Bankruptcy Act and the Farmers' Creditors Arrangement Act, but the Province has now purported to set up a rival or competing system based, however, upon administrative discretion rather than upon established rules of law.

The Act also provides in effect that time shall run, for the purposes of the Statute of Limitations (prescription), during the period when proceedings are prohibited by the Debt Adjustment Act. The introduction of this pernicious principle indicates that the legislature was no longer concerned with debt adjustment or moratory legislation, but engaged in a scheme of repudiation as will hereinafter appear.

Mr. Lapointe felt, however, that disallowance on these two acts could safely be deferred. The objectionable provisions appeared to be clearly *ultra vires*, and the fact that they set up, in the instance noted above, a system based "upon administrative discretion rather than upon established rules of law," would not strengthen their appeal to the courts. If the aggrieved groups were unable to assert effective legal remedies against these provisions, sufficient time remained, it was implied, for the question of disallowance to be reviewed by the Department of Justice.

Another act under attack was the Limitations of Actions Act, 1935, Amendment Act, 1938. It provided that actions for the recovery of debts contracted prior to July 1, 1936, must be commenced before July 1, 1940. Such debts would be enforceable after that date only if and to the extent that new agreements had meanwhile been entered into by the parties. "The application of this enactment," the Minister observed, "is not certain but it appears to relate to debts which will not even have matured on the 1st of July, 1940, as well as to matured obligations. A statute of Limitations ordinarily deals with stale claims. This statute, however, deals with claims which are not even matured, and, therefore, are not properly the subject of a Statute of Limitations." Disallowance, however, was not recommended, on the ground that the effect of the Act as a debt cancellation measure would not be felt until 1940. It would be up to the courts, presumably, to decide at that time how far it went beyond the proper sphere of such legislation.

Two of the acts petitioned against were, the Minister considered, evidently drafted to penalize non-resident institutional creditors. The intention of the Home Owners' Security Act was to prevent the commencement or continuation of foreclosure proceedings or sale of a farm home, that is, the quarter section on which the owner's house is located. Similar prohibition was enacted against urban homes, unless the creditor was prepared to deposit $2,000 which would be payable to the debtor on the final order of foreclosure or sale. This act, the memorandum pointed out, made

no distinction between the debtor who is able to pay, according to his contract, and the debtor who is unable to pay. Viewing the Act from the point of view of the relief of debtors, it should be observed that it does not extend to agreements of sale which constitute the security ordinarily taken in Alberta by an individual who sells property to another individual. Thus, one security holder, the mortgagee who is often a lending institution, is treated very differently from the vendors of property, notwithstanding that the respective debtors stand in virtually the same relationship to their respective creditors. The Act is extremely vague; nothing is said as to the rights of the mortgagees if and when the home ceases to be occupied by the owner.

The Security Tax Act, 1938, imposed a tax of 2 per cent on the principal sum of all mortgages. There were heavy penalties both for failure to disclose holdings and for failure to pay the tax on the due date. The tax was imposed on all holders of Alberta mortgages regardless of residence or domicile. Certain exemptions were provided in the case of mortgagees who were natural persons and who came within the terms of the provincial Income Tax Act, that is, were residents of Alberta. To the Minister both these Acts constituted "the central part of the scheme of oppression and repudiation," and he recommended that they be disallowed.

Three other statutes were considered in the Report. The Debt Proceedings Suspension Act, 1938, allowing suspension of proceedings on many kinds of debts, was objectionable on the ground that it applied only to certain debts (debts due the Crown were exempted, and in effect the Act suspended proceedings with regard to debts owing to corporations and not to the debts they owed). However, the Act was intended to be brought into operation only if certain other debt suspension statutes were cut down either by disallowance or by the courts. Since it had not been proclaimed at the date of the memorandum it had not created any damage that required remedy, and disallowance was therefore not recommended.

The two remaining statutes were taxing statutes. The Minister recommended that action be deferred on the Banking Corporations Temporary Additional Taxation Act, 1938, on the ground that the Bank Tax Act of the preceding year was before the courts. The latter had already been found to be *ultra vires* by the Supreme Court of Canada and there seemed little reason, it was inferred, why that decision would not be upheld by the Judicial Committee of the Privy Council. At any rate it is probable that disallowance was deferred in the expectation that if a remedy were provided by the courts in the latter case, the Act under consideration would fall also.

The Tax Recovery Act, 1938, had been objected to by the petitioners on the ground it was "an inducement to the owner of real property to default in his taxes in the hope that the mortgagee may not have sufficient funds to prevent forfeiture and thus furnishes the owner with an easy method of acquiring title clear of his liabilities." This result was not clear from the Act itself, however, and the memorandum recommended leaving it to its operation.

The Minister found that the majority of these acts were part of a grand scheme to alter the legal context in which a large part of Canadian business operated:

Under the guise of establishing a moratorium and of barring stale claims and of taxing property in the province for provincial purposes, the legislature has sought to bring about a general clearance of mortgage debts of the province. Proceedings against the debtor are prohibited or penalized or so controlled by the Debt Adjustment Board that the creditor is practically deprived of all legal remedies. Then his claims are forever barred unless he comes to terms with the debtor and the Debt Adjustment Board before July 1st, 1940. Creditors largely affected are Dominion Corporations, namely, chartered banks, insurance companies, trust and loan companies, established under laws of Canada. These lending institutions carry on business throughout Canada and their depositors, policyholders, debenture holders, creditors and shareholders, most of whom reside outside of Alberta, must bear the burden cast upon mortgagees by this scheme of repudiation and debt clearance. The tax of two per cent upon the principal of all mortgages similarly, is designed to provide the Province of Alberta with a revenue derived to a large extent from outside the Province.

Mr. Lapointe's memorandum then went on to quote at some length from a report of the Dominion Superintendent of Insurance which dealt with the effect of Alberta legislation on the solvency of the insurance companies under the jurisdiction of the Dominion government.

If the legislation remains [the Superintendent asserted] it will be impossible to avoid an impairment of confidence throughout Canada in the institution of life insurance, but that impairment will be felt more particularly by the Canadian companies nearly all of which have substantial assets in Alberta. Canadian policyholders of British and United States companies are secured to 100% of their reserves by deposits in the hands of the Receiver-General or Canadian trustees of which Alberta farm mortgages form no part and Alberta urban mortgages only to the extent of $171,000., while Canadian companies have loaned to the extent of approximately $13,800,000 on Alberta farms and on Alberta urban properties $5,600,000. It is inevitable from these facts that an impairment of confidence will affect Canadian companies to a greater extent than British and foreign companies and the invisible import represented by life insurance will increase.

The report of the Superintendent went on to refer to the adverse effect that Alberta legislation was having on the competitive position of Canadian companies for business outside Canada.

> On the other hand the Alberta legislation has received such prominence outside of Canada, particularly in Great Britain, that the large business of Canadian companies in other countries will be adversely affected. The invisible export represented by life insurance will therefore decrease.
>
> In other words, these imports will increase and exports decrease, which, apart from the inherent unfairness to Canadian companies, must have some consideration from the standpoint of national economy.

The legislation would, in addition, result in so impairing their assets that some companies would inevitably be driven out of business. It was the duty of the Department of Insurance to require financial statements from insurance, trust, and loan companies. As a result of Alberta legislation the Department had been forced to revise these statements either by reducing downward the values of their assets or by increasing their reserves held against them, so that the margin of security on the statements of some companies was uncomfortably narrow. The Superintendent referred to two companies which, as a result of the effect of the legislation under review, had suffered such an impairment of their assets that they would probably be unable to continue in business. The report concluded:

> The Department has been anxious to overlook the Alberta situation as merely a temporary disturbance, and has up to date done so probably beyond what is justifiable. The cumulative effect of this year's legislation with its implications of a permanent policy of confiscation is such as to make it necessary to face the facts before the public must lose their protection.
>
> If this legislation is allowed to remain the task of the Department becomes an impossible one and we might as well say at once that financial supervision by a Government which lacks the power to restrain confiscatory acts of other Governments is an illusion.

Mr. Lapointe's memorandum concluded with the following observations:

> These enactments are unjust in that they confiscate the property of one group of persons for another group; they authorize and encourage repudiation by debtors regardless of their ability to pay their debts. They discriminate in that they seek to relieve Albertans at the expense of Canadians generally. They impose such a burden on Dominion corporations as will drive them out of Alberta, thus depriving Canadian citizens in Alberta of the services rendered by such corporations. If allowed to operate they will injure public and private credit in Canada.
>
> It is one of the cardinal principles of the Act of Confederation that the Provincial legislatures should be confined to the exercise of their sovereign

legislative powers to the enactment of laws, provincial or local, in their operation and objects. The provinces may legislate in relation to "Direct Taxation within the Province . . . " i.e. taxation which shall not directly or indirectly bear upon persons outside the province; "Property and Civil Rights in the Province"; "The Incorporation of Companies with Provincial objects" and "Matters of a merely local or private Nature in the Province." The Legislature of Alberta has not, in the opinion of the undersigned, in enacting these statutes, engaged itself genuinely and in good faith in the legislative field thus assigned to it by the British North America Act, but on the contrary, has deliberately legislated in a matter injurious to the public interest of Canada and contrary to the clear intention of the Act of Confederation.

The memorandum then recommended the disallowance of The Home Owners' Security Act and the 1938 Security Tax Act on the ground that they "constitute the central part of the scheme of oppression and repudiation."

Circumstances had driven the Minister to an exceptionally clear statement of the limits of provincial jurisdiction. He revived the criteria "unjust, discriminatory, and confiscatory" as grounds for disallowance and seemed to impose on the Dominion government the duty of enforcing uniformity of treatment of all Canadians and protecting them against local discrimination. In reaching his conclusion he relied heavily on the stern warning of the Superintendent of Insurance about the effect of Alberta legislation on the national welfare. Taken at face value it gave good ground for federal intervention. The Superintendent had said in effect that a large part of the business of the country could be ruined by the action of a single province, and that it was the duty of the federal government to prevent such a thing from happening. Yet the argument of the Superintendent of Insurance begged the whole question. It was his business to police the insurance field and to make sure that the assets of the companies under his supervision were so employed that all the contractual rights of insured persons would be protected. His task was to watch over the solvency of the insurance business and not to worry over the effects of its actions on the rest of the economy.

It was impossible to imagine that such a titanic struggle over the conditions of sale in the agricultural capital market could continue without a resulting alteration in bargaining power and a significant change in the rules. The Alberta situation was no "temporary disturbance," but a manifestation of emerging economic maturity.

The basic question at issue was who should bear the burden of adverse price changes for agricultural products. This was not a situation in which responsibility could readily be indicated. To some extent the debt problem was not the result either of the market or of the inefficiency of the stranded debtors. It was possible for many westerners to argue that the creditor interests themselves had contributed to the magnitude of the debt problem. The expansion of Canadian life insurance business had been greatly aided by the high earnings of its western assets, and these "assets" had been created in part by the tenacious salesmanship of company officials who encouraged borrowing on land and in areas which might better have been left alone. A good part of the expansion of the last land boom in the West had been caused by the too great availability of capital. The implement companies had also contributed to the problem. They were able to produce only on a basis of large-scale operation and their continued operation depended on high turnover. Around this fundamental need their sales organization was set to sell their product in the desired volume.

But while in economic terms the mortgage and implement people must bear their share of responsibility for an economy in the griping agony of economic contraction, and while they took some punishment in a diminution of their assets, it was the failure of the law which lay at the root of the problem. The courts were applying rules which were appropriate in a period of expansion or even of stability. Under those conditions the law relating to debt rewarded the enterprising and to a less extent the merely competent and industrious, while it weeded out the inefficient, and shiftless, and the lazy. The concept "Act of God" is a helpful recognition that, under circumstances which no reasonable man would be led to expect, the ordinary rules simply fail to promote either justice or economic progress. In essence the shadow of a monstrous Act of God lay across nearly every contractual obligation in western Canada. But the rules had not been changed to mitigate the severity of often impossible obligations and the changed conditions robbed the rules of much of their social validity. If the Alberta legislature attempted a somewhat extreme adjustment of the rules, the mortgage interests for their part continued to resist all modifications. They were, if anything, astonished by the success of their appeals for disallowance and, with petition and court action, continued hopefully to resist all legislative attacks on their assets.

Mr. Lapointe, in his memorandum of June 15, 1938, had promised further study of several Alberta statutes for which disallowance had been requested, but on which he had chosen to defer action. In accordance with this undertaking he reported on March 21, 1939.[30] With regard to the Debt Adjustment Act, 1937, Amendment Act, 1937, the

[30]Memorandum attached to Order-in-Council P.C. 676, March 25, 1939.

Minister decided against disallowance. The petitioners, he said, had urged that the Act was *ultra vires* and he was inclined to share that view. Since that was the case the courts could be relied upon to relieve the petitioners. He was, however, prepared to disallow the Limitation of Actions Act, 1935, Amendment Act, 1938, on the ground that it provided for "wholesale repudiation." He felt that the Banking Corporations Increased Taxation Act, on the other hand, was on all fours with the earlier Bank Tax Bill which Lord Maugham, for the Judicial Committee of the Privy Council, had recently found *ultra vires*. The phrases applied to the earlier enactment by Lord Maugham, "highly selective measure," "discriminatory," "prohibitive," and "singling out," seemed to apply also to the Act under review, and "in these circumstances, it would seem probable that the courts would hold this statute to be *ultra vires*."

By September, 1939, important events elsewhere diverted attention in Alberta from the struggle with "the interests." The period of relative political quiescence which followed in the affairs of the province was partly a result of the war, partly a result of the complete frustration of the earlier Social Credit and debt adjustment phases of the party's programme. It became necessary, as the Social Credit Board put it, "to pursue the struggle for reform by other methods."[31] These other methods—as revealed in the Board's *Report* for 1939—were of two kinds: certain palliative measures which went under the name of the Interim Programme, and a new propaganda line aimed at advancing the political future of the movement in the great social changes which might be brought about by a long war.[32]

The Interim Programme aimed at weakening the monopoly of outside financial interests by reducing the dependence of the province on large financial institutions and strengthening its economy through government-supported economic development. The first of these objectives was to be sought by encouraging the public to use the Treasury Branches of the Alberta government for a variety of financial transactions, for it was felt that "given the alternative of institutions under their own effective control, through which they could obtain the necessary facilities for doing their business . . . the people would be in a position to gradually discard the use of the private institutions whose domination they have had to accept."[33] Economic development

[31]*Annual Report of the Social Credit Board, 1939* (Edmonton, 1940, mimeo.), p. 10.

[32]The significance of this change in propaganda is discussed in chapter VIII, *infra*.

[33]*Annual Report of the Social Credit Board, 1939*, p. 11.

was to be encouraged by the Marketing Boards operating under the Department of Trade and Industry.[34]

There was a lull in legislative activity after the spring of 1939. Only one contentious piece of legislation appeared in the next two years. In the 1939 session the Limitation of Actions Act, 1935, Amendment Act, 1938, was re-enacted nine days after it had been disallowed. It was again disallowed in October.[35] Then in the 1941 session the legislature turned again to the debt problem and passed several new measures which prevented legal proceedings against certain types of debtors.

Eight acts passed in the 1941 session were the occasion of a petition for disallowance presented by the Dominion Mortgage and Investments Association, dated January 15, 1942. Already remedial action had been obtained in the courts against some of these, but the petitioners sought, by a detailed consideration of Alberta legislation, to establish that the legislature was engaged in a design to "break down the existing credit system of the country." The petitioners requested the disallowance of four acts. The first of these was the Debt Proceedings Suspension Act. This Act was objected to both on the ground that it purported to cover debts under the jurisdiction of Parliament, such as bank debts and debts payable outside Alberta, and on the ground that it was discriminatory. Since the Act did not apply to any debts owing by a company or by an "individual" to an "individual," it was clearly aimed solely at debts owing by individuals to companies. Since a company must pay its own debts even when the debts owing it are unenforceable in the courts, this provision was taken to indicate that the Act was intended primarily to embarrass banks and mortgage lending institutions. "It is common knowledge," the petition pointed out, "that trade and commerce is carried on largely through incorporated companies, and in discriminating against them the Act is a direct attack upon the existing system of finance and industry." While the Act had not been proclaimed, and was presumably being held in reserve in case other legislation was successfully attacked in the courts, the petitioners asked that it be disallowed, lest remedial action be barred by lapse of time.

The second Act on which disallowance was requested was the Orderly Payment of Land Debts Act.

> This Act [the petitioners alleged] is another attempt to achieve the same result as in previous legislation which has been held to be invalid

[34] *Ibid.*, pp. 11–12.

[35] By Order-in-Council P.C. 2949, Oct. 4, 1939.

> or has been disallowed. The method adopted in this case is to determine what is "default" on a contract. In previous statutes, such as the Reduction and Settlement of Debts Act, the Securities Tax Act, the Home Owners' Security Act, the legislature attempted to deal with contracts by changing their terms, imposing special taxation, denying access to the Courts or outlawing them. As these attempts have not been successful, a new method is attempted by this Act which gives a special definition of what constitutes default. . . .
>
> What the legislature is seeking to do, in lieu of barring access to the Courts, which it fears cannot be done, is to define what is default on a contract and so seek to prevent a right of action accruing. This is an indirect method of achieving the same result it has sought by other legislation.

Equally objectionable was the Limitation of Actions Act, 1935, Amendment Act, 1941. "The normal purpose of a Statute of Limitations is to prevent parties being harassed by stale claims when witnesses might be dead and the evidence no longer available. Without a Statute of Limitations the administration of justice would be hampered in that persons might sleep on their rights indefinitely and there would be interminable litigation with great difficulty in determining the truth or justice of respective claims." But "the Act in question here is not of that type" but a "disguise in seeking to wipe out debts." It reduced the limitation of time in which actions on mortgages and judgments could be brought from ten to six years, and applied not only to future contracts but to all existing judgments, mortgages, and agreements for sale. This Act was a serious hardship because

> in a federal system such as that of Canada, the citizens of one part have a right to expect that when they do business with citizens in other parts they will receive reasonable and fair treatment. Trade and commerce could not satisfactorily be carried on throughout Canada if a province is permitted to enact statutes unreasonably curtailing the period in which actions must be brought. While residents of a province may become aware of drastic provincial laws of this character those in other parts of Canada are not likely to be so well informed. And they would not anticipate that interprovincial obligations would be affected by an extraordinary reduction in the period of limitation.

According to the petitioner, the real purpose of the legislation did not appear on the face of the statutes.

> It is submitted that these four statutes have not been passed to deal bona fide with matters under provincial jurisdiction but they are a continuance of what has been a general attack on the existing credit system of Canada. Institutions, such as Canadian life insurance companies, loan companies, and trust companies are the chief source of long-term credit in Canada and with the chartered banks constitute the central structure of the established

economic system of Canada as it existed at the time the British North America Act was passed and continuously since. Most of these institutions are federally-incorporated companies. They receive savings from citizens throughout the whole of Canada, and re-invest such savings to a great extent in mortgages. The mortgages and agreements for sale secured on real estate in Alberta held by such institutions aggregate over $50,000,000.

The petition concluded by quoting from the Report of the Superintendent of Insurance on which Mr. Lapointe had relied in recommending the disallowance of Alberta legislation in 1938.

The Minister, in his memorandum, was disposed to accept the argument of the petitioners as to the nature of several of the acts attacked. "While the Debt Proceedings Suspension Act, 1941, purports merely to effect a moratorium," he said, "it is so discriminatory in character that it may properly be described as being 'part and parcel' of the unconstitutional scheme of debt repudiation. Like the Debt Adjustment Act recently held by the Supreme Court of Canada to be ultra vires, this statute enables the executive, contrary to constitutional principles, to deny access to the courts."

Altogether three of the acts petitioned against were disallowed, the Debt Proceedings Suspension Act, the Limitation of Actions Act Amendment Act, and the Orderly Payment of Land Debts Act. No action was taken on the Municipal District Act Amendment Act which the petitioners had alleged would tend to force creditors to assume liability for their debtor's taxes.[36]

This was almost the last disallowance of Alberta legislation. The only other, of the discriminatory Land Sales Prohibition Act of 1942, had nothing to do with the agrarian problem as such and does not concern us here. The long struggle over debt adjustment was brought to a conclusion with the final disposition by the courts of the keystone of the legislative programme, the Debt Adjustment Act itself. On December 2, 1941, the Supreme Court of Canada had declared the Debt Adjustment Act, 1937, Amendment Act, 1941, to be *ultra vires* of the legislature of Alberta. This decision was appealed to the Judicial Committee of the Privy Council and the province, pending the appeal, anounced that the Act would remain in force.[37] Early in 1943 the Privy Council handed down its decision. The judgment of the Supreme Court of Canada was upheld and the Act declared to be *ultra vires*.

Their Lordships [said Lord Maugham, the Lord Chancellor] have come

[36]Order-in-Council P.C. 2350, March 27, 1942.
[37]*Edmonton Journal*, Jan. 19, 1942.

to the conclusion, in agreement with the Supreme Court on the one hand, that the Act as a whole constitutes a serious and substantial invasion of the exclusive legislative powers of the Parliament of Canada in relation to bankruptcy and insolvency, and on the other hand, that it obstructs and interferes with the actual legislation of the Parliament on those matters.[38]

The effect of this decision was not entirely favourable to creditor interests, since the destruction of the main Debt Adjustment Act meant that many claims which had been postponed under its operation were now permanently barred by the limitation of time.[39] A further unwelcome effect was that it suggested that the Manitoba and Saskatchewan Debt Adjustment Acts might also be invalid. Not only would this involve the loss of claims deferred under those acts by the Statute of Limitations, but the operation of the acts themselves had not been disadvantageous to creditor interests. According to the *Financial Post*,

Powers of debt adjustment boards in Manitoba and Saskatchewan have been narrower than those which the Alberta Act sought to convey. Broadly speaking the principle was that a provincial debt adjustment board might refuse a claim if the debtor made, and continued to make, such payments as the board might specify but in some cases creditor interests found the procedure operating to their advantage, as they were able to secure what was in fact, although not in form, an order for a debtor to make such payments as were actually in his power.[40]

Nevertheless, the defeat of the Alberta debt adjustment programme, for that is what the decision meant, was a cause of great satisfaction to the creditor interests. Mr. J. M. Macdonnell, then an official of the Dominion Mortgage and Investments Association, announced that the chief beneficial result of the decision would be to permit creditors access to the courts to assert their claims. The denial of this right by means of arbitrary decisions of a non-judicial body, the Debt Adjustment Board, he said, had been one of the greatest objections to the Alberta Act. The way in which the Act had been administered in recent years, he felt, had enabled persons well able to pay to evade their obligations. He continued:

In some quarters there may be a feeling that there will be a great rush of foreclosure actions in Alberta, but there is no reason why this should be the case. It is to be expected, of course, that some actions will be taken in troublesome cases where borrowers who are able to pay have been taking advantage of the legislation.

[38]*Reference re the Debt Adjustment Act, 1937 (Alberta): Attorney-General for Alberta* v. *Attorney-General for Canada*, [1943] 2 D.L.R. 1, *per* Lord Maugham L.C., at p. 14.

[39]*Edmonton Journal*, Feb. 3, 1943.

[40]*Financial Post*, Feb. 13, 1943.

The number of debtors in Alberta who will be threatened with court actions as a result of the Privy Council decision represent a very small percentage of the total. After all, the great majority of debtors in Alberta, despite the legislation passed by the Alberta government, are honest and made a sincere effort to meet their obligations.[41]

Had western agriculture in 1943 been as depressed as it had been in 1936 and 1937 the reception of this decision might have been far different, and its effect on both party politics and Dominion-provincial relations in the West might have been profound. But by 1943 a combination of improving crops and steady markets at better prices was gradually pulling western Canada back to economic parity with the rest of the country. As it was, real benefits in transitional protection had been gained from the debt adjustment legislation and its destruction by the courts came at a time when the necessity for it had largely passed. Thus it no longer played an important role in the relations between the Dominion and the province of Alberta.

In fact the restoration of prosperity to the West—even on a modest scale—did much to heal the breach between the Dominion and the province of Alberta. A further factor of importance was the death of Aberhart himself and the passing of the leadership of the party into the hands of men with a less acutely subjective approach to politics. Aberhart's death in 1943 coincided with, and to some extent caused, a shift in the relation of the Social Credit party to the main stream of the western agrarian movement and to Canadian politics. The precise nature of this shift will be examined elsewhere.

The question remains why the struggle between the province and the creditor interests was waged so bitterly and so long. To many Albertans it was a holy war against soulless and foreign corporations which had ruthlessly destroyed and drained off the wealth of the province. To the creditor interests it was more than a struggle to protect imperilled assets. It was a vigorous crusade to defend the constitution from attacks on the most sacred of human relationships. They managed to convey the impression that they were being practically expropriated by numerous varieties of "confiscatory legislation."

Yet, thanks largely to the revival of western agriculture during the war, it is unlikely that they suffered any severe diminution of assets. There were some losses which fell on mortgagors as a result of drought or excessive borrowing. But their losses were negligible in contrast with the social costs of the period of the West. The real

[41]*Ibid.*

losses were endured in the human suffering of families whose fields had turned to dust, who lived in a drought in which the flow of cash had been cut off like the rains, where everything had failed them but their courage.

At bottom the struggle was one of opposing legal principles; it was an attempt to modify the rules by shifting the balance of power in the community. The priority of desirable social ends had altered in western Canada but it was difficult to transmute this new scheme of social values into the law. Simply because these values were different they met resistance from the inanimate body of legal principles which already existed. This resistance was exploited by groups who stood to lose by a modification of the status quo. But in the memoranda of ministers of justice and in the opinions of judges the question was resolved on a plane of abstraction. To them it appeared simply as an attempt to introduce novel, inconsistent, and illegitimate rules and remedies into the law.

CHAPTER SEVEN

# Public Finance and the Public Debt

"PERHAPS the outstanding feature of the great depression in Canada," says the Sirois Report, "was the enormous strain which was placed on the public finance system."[1] Three factors contributed to this strain: the nature of the Canadian economy, the division of powers and responsibilities between the Dominion and the provinces, and the economic policies adopted by the Dominion government. Canada, dependent on the highly variable income from the export of bulk staples and relying for its capital on foreign investment, was bound to suffer a great reduction in national real income as a result of the slump in export prices, the worsening of the terms of trade with other countries, the accompanying increase in the already heavy burden of external debt, and the collapse of investment. Canada was thus in the position of all debtors whose liabilities exceed their current assets. If governments cannot pay their own way they cannot hope indefinitely to retain their independence. Just as private law permits the creditor to limit the freedom of action of the debtor, so also the institutional pressures on the freedom of debtor governments is strong. Already as a result of the report of the Amulree Commission which had been appointed in 1933 the colony of Newfoundland had been placed in the hands of the political equivalent of receivership, and the impact of the depression on Canada and its provinces was such that similar political and economic bankruptcy was a very real possibility in the depression years.

Moreover, the reduction in income was distributed very unevenly over the various regions, industries, and classes within the country. Had it been distributed evenly, the burden might have been borne. But in a federal state where both the load and the ability to bear it differed widely the result was that in some provinces the weight was staggering whilst in others it was relatively slight. The decentralization of the Canadian system of public finance made it extremely vulnerable to the uneven incidence of the depression, since

[1]Royal Commission on Dominion-Provincial Relations, *Report* (Ottawa, 1940), Book I, p. 160.

the increased burden on the public services was intensified by the declining productivity of provincial revenues. In the areas where the load was greatest the public finances were so imperilled that the political survival of the provinces was threatened, with consequent repercussions on the delicate balance of the whole financial and constitutional struggle.

The Dominion government, through its control over tariffs and monetary policy, might have done much to modify the varying incidence of depression in the different provinces. However the monetary orthodoxy of that age of economic innocence dictated the adoption of policies which "did little to improve this situation and in some respects intensified it."[2] The depression impelled considerable transfers of income between both governments and regions. The transfers were almost involuntary. Frowned on by the accepted monetary theorists, they were initiated, not for reasons of economic policy with reference to their productivity, but to meet demands created by irresistible political pressures. In any state a theoretically sound monetary policy has to be modified in its application by considerations of political acceptability. In a federal system these considerations will result in extensive modifications to fit both the constitutional allocation of powers and the balance of power between constituted authorities. Such modifications are bound to reduce considerably the effectiveness of the policy adopted. During the depression the overriding considerations in Canada were economy and fiscal autonomy. Neither of these was relevant to the situation and the result was that such transfers of income as took place were frequently too niggardly to be useful or else benefited the more insistent rather than the more productive or the more needful.

In fact the monetary policy of the Dominion further distorted the disequilibrium in the economy which had been brought about by the depression. The cautious observation of the Sirois Commission that Dominion monetary policies "in some respects intensified" the situation grossly understates what actually happened. The commission should not be blamed on this count. They were making policy recommendations which they considered vital and necessary. They realized that needless ruffling of feelings would not advance the national welfare.

The economic problem faced by the government of Alberta was a reflection of the factors mentioned above. The Alberta economy was hard hit by the depression and after 1935 efforts to extricate it were frequently vitiated by the extreme differences between the govern-

[2]*Ibid.*, p. 160.

ment of the province and the Dominion government over the proper principles of public finance and monetary policy.

The problem of unemployment relief was not exceptionally severe in Alberta, being approximately equal, according to the Sirois Commission, to the average for all Canadian provinces. On a per capita basis the outlay in Alberta was the lowest in Canada with the exception of Quebec and the Maritimes. Alberta's relief expenditures arose largely out of unemployment prevailing in the cities, principally Edmonton and Calgary. The city dwellers were mainly dependent for their employment and income on the distributive trades and on investment resulting from rapid frontier expansion. The collapse of agricultural purchasing power reduced employment possibilities, and the number of unemployed was increased by workers and farmers who were refugees from the land. The expenditures on unemployment and on agricultural aid in Alberta amounted to only slightly more than one-quarter of that in Saskatchewan and three-quarters of that in Manitoba. There were relatively few crop failures and the area seriously affected by drought was small. Average yields per acre of wheat during the period 1930–7 were only slightly below normal and were 60 per cent greater than in Saskatchewan. The main cause of distress among the farming population was ruinously low prices. Alberta had been the last frontier, and as a result its fixed debt charges for development were the highest in Canada. The initial overheads of establishment had not been fully met by the Alberta farmers when the bottom dropped out of their market.[3]

The public debt of the province of Alberta was, as a result of financing development in a period of high interest rates, not only very large but very burdensome to carry. The debt charges of the province were the highest of any province in Canada. In 1930 the net debt charges on the provincial budget were $4,300,000, and in 1937 at full interest rates would have been nearly five and a half millions. Only 22 per cent of the funded debt of the province was payable in Canadian currency only, and more than half of the debt bearing coupon rates of 4½ per cent or over did not mature until after 1950. "It is consequently evident," as the Sirois Report said, "that the provincial debt at its original coupon rates was in a technically rigid and vulnerable position, and only small reductions in carrying charges would have been possible through orderly refunding."[4]

It is therefore not surprising that the provincial debt was singled

[3]*Ibid.*, pp. 170–1.
[4]*Ibid.*, p. 239.

out for attack by the provincial authorities. When the Social Credit party took office in August, 1935, the U.F.A. government had already survived over four years of depression. But during that period it had been gravely weakened by losses of leadership and a deterioration of morale, and in its last year in office the magnitude of the problems which it faced had driven it to a hand-to-mouth improvisation in the absence of policy. Thus, the financial problem which the Social Crediters faced was serious, though perhaps not as black as they painted it. It was the first problem to be met before "any steps could be taken to introduce the necessary reforms in obedience to the people's mandate." The Social Credit Board, in its *Annual Report* for 1939, described the situation that had confronted the party on its accession to power:

> The Savings Certificate Fund was bankrupt; no adequate provision had been made for maturing obligations; interest on the public debt absorbed 45.47% of the total revenue; the revenue was quite inadequate to meet current expenditures; the finances of the province had been bolstered up for years by a continuous policy of borrowing which had inflicted a net funded debt of over $153,923,027.49 on taxpayers; and, in short, the affairs of the Province had been permitted to drift into a highly unsatisfactory state.

The *Report* went on to summarize the steps taken to deal with the situation:

> Because it was evident that the democratic reforms demanded by the people would call forth considerable resistance from the financial interests, who alone were the beneficiaries of Alberta's stupendous debt structure, it was necessary to order the finances of the Province so as to render it independent of the financial interests. A halt was called to the policy of borrowing; revenue was stepped up to meet expenditures; bond-holders were called upon to make their contribution towards the reorganization of the Province's finances by accepting a cut of 50% in interest to bring this within the ability of the Province to meet its obligations; the entire field of Government administration was overhauled; sweeping economies were introduced where unnecessary laxity had existed; and generally steps were taken to place the affairs of the Province on a sound basis for proceeding with the reforms to be introduced.[5]

The sequence of events was as follows. Mr. Aberhart's first official act was to appeal to the federal government for a loan of $18,389,000. Mr. Bennett responded by granting a loan of $2,250,000, which he felt was adequate to meet the urgent needs of the province until the date of the federal general election. On that date the matter could be

[5] *Annual Report of the Social Credit Board, 1939* (Edmonton, 1940, mimeo.), p. 1.

reopened. A positive step was taken to reorganize the financial structure of the province by the appointment of Mr. R. J. Magor of Montreal, an actuarial expert, as financial adviser to the government. Mr. Magor had recently served in a similar capacity in Newfoundland. As we have seen his appointment roused a considerable amount of speculation and some criticism within the party.

Meanwhile the government attempted to reduce the interest on the provincial debt by seeking a voluntary refunding of the debt at a lower rate of interest. On December 5, 1935, a letter from Mr. Manning, the Acting Premier, was addressed to the principal bond dealers in the country stating the problem from the government's point of view and making tentative suggestions for its solution. "Since the present Government came into office on the 22nd of August last," the letter said, "it has carefully reviewed the financial affairs of this Province, and has been forced to the conclusion that an adjustment in our debt charges seems unavoidable if we are to meet our necessary obligations and balance our Budget." It would be necessary to reduce the fixed charges, but the province would at the same time "apply the maximum of economy and efficiency," and seek to increase its income by exploring new sources of revenue. The government and people had no thought of repudiating their obligations "but what they would like the holders of their securities to consider is a rearrangement which would bear less heavily in the way of service charges and compensate by an alteration of maturities and increased assurance of security." No complete plan was offered as the government wished first to consider the views of the security holders. However, as a basis for discussion, the government suggested that it might issue a perpetual security of the "British Consols" type covering one-half of the provincial debt of $160,000,000. The remainder of the debt would be replaced by serial bonds. On these two securities the government felt that a rate of 2¾ per cent "would approximate the annual capacity of the Province to pay on debt account." In exchange for the reduction in interest the government offered to strengthen the security of these issues by earmarking the whole of the Dominion subsidy of about one and three-quarter million dollars together with certain other sources of revenue.[6]

This letter did not receive an encouraging response from the creditor interests. No steps were taken to meet with the government or to consider the proposals which had been made. For much of the

[6]This letter and a summary of the events which followed are contained in the *Report of the Alberta Bondholders' Committee* (Edmonton, 1936). This report was prepared for the Committee by J. Courtland Elliott and J. A. Walker.

acrimonious struggle that followed the investment dealers must bear some share of the blame by their refusal to take seriously a proposal which in these days of low interest rates does not seem as preposterous as it may have seemed at the time. Messrs. Elliott and Walker seem a little uncomfortable about this and suggest rather lamely that no action was taken pending the outcome of Dominion-provincial discussions on the subject of finance: "By the time this letter had been received in the East a Dominion-Provincial Conference in Ottawa was in progress and it became apparent that the Dominion Government would issue proposals looking to the formation of loan councils. Under these circumstances it was apparently considered unwise to intrude into intergovernmental plans and no complete replies to the Government's suggestions were received."[7]

When the Liberal party took office in 1935 one of its first steps was to grapple with the problem of Dominion-provincial finance. The Dominion-provincial conference summoned to Ottawa for December 9–13 intended to consider the general problem of recovery as it affected the Dominion and the provinces. The conference was concerned with six different topics, all related to the general problem: Mineral Development and Taxation, Unemployment and Relief, Constitutional Questions, Agriculture and Marketing, Financial Questions, and Tourist Traffic. It was not a conspicuously constructive conference, but the subcommittee on Financial Questions reached agreement in principle on the main problems which affected government finance.

Mr. Dunning, the Minister of Finance, reported that considerable progress had been made in this committee. Three sessions had been devoted to a discussion of (1) the financial position of the provinces, (2) a National Loan Council, and (3) duplication of taxation and a possible reallocation of tax sources between the Dominion and the provinces. No statement was made of the exact stage that these discussions had reached but it had been agreed "that with a view of building on the foundation which has already been laid a permanent committee should be established, consisting of the Dominion Minister of Finance and the Treasurer of each province." Moreover, "the subconference was unanimous in regard to the necessity of reducing governmental costs to the minimum and also recognized that the fundamental solution of the problem of public finance is an increase in the national income, and stressed the necessity of making every effort to shape national economic policies in such a way as to promote the

[7]*Ibid.*, pp. b1–b2.

growth of national income from which all governments must draw their revenues."[8]

The proposed Loan Council was intended to facilitate the reduction of the public debt charges of the provinces through conversion of existing debt into bonds, guaranteed by the Dominion, bearing substantially lower rates of interest. For each province there would be set up a Loan Council, consisting of the Dominion Minister of Finance and the Provincial Treasurer (or their representatives) advised by the Governor of the Bank of Canada, which would have the power to approve both schemes of refunding existing debt and proposals for new provincial borrowing. In exchange for this curtailment of its freedom to borrow, the province would gain the great advantage of being backed by the credit of the Dominion. Such an arrangement would, of course, require a constitutional amendment, the form of which was worked out in the discussions.

In the negotiations which followed the principal obstacle to general agreement proved to be the government of Alberta. It is said that during the conference in Ottawa the discussions regarding the Loan Council were in the hands of Mr. Cockcroft, the Provincial Treasurer, and that the Premier did not concern himself with it at all. Thus Mr. Aberhart's later intransigence was surprising to Mr. Dunning and rather disconcerting to Mr. Cockcroft.

As long as the Loan Council discussions were in progress the Dominion had been prepared to be accommodating in making advances to the Alberta government to aid in meeting maturities as they fell due. But Mr. Dunning hoped that the Loan Council scheme could be put through in time to avoid further *ad hoc* assistance to the provinces after the end of the fiscal year on March 31, 1936. But agreement with the Alberta government was not to be easy.

An Alberta debenture issue of $3,200,000 was to fall due on April 1, 1936, and on March 12 Mr. Cockcroft wrote to Mr. Dunning requesting assistance in meeting this obligation. The provincial treasury, he said, had available $354,000 in sinking funds against this issue and could raise in addition $196,000, or a total of $550,000. He requested a loan from the federal treasury of the remaining $2,650,000. He pointed out that the government had made great efforts in the direction of both economy and increased revenue, and he felt sure that it would not again be necessary to borrow from the Dominion, except for unemployment relief.[9]

[8]*Ibid.*, p. b2.
[9]*Report of the Alberta Bondholders' Committee*, Appendix "B."

Mr. Dunning's reply was far from favourable. A further loan could not be expected, and the Minister of Finance referred to the serious effect which the province's threat of repudiation constituted to the position of all Canadian governments in the capital market. The telegram continued:

> Your letter requesting dominion loan to assist you in meeting April first maturity reached me simultaneously with premier's newspaper announcement that province was about to introduce legislation reducing interest rates on outstanding debt apparently without reference to proposed loan council arrangement. Announcement has already had serious adverse effect on market particularly for western provincial bonds and proposal if carried out would nullify all efforts already made and proposed to be made by Dominion to protect the provinces and the Dominion as a whole. In view of action contemplated by province I do not see how I could justify to parliament and the country the loan for which you are now asking.[10]

The implication of this telegram was clear. If the province persisted in compulsory interest reduction no loan would be forthcoming. Taken together, Mr. Cockcroft's letter and this telegram put the provincial government in a bad light. It looked as if the province was trying with one hand to welsh on its creditors and then, having done so, to reduce the burden of the rest of its liabilities by sharing them with the Dominion under the Loan Council scheme. This was the very thing which Mr. Dunning's scheme was intended to prevent and he was naturally annoyed at the Alberta government for wanting to have it both ways. What had happened was that Mr. Aberhart had not fully appreciated the implications of the agreement which Mr. Dunning and Mr. Cockcroft, in discussion and correspondence, had already reached in principle. The unfortunate coincidence of the Premier's press announcement and Mr. Cockcroft's letter revealed the divergence at the last minute and placed the Alberta Treasurer in a most invidious situation.

Gradually Mr. Cockcroft's position in the cabinet became untenable. He had worked hard to secure the adherence of the government to the Loan Council agreement and he had done much to improve the financial practices of his department. But he was to learn that no minister, except possibly Mr. Manning, had the complete confidence of the Premier. He had to acommodate himself at times to abrupt changes in policy in which his own views were not likely to be important. He was not a Social Crediter by conviction but, like Mr. Hugill, had joined the government because it promised reform. By the end of 1936, at the time of the revolt of the back-

[10]*Ibid.*

bench ginger group, there were repeated rumours that he was about to resign and his resignation, when it came at the end of January, 1937, was not unexpected.

Mr. Dunning seems to have sensed a difference in attitude between the Premier and his Provincial Treasurer over the Loan Council plan, for two days after his telegram to Mr. Cockcroft he addressed, on March 19, 1936, a telegram to Mr. Aberhart. While this telegram was addresed to all the western provinces it was primarily aimed at Alberta. The Minister of Finance repeated his declaration that the Dominion would not, after the end of the fiscal year, offer to assist the provinces either to meet maturing obligations or for general provincial purposes. The Loan Council agreement, he said, implied "virtually unanimous approval" of the provinces, and he wished, since some provinces had raised difficulties, to make the position of the Dominion government clear. He was prepared, if necessary, for an immediate conference with the four western premiers the following week.

To this Mr. Aberhart replied by stating that he would be unable, since the legislature was in session, to attend such a conference until after the beginning of April. Meanwhile, he suggested, arrangements should be made for federal assistance in meeting the April 1 maturity.

Mr. Dunning responded by wearily repeating that five months had already been spent in arriving at an acceptable solution to the financial difficulties of the provinces. It had been made abundantly clear, his telegram pointed out, that the Dominion could not consider making further loans for the purpose of meeting provincial maturities and could not possibly consent to any plan which removed the absolute control of Parliament of the extent to which guarantees and loans could be made to the provinces. A plan had been agreed in conference with the provinces to provide for the refunding of maturities under a Loan Council arrangement. With the unanimous consent of representatives of all provinces, the Dominion had undertaken to initiate steps to secure enabling powers by constitutional amendment, and the requisite legislation was already before Parliament. The January maturity had been met with Dominion assistance in order to allow time for full consideration of the proposals by the province. That reason no longer applied, since two more months had elapsed. "It may be," the telegram concluded, "that the views of the Dominion and Alberta cannot be reconciled but my telegram of yesterday was intended to invite a final effort to avert serious impairment of the credit of Alberta and other western provinces which default on your impending maturity would inevitably cause. Regret impossible for me to suggest any other course."

To this final appeal Mr. Aberhart replied that his government was unable to agree to the Loan Council proposals since the Parliament of Canada had not defined the terms of the agreement; section 1 of the proposed bill in a form acceptable to the Alberta legislature would be necessary before the agreement could be ratified by the province. Mr. Dunning in his reply pointed out that the only thing which was not presented in detail in the legislation was the constitution and powers of the individual loan councils. This, however, had been made perfectly clear in the minutes of the committee on Financial Questions which was attended by all the provincial treasurers. The "sum and substance" of this agreement was that there would be "a council consisting of representatives named by the province and the Dominion Minister of Finance with the Bank of Canada governor acting as technical adviser," which would have the power to approve any programme for refunding existing provincial debt and any future borrowing before a Dominion guarantee would be given. On the same day, March 23, Mr. Dunning wrote to Mr. Aberhart to say that the Dominion government was not prepared to go ahead at that time with the Loan Council amendment if any province objected to its provisions. He therefore requested the Premier to be good enough to tell the Dominion government whether or not his government objected to the terms of the amendment.

Meanwhile on the twenty-fifth Mr. Aberhart had replied by telegram to Mr. Dunning's telegram. The position taken by his government was that "conditions outlined inapplicable to assistance by dominion which does not extend to entire funded indebtedness of province." He then re-stated Mr. Manning's proposal to the bondholders of refunding by the issue of perpetual stock. The following day Mr. Dunning replied that it was already clear from the earlier discussions that a province could, if it wished, make arrangements for the refunding of its entire debt. The method proposed by the Alberta government was one for discussion at the technical level. He concluded by pointing out that his question as to whether the province wished the Dominion to continue with the amendment had not been answered.

To this request at least a categorical reply was sent on the following day. Alberta had no objection to proceeding with the amendment, but it was still felt that the province could not agree "to future loan council regulations controlling future borrowings" in exchange for "a refunding advance of this character." This was the crux of the matter. Mr. Aberhart would not consent to the future supervision of provincial borrowing by the Loan Council, and without it, as Mr. Dunning's telegram of March 30 made clear, the Dominion would not assist the province in meeting its obligations.

This was really the end of this exchange but Mr. Aberhart, on the same day, came back with a further proposal to meet the maturity. He would, he said, agree to reimburse the Dominion out of Alberta's share of the natural resources award which was then pending. He pointed out that in his government's view the natural resources award "would have to be offset against debts already owing by provinces to the dominion amounting in Alberta's case to twenty-four million seven hundred and forty-nine thousand dollars."

It is impossible to escape the conclusion that this lengthy negotiation between these two strong-willed antagonists was bound to fail. It is evident that Mr. Aberhart was trying to use agreement to the Loan Council scheme as a bait to gain Dominion assistance for his maturity. And yet it is equally clear that he would never accept the agreement as it stood. But Mr. Dunning called his bluff, forced him to come into the open and make his position clear, and then left the province to default unassisted two days after his final telegram.

The reasons why Mr. Aberhart objected so strongly to the Loan Council were not difficult to perceive. The provincial debt was incurred by his predecessors. It was an excessive burden and impaired the ability of the government to serve the people of the province. While it must if possible be repaid the carrying charges presented a heavy drain on current revenue. The interest—and to the Social Crediter excessive interest was not on all fours with honest debt—was heavy and it was incumbent on the creditors to recognize this fact. If the burden could not be shifted to the country at large by a Dominion loan then it must be borne by the creditors alone.

To agree to borrow in future only with the consent of the Dominion Minister of Finance advised by the Governor of the Bank of Canada would be bad on grounds of both principle and expediency. It would, in Social Credit terminology, turn over a portion of the sovereignty of the people to the bankers and the money power who controlled both the Dominion Minister of Finance and the Bank of Canada. Politically, too, the step would be dangerous. The Loan Council agreement had already been denounced by Douglas and it could be exploited with deadly effect by those members of the party who were suspicious of every government measure which was not in the nature of an open defiance of the money power.

There were equally strong reasons why Mr. Dunning would be unwilling to budge from his prepared position in the Loan Council agreement. He was a Minister of Finance who was acutely sensitive to adverse changes in the capital market. His own government's ability to borrow and to refund its obligations as opportunity permitted depended on the general attitude of the market, both in Canada and abroad, towards Canadian governments. The capital market, perhaps even more than most markets, is not a place where buying and selling take place as a result of reasoned calculation. Any action, no matter how ill conceived or unlikely of ultimate execution, which promises to improve the lot of lenders is accepted with innocent enthusiasm. Disasters like wars and explosions, which enhance the gloom of the historian and the humanitarian, cause optimism. Equally irrelevant considerations, rumours, and slogans will cause despondency which may drive liquid funds deep into funk-holes.

Moreover, Mr. Dunning believed in balanced budgets and financial orthodoxy. Under this enormous intellectual handicap he was in charge of the finances of a country in the depths of a major depression. The future financial commitments of the Dominion for relief alone were likely to be heavy and incalculable. Every measure which further tied the hands of the government weakened its chance of fiscal recovery. Responsibility for mounting provincial debt without the means of controlling its growth would only worsen matters.

In spite of the intransigence of Alberta the Dominion government proceeded in due course to seek an amendment to the British North America Act which would implement the Loan Council proposals. A resolution was moved in the House of Commons on May 14, 1936, that a joint address be presented to the British Parliament seeking such an amendment. The first part of the amendment proposed to add to the provincial powers certain rights of indirect taxation. The need for additional revenue had already driven the provinces to numerous "direct" taxes which were in reality the kind of indirect imposts which were reserved to the Dominion by the British North America Act. The amendment proposed to allow provincial indirect taxes except on such commodities as were already subject to customs or excise duties, or were destined for interprovincial trade. This would both increase dwindling provincial revenue and also retroactively protect a number of highly doubtful existing taxes. The amendment further authorized the Dominion to guarantee the principal and interest of provincial bonds. As security for this guarantee the Dominion might, where any default by a province had occurred on payment of interest, principal, or sinking fund of such guaranteed securities, (*a*) withhold the subsidy transfer payments made to the province under the British North America Act and subsequent revisions, (*b*) pay over to the creditor any of such subsidy payments withheld, (*c*) reimburse the creditors of the province out of any taxes collected by the Dominion on behalf of the province.

Mr. Lapointe explained that the resolution was the result of discussion which had taken place during and since the Dominion-Provincial Conference of 1935. The two subjects dealt with were of particular urgency because of the serious financial difficulties in which some of the provinces had found themselves in the preceding two or three years. The motion was adopted on division without a recorded vote.

On May 19 the same proposal was laid before the Senate on the motion of the Honourable Raoul Dandurand. After some debate the motion was put on June 10 and lost.[11] The Liberals were still in a minority in the Senate and the proposal was defeated by the Conservative majority. This was the end of the Loan Council proposals. The situation with which they were intended to deal remained serious, but later approaches to the problem proceeded differently.

Meanwhile in April the Alberta legislature had passed the Provincial Loans Refunding Act, which provided for the compulsory refunding of the existing provincial debt at a lower coupon rate. The Act was not, however, proclaimed. In its stead an order-in-council of May 30 provided that interest should be paid on Alberta securities at one-half the coupon rate, commencing on June 1.

At last the bondholders, who had been confidently awaiting Dominion action to protect their interests, realized the danger of their positions: the Alberta government having defaulted once might default again. With the failure of the Loan Council proposals some alternative method must be found to protect their interests, and accordingly a committee of bondholders was formed for the purpose of negotiating with the Alberta government.

The action to reduce interest payments accomplished in two weeks what Mr. Manning's letter had failed to accomplish in nearly six months. It brought the bondholders of the province to Edmonton in a mood to negotiate. The character of the delegation emphasized the contrast between the social credit stereotype of the top-hatted bondholder and the bondholder in real life. There were, it is true, representatives of the chartered banks and the trust and life insurance companies on the committee, as well as representatives of United

[11]*Canadian Annual Review*, 1935–6, pp. 125–7.

States and British bondholding groups. But provincial bonds are a trustee list security. They are expected to possess almost the liquidity of cash and the certainty of income of the goose in the fable. Consequently they are widely employed for endowment purposes by a great variety of charitable, religious, and educational organizations. The organizers of the committee had been careful to stress this aspect of bondholding by including in their number the Treasurer of the United Church of Canada and the President of Manitoba College. No doubt they hoped by this visible illustration of the social effects of interest reduction on religion and education to appeal to the Premier who was known to be prominent in both fields. Unfortunately they forgot that ideology is more important than rational class and occupational interest.

Mr. J. M. Macdonnell of the National Trust Company acted as spokesman for the committee which met with a committee of the cabinet on June 11 and 12. After emphasizing the representative character of his committee Mr. Macdonnell referred to the serious results which were accruing from the action of the province.

> I am sure [he said] it is not necessary to stress the serious consequences which have already flowed from the fear of partial repudiation on the part of Alberta. In the first place, there is the delisting of Alberta bonds in London. In the second place, we have reports of widespread disquiet among American holders. In the third place, there is the effect already apparent on the debentures of the Dominion itself. Then there is the more immediate effect on those funds—Church, school and university pension funds and other similar funds, which will suffer a loss of income. Dr. Robert Laird, who will speak to you later, will illustrate in a very definite and striking manner how close home the results come. Those who follow me will emphasize the effect of the fear of repudiation upon the capacity of individuals in the Province to borrow.

There were two reasons why this eloquent and well-presented appeal should fail to arouse the desired response in the Alberta cabinet. For one thing the evidence of damage was largely external to Alberta. It might bring hardship to many worthy and godly persons, but most of them were not voters in the province of Alberta. Second, and more important, the Social Crediters did not care whether or not they permanently impaired their ability to borrow. Debt to them was bad. It was the source of evil and the nexus which bound the people to the designs of the money power. The essence of Social Credit was that credit should be freely provided by the state. Borrowing from private sources, no matter how eminent, involved the double price of usury and subjection to the money power. Thus in their whole attack on the debt problem they were not hampered by fears about long-run consequences. They were the vanguard of a revolution which would free the world from the evil habit, debt.

Mr. Macdonnell turned from his introduction to definite proposals. "The debenture holders in the mass naturally find it hard to believe that a great Province like Alberta, with its vast and varied resources, cannot pay its debts. The debenture holders in the mass naturally believe that there is a *prima facie* case for payment in full, and you will realize that they have had no information presented to them to indicate that there is any necessity for them to accept less than the amount contracted to be paid. Nevertheless debenture holders are reasonable men and we believe that they will be ready, as sensible crditors should be, to examine the situation, through their representatives, with an open mind." Accordingly the committee proposed that the debenture holders "should be allowed to make a full study of the situation in order to reach a conclusion, based on a full knowledge of the situation." The committee wished to have such a study commenced at once by Mr. Courtland Elliott, who had accompanied them. It was further requested that no attempt be made to reduce interest payments until the study had been completed—a date set tentatively at August 1.

The government announced that it was quite willing that the study should be made, but was not prepared to defer the reduction of interest payments as the committee had wished. Accordingly Mr. Elliott proceeded, assisted by Mr. J. A. Walker, to prepare a study of the ability of the Alberta economy to meet its collective obligations. This study was completed on July 17, 1936.

In their conclusions Messrs. Elliott and Walker referred to the productive and necessary character of the provincial debt. "As far as government finance was concerned, recourse to public credit was had to bring to the people of the area the amenities of life which seemed to be warranted by the rapid development of private enterprise." This borrowing, while proportionately heavier than that in the East, was not injudicious. In fact most of it "was imperative and Alberta could not have achieved the degree of development and the standard of living it subsequently attained without it." Thus the public debt of the province was not, in 1929, materially out of line with the rest of Canada.

The Alberta economy was, however, highly vulnerable since agriculture had been responsible for about 70 per cent of the net value of production in the years 1920–34, and the fall in agricultural income had been a major feature of the depression in the West. While the fall in money income had been to some extent offset by a much less steep fall in real income, the effect of the depression upon Alberta had been severe.

Nevertheless, Alberta had not been exceptionally hard hit. In fact, "the only conclusion that can be derived from the official statistics is that, while Alberta has borne a full share of depression burdens, there is no especially marked indication that the plight of Alberta is unduly more severe than elsewhere. There is, therefore, no apparent reason why Alberta should be singled out for any preferential treatment except in special distressed areas. Proposals for national reconstruction can seldom proceed on a basis of sectional discrimination."

The effect of reduced interest payments, it was pointed out, would merely be to reduce fixed charges on the 1937–8 budget by a little over three and one half millions, "an amount which could hardly represent any relief in the daily lives of Alberta citizens." Indeed, this benefit would be more than offset by "the incalculable economic and financial damage that would be wrought both within and without the borders of Alberta." Instead of fastening on interest payments which were a small part of Alberta's problem it would be much more useful to devote attention to "the vital problems of loss of earned income and capital values." Stress was laid in the report on the desirability of relying as far as possible on the natural recuperative forces of the economy which would achieve a more stable long-run equilibrium than any which could be brought about in other ways. "The processes of economic adaptation are slow and impatience for better days is thoroughly understandable. Yet statistical analysis of the events of recent years has shown an astonishing ability on the part of the economic organization to sustain successive shocks and, when the crisis has passed, to become slowly adapted to the new and altered relationships. The danger is that public opinion, failing to perceive the extent of the readjustments achieved, will accept short-cuts and short-sighted policies which can only retard the process of adaptation."

Consequently, it was concluded, "the solution of Alberta's problem lies in the enlarging of income. Already substantial progress has been achieved. It seems apparent, therefore, that from an economic standpoint reduction or even total suspension of provincial interest payments can bring no appreciable temporary or permanent advantage to the people of Alberta."[12]

[12]The above quotations are taken from the *Report of the Alberta Bondholders' Committee.* Chapter II of this mimeographed report (commonly referred to by the names of its authors as the Elliott-Walker Report) gives a summary of events leading up to the commissioning of the report; the conclusions quoted are from chapter IV, and the Dunning-Aberhart correspondence is reproduced in full as Appendix "B."

The government of Alberta was unmoved by the arguments of the Elliott-Walker Report and continued its determination to use interest reduction as a method of budget balancing. Although the statutory basis of interest reduction was declared *ultra vires* when the Provincial Securities Interest Act was rejected by the Canadian courts and ultimately by the Judicial Committee of the Privy Council,[13] the province continued to tender interest to holders of its bonds at a reduced rate without any sign of a settlement being reached. By August, 1939, the defaults on principal and interest had reached about twelve million dollars.[14]

The Bondholders' Committee were not alone in commissioning outside investigations of the financial affairs of Alberta. As part of a systematic attempt to place Dominion-provincial financial relations on a sounder footing—of which the Loan Council negotiations had been the beginning—Mr. Dunning, the Minister of Finance, commissioned the Bank of Canada to prepare reports on the finances of the three prairie provices.

On February 11, the report on Manitoba was submitted to the Dominion government and on March 6 and April 7, respectively, the reports on Saskatchewan and Alberta were presented. Saskatchewan "for reasons largely beyond its control" was reported by the Bank to be in a particularly unfortunate position. Total relief expenditures up to the end of 1936 had been $110 million, of which municipalities had contributed $5 million and the province $13 million together with another $5 million in guaranteed loans to municipalities. The remaining $87 million had been contributed by the Dominion—$40 million outright and the balance in loans and guarantees. "As in the case of Manitoba," the report said, "we do not see any solution other than that which might be provided by a complete inquiry into the financial powers and responsibilities of all our governing bodies." Any workable solution was bound to be expensive because "in no section will credit be so necessary in the future and in no other section is it now so important to maintain confidence in the good faith of borrowers."

If Alberta had continued to pay its interest obligations in full, the Bank found, it would also have been forced to borrow from the Dominion, and its position would have been "a little worse than that of Manitoba but distinctly better than that of Saskatchewan." While the reduction in interest payments had put the province in a position

[13]This was the lengthy litigation between the Order of Foresters and the Lethbridge Irrigation District. Cf. chapter VI, above.

[14]*Edmonton Journal*, Aug. 21, 1939.

where it was not dependent on assistance by the Dominion the repercussions of default would in due course affect its situation adversely. The Bank's report differed from the Elliott-Walker Report in assessing the immediate value of interest reduction. It found that "Alberta's budgetary position differs materially from that of the other provinces, by reason of the fact that interest payments have been reduced by 50 per cent, or $3,400,000, and, other things being equal, its cash requirements have been reduced by the same amount."[15]

After the submission of the Bank's report on Manitoba, the government had acceded to its recommendation by announcing that it would launch a thorough investigation of the whole range of Dominion-provincial financial relations. By Order-in-Council P.C. 2880, dated August 14, 1937, a Royal Commission on Dominion-Provincial Relations was appointed for the purpose of "a re-examination of the economic and financial basis of Confederation and of the distribution of legislative powers in the light of the economic and social developments of the last seventy years." This Commission was originally made up of Chief Justice Newton W. Rowell of Ontario, Mr. Justice Thibaudeau Rinfret of the Supreme Court of Canada, Mr. John W. Dafoe, of Winnipeg, and Professors R. A. MacKay of Dalhousie University and H. F. Angus of the University of British Columbia. Resignations through ill-health deprived the Commission of Mr. Justice Rinfret and the Chairman, Chief Justice Rowell; Professor Joseph Sirois of Laval University was added to the Commission and became its Chairman.[16]

While no government willingly makes itself a hostage to fortune by giving investigating powers to a royal commission of persons known to be hostile to its views, the government had on this occasion commissioned a body of men of unusual ability and known independence of judgment. The reason for this lay in the fact that, although royal commissions are usually appointed either to delay action indefinitely or to provide an acceptably innocuous solution for partisan ends, the problem faced by this particular Commission was one which the government was anxious to solve on a lasting basis. Although an exhaustive investigation would provide a welcome breathing space for the government, there can be no doubt that the conclusions of the Commission were intended to be taken seriously.

The personnel and purpose of the Commission did not, however,

[15]*Canadian Annual Review,* 1937–8, pp. 12–13.

[16]Royal Commission on Dominion-Provincial Relations, *Report* (Ottawa, 1940) pp. 9–10.

make a strong appeal to the government of Alberta. Premier Aberhart promptly issued a statement declaring that the Commission was biased, having views for the most part known to be in direct conflict with the policies of the Alberta government. "This government," he said, "cannot believe that a Liberal government at Ottawa actually is selecting an obviously biased commission to recommend an entire revision of our constitution." The personnel of the Commission meant that its recommendations were certain to be "rigidly within the framework of the present antisocial financial system" and its recommendations, if adopted, "would inevitably mean tearing up the B.N.A. Act and substituting for it a charter drafted in the interests of finance."[17]

Major Douglas had repeatedly warned the Alberta government that attempts would be made to frustrate its programme by constitutional amendment aimed at reducing the fiscal autonomy of the provinces. The centralization of financial burdens and responsibilities, in his view, was bound to be a method by which international finance would attempt to protect its interests and strengthen its control over the credit of the people. According to the first *Annual Report* of the Social Credit Board:

> On July 20th, Major Douglas warned the Board as to the probability of both the composition and the terms of reference of the Royal Commission on Dominion-Provincial Relations which was likely to be set up. At the same time he pointed out that the recommendations of any such commission were absolutely certain to suggest a strengthening of the grip of the Bank of Canada upon the provinces.
>
> Subsequently when the commission was hurriedly appointed following disallowance of Alberta's legislation, Major Douglas' warning was vindicated, as Honourable Members now appreciate.
>
> In carrying out this warning from Major Douglas, your Board recommended no submission be made to the Royal Commission on Dominion-Provincial relations but that every effort be made to bring together the western provinces in an enquiry conducted by a commission of their own selection, and under conditions commanding the confidence of their own people. The force of this will be appreciated when it is realized that the essential nature of the struggle in which Alberta is engaged is the Individual versus the Institution, and any submission made of the people's case which is presented should be to a court which is fully cognizant of the nature of the issues involved.
>
> Your Board would like to place on record before the Legislature a warning that every action which can be taken towards weakening provincial autonomy, and centralizing control in the interest of the Bank of Canada, will be taken in every sphere of our national life. It is the consistent policy of your Board to watch the developments throughout the Dominion and to

[17]*Edmonton Journal*, Aug. 18, 1937.

draw the attention of your Government to any attempts made to weaken the Province and strengthen that of centralized Dominion control.[18]

Undoubtedly two factors, in addition to the fiat of Major Douglas, induced the Alberta government to exhibit consistent hostility to the Royal Commission. While its aggressive legislative programme gave it the appearance of an embattled champion of the people against the interests, the unqualified failure of its measures to survive without either being disallowed or held *ultra vires* by the courts was bound to bring a certain loss of prestige. Thus a fresh campaign against the hypothetical conclusions of a royal commission then sitting would be good evidence of the eternal vigilance of the government and the multiplicity of its enemies. Here, at least, no reverses were possible since there was no concrete issue involved. In addition, as it became clear that the task of attaining power nationally was going to be formidable it seemed good tactics to press the powers of the legislature of Alberta to the limit, for it was from Alberta that the ultimate sally would have to be made.

Accordingly the government refused to give evidence before the Commission and instead prepared, in *The Case for Alberta*, a lengthy brief describing its position, addressed "to the Sovereign People of Canada and their Governments."[19] In the introduction to this work they set forth a theory of provincial rights as the basis of their case against fiscal reform. "The Government of Alberta does not concur in the view that the constitutional structure so carefully planned by the Fathers of Confederation has materially failed, that is in so far as the distribution of legislative powers is concerned. Neither does it share the view taken by some that in order to meet adequately the problems of the day there is any need for a wide transference of powers and legislative authority from the Provinces to the Dominion or from the Dominion to the Provinces."[20] The true solution to the problem lay not in a revision of the financial relationships now existing between the Dominion and the province but in "a fundamental reform of the financial system."[21]

*The Case for Alberta* is divided into two parts. The first part is a survey of the problems of the Alberta economy and concludes with a series of policy recommendations which were made "within the limi-

[18]*Annual Report of the Social Credit Board, 1937–38* (Edmonton, 1938, mimeo.), p. 12.
[19]Edmonton, 1938.
[20]*Ibid.*, p. 9.
[21]*Ibid.*, p. 10.

tations of the present defective monetary system and its adaptation to meet the transition period to a new economic order."[22] Thirteen recommendations were put forward: (i) the Dominion should cancel the portion of outstanding provincial treasury bills which represented relief expenditure; (ii) the Dominion should at least share the responsibility for drought relief, irrigation development, and provincial railway development, and share the loss resulting from the alienation of natural resources; (iii) because of the adverse effect of tariff, high interest rates, and Dominion monetary policy, the Bank of Canada should underwrite the refunding of the balance of the provincial debt at a rate of interest of 2 per cent or less; (iv) the Dominion should either deal with the problem of civic, municipal, and private debt or allow the province to do so; (v) the Dominion should assume responsibility for relief and old age pensions; (vi) the Dominion should inaugurate and maintain adequate grants for public health services, education, mothers' allowances, and highway construction and maintenance; (vii) the Dominion should undertake the construction and maintenance of a properly surfaced transcontinental highway; (viii) the Dominion should provide an arterial highway from the United States border to the northern areas with branches to the national parks at Banff and Jasper; (ix) the Dominion should construct and maintain water storage reservoirs in the foothills and assume the cost of rehabilitation of the drought area; (x) agricultural credits at low rates and for long terms should be provided through the Bank of Canada; (xi) the Dominion should provide "adequate monetary facilities" for an extensive home-building programme: (xii) the Dominion should actively assist in promoting markets for Alberta products and also provide for minimum prices for wheat and livestock; and, finally, (xiii) the freight rate structure should be revised on a more equitable basis.[23]

In the aggregate these recommendations were a repetition of the usual demands of western agrarianism, leavened by expansionist measures copied from the New Deal in the United States. A good many of them have now passed into the realm of national policy or of national policy objectives. As stabilization measures they were in most cases useful and well within the means of the Dominion to perform.

And yet they were very one-sided. They consisted entirely of suggestions for further Dominion responsibilities without facing the ques-

[22]*Ibid.*, p. 377.
[23]*Ibid.*, pp. 375–7.

tion of adequate Dominion powers. Here lay a problem which was distinguished clearly by the Rowell-Sirois Commission. To carry these responsibilities the Dominion needed to be assured of elastic and controllable sources of revenue. This meant that the double taxation in both direct and indirect fields which reduced the productivity of tax revenues would have to be eliminated and that the Dominion's uncontrollable responsibilities for baling out unseaworthy provincial governments would have to be defined if not reduced. Furthermore, in order for the Dominion measures to be effective, the whole structure of public finance in the country would have to be integrated. Fiscal policy is not merely a matter of raising revenue and spending it. The way in which revenue is raised and the timing of taxation and expenditure are important. The provinces were in a position to vitiate completely, by regressive taxation and ill-timed borrowing and spending, any fiscal or monetary measures which the Dominion might initiate. The most important change in the constitution since Confederation was the enlargement of provincial responsibilities which destroyed the monopoly of fiscal and monetary policy, explicity or implicity assigned to the Dominion in the British North America Act.

To the Social Crediter, however, the problem of boom and depression was not to be resolved by fiscal and monetary measures. It could only be solved by attacking the central evils of society as envisaged by social credit theory. The implications of this view are fully developed in Part II of *The Case for Alberta.* Here the thesis is expounded that the root cause of the economic troubles of the time stems from the fact that financial policy, instead of being controlled by the people, is exploited for profit by a financial monopoly. The principal need is to establish democracy, "that is democracy in the correct sense of the term."[24] Specifically it recommended that the province be confirmed in the powers over credit control and debt adjustment which had been denied it by judicial interpretation and disallowance, and urged the calling of a Dominion-provincial conference to discuss its proposals. The government of Alberta was prepared to test the soundness of its economic proposals by putting them to the test. All it asked was non-interference. "Is it too much to ask that our Province be afforded the privilege of leading the way out of the present chaos of poverty, debt and crushing taxation in a land of abundance and promise?"[25]

"These recommendations," said the *Annual Report of the Social Credit Board* for 1939, "will stand out in contrast to those which are

[24]*Ibid.*, p. 51.
[25]*Ibid.*, p. 55.

likely to be submitted by the Royal Commission on Dominion-Provincial Relations for transferring to the Federal Government certain responsibilities at present assumed by the provinces, in return for the centralization of powers in the Federal Government and the Bank of Canada, the adoption of which would lead to an intensification of our present difficulties." It was "fantastic" to suggest that the present difficulties could be solved without radical reform, merely by exchanging a number of provincial problems for one huge national problem. More important still, such changes would reduce the provinces to the status of glorified municipalities "rendered helpless to order their own affairs within their own boundaries in such important matters as wages, hours of work, debts, transportation and everything else of an essential nature to their economic welfare. Gone would be the last venture [*sic*-vestige?] of their constitutional provincial property and civil rights, for all practical purposes."[26]

There was plenty of evidence, in the Board's view, that a carefully planned campaign of propaganda directed towards gaining support for a centralization of control was being developed "as a build-up" for the report of the Royal Commission. "It can be assumed with certainty," the Board's *Report* said, "that the banks and other financial institutions will not sit with folded hands and watch the people of Alberta gain their freedom from financial bondage." Strong financial pressure would be placed on the people by these institutions, and attempts would be made to wreck the Treasury Branch programme; "threats of curtailed credit to persons co-operating under the Interim Programme, pressure on merchants through wholesale houses, an organized boycott of Alberta products, exorbitant exchange rates on cheques" were some of the expedients that might be expected. The main attack, however, would be a bold and determined effort to divest Alberta, and incidentally the other provinces, of the constitutional power to carry out any reforms or "to protect itself from the ravages of financial tyranny." In the national field this would be accomplished through the recommendations of the Royal Commission; the report would probably "be carefully prepared to give the impression that it is favourable to the provinces," but the effect of its recommendations would be "the centralization of all effective power in the Federal Government and the Bank of Canada." The beneficent results of centralization to the financial interests would be twofold. It would on the one hand "dispose of Alberta" and on the other would entrench these same interests more strongly than ever. The provinces would

[26]*Annual Report of the Social Credit Board,* 1939, p. 23.

be weakened as laboratories of experiment. "At present if the people of Alberta or of any other Province desire reforms in regard to any matter coming under the jurisdiction of their own legislature, they can easily unite to bring pressure on their Provincial government to get these reforms. But if the legislative authority was vested in Parliament they would be helpless to gain the reforms they wanted within their own province unless the majority of the people in the country could be induced to press for them. In other words, the power of the electorate is weakened and the power of the financial interest to defy the electorate would be strengthened."[27]

It is thus reasonably clear why the government of Alberta did not regard the Royal Commission as an instrument likely to produce an acceptable solution to the problem of Dominion-provincial relations. Consistent with this attitude they did nothing whatever to assist the Commission in its work. Incidentally, this is remarkable since they claimed to have co-operated fully with other studies of the province, including that leading to the Elliott-Walker Report. Not only did the government refuse to appear or submit a brief to the Commission, they refused to permit any officials to appear before it. The result was that the only substantial brief presented at the Edmonton hearings was submitted by the Edmonton Chamber of Commerce. It must be recalled that this melancholy incident was not the only rebuff suffered by the Commission. It was received more courteously, but not much more helpfully, by the governments of Ontario and Quebec.[28]

Alberta and the Dominion had now reached a high point of mutual frustration. The conflict ranged over the areas of debt and monetary policy, and across the whole field of intergovernmental relations. During 1939 the province revived the proposal that the part of the Northwest Territory lying between its northern boundary and the Arctic seas be transferred to the province. This was an old proposal, said first to have been made to the province in the time of the U.F.A. government. At that time the province rejected the proposal on the ground that it involved more expense than advantage. However new discoveries of mineral wealth and improvements in air transport had altered the immediate, as well as the potential value of the North. In the 1939 session a resolution was passed by the legislature approving the opening of negotiations for the transfer from the Dominion of the territory between the northern boundary of the province and the Arctic circle, an area of half a million square miles which would have doubled

[27]*Ibid.*

[28]Royal Commission on Dominion-Provincial Relations, *Report*, Book I, p. 16.

the size of Alberta. Negotiations were subsequently opened with the Dominion government.[29] Apparently these negotiations were in some degree involved with the question of the Rowell-Sirois inquiry, for after the breakdown of the Dominion-provincial conference of January, 1941, the attitude of the federal government cooled considerably and the proposed agreement fell through.[30]

In May, 1940, the Royal Commission on Dominion-Provincial Relations, after having held hearings across Canada and digested over ten thousand mimeographed pages of evidence, presented its report to the federal cabinet. This report was a massive document, including a definitive study of the history and development of intergovernmental financial relations and a series of proposals for their modification. It was the hope of the Commission that these proposals would "enable Canada to withstand the stresses and strains of today and tomorrow without undue peril either to reasonable national unity or to legitimate provincial autonomy."[31]

Little time was lost in summoning a Dominion-provincial conference to consider its recommendations. On November 2, 1940, Mr. King wrote to the nine provincial premiers stating that the Report of the Royal Commission commended itself strongly to the judgment of his cabinet and that in their view a conference should be arranged with the provinces to secure, if possible, the adoption of its recommendations. This letter was tabled in the House of Commons on November 7 and replies were received at the same time from all the provincial premiers agreeing to attend a conference in January.[32]

Accordingly, on January 14, 1941, the conference assembled in the House of Commons Chamber to hear Mr. King's opening address. The Prime Minister pointed out that while the locus of the problem of Dominion-provincial finance had shifted as a result of the war it remained in as acute form as before. Though the burden of relief was gradualy being reduced as the war economy got under way the problem of revenue to finance war operation had become more serious than ever. "We feel too that while our energies at present must be concentrated upon the prosecution of the war, neither the federal nor the provincial governments can afford to neglect the future. The perpetuation of the existing inequality, inefficiency and duplication of our governmental financial structure wil leave us in no position to

[29]*Edmonton Journal*, Aug. 21, 1939.
[30]Edmonton *Bulletin*, March 14, 1941.
[31]*Report*, Book II, p. 10.
[32]*Dominion-Provincial Conference, January 14th and 15th, 1941* (Ottawa, 1941), pp. v–x.

make the social and economic adjustments which will be necessary after the war. The war will inevitably be followed by a period of reconstruction which will impose new obligations and burdens upon all Canadian governments."[33] Accordingly, he felt that adjustments in intergovernmental financial relations would make the country better equipped to meet the needs of both war and reconstruction.

The essence of the Commission's proposals, he said, were (1) that the Dominion take over the whole burden of provincial net debt; (2) that the Dominion relieve the provinces, and therefore also the municipalities, of the whole burden of relief for unemployed employables and their dependents; (3) that the Dominion be conceded exclusive rights to levy succession duties, and taxes on corporate and personal incomes; (4) that existing provincial subsidies should be abolished, and where necessary the Dominion should make to the provinces national adjustment grants, calculated to maintain an average Canadian standard of both services and taxation.

In speaking of the advantages of these various proposals he made a reference to the debt problem that was particularly relevant to Alberta. While the proposed plan would impose a heavy burden on the federal government it would confer three important advantages. It would lift the burden of debt from people living in areas incapable of bearing it, whether from loss of population, loss of markets, "the calamity of drought and pestilence, or over expansion consequent upon the reasonable but unfulfilled expectation of growth." It would strengthen the credit of the whole country by removing the danger of provincial default. In strengthening the credit of Canada, he said, it would also strengthen the public and private credit of the industrial provinces. "For the financial difficulties of one province are bound," he added, "in the long run, to be a burden upon, and a threat to, the financial position of every other province."[34] At the same time the pooling of debts would effect considerable savings by the refunding of maturities on the credit of the Dominion.

He concluded by dealing with the objection, which had been raised in several quarters, that the centralization of borrowing and taxation would destroy the autonomy of the provinces. This was not valid for the Commission had adhered to its terms of reference in framing recommendations which would, if anything, enhance provincial autonomy. "The substance of provincial autonomy," he said, "will become only a shadow if provinces are not in a position to discharge the financial obligations without which the other duties of government

[33] *Ibid.*, p. 7.
[34] *Ibid.*, p. 7.

cannot be performed. The best way to preserve provincial autonomy is to maintain provincial credit."[35]

Mr. King was then followed by the provincial premiers in order of seniority of provinces, beginning with Mr. Hepburn of Ontario. Mr. Hepburn's remarks did not promise the co-operative spirit for which Mr. King, in his opening remarks, had hoped. Ontario, said Mr. Hepburn, had co-operated and was co-operating with the Dominion. But "we were not informed nor consulted with regard to the terms of reference contained in the order in council passed by the dominion cabinet which gave life to the commission itself." He continued: "When Ontario's presentation was made we asked for nothing. When the findings were agreed upon by the commissioners, Ontario had no representative,[36] Mr. Rowell having long before retired because of ill-health. But later on we were presented with a costly five hundred thousand dollar report—the product of the minds of three professors and a Winnipeg newspaper man, none of whom had any governmental administrative experience, and whose opinions all of us cannot share."[37] Mr. Hepburn had no love for professors, possibly because they, like many journalists, are comparatively immune to spectacular and oratorical appeals.

In his view the report was a sinister attempt to create windfall capital gains for the financial interests. He quoted from an editorial in the Toronto *Star*[38] in support of this allegation, and went on:

[35]*Ibid.*, p. 11.

[36]Actually, this was not the case. At least two of the commissioners in addition to Mr. Justice Rowell had been born in Ontario, and in view of the unwillingness of Nova Scotians to regard all those not born in the province as anything but outsiders, Dr. MacKay could hardly be regarded as representative of the province in which he resided.

[37]Quotations from Mr. Hepburn's speech are from *Dominion-Provincial Conference*, pp. 11, 15.

[38]"The report has, naturally enough, strong backing. Great financial concerns and wealthy individuals who are holders of provincial bonds support a project which would place the credit of the dominion behind provincial securities whose market value has greatly deteriorated. A Toronto broker has estimated that adoption of the report might add as much as $20,000,000, $40,000,000 and $60,000,000 to the value of the bonds of Manitoba, Saskatchewan and Alberta, respectively. This gift to the bondholders would be more costly to Ontario than any other province. Ontario's own bonds would not be increased in value to any marked degree, as its credit closely approaches that of the dominion. A feature of the arrangement not generally realized is that in the case of Alberta the dominion would assume not only the provincial debt, but the defaulted interest on the same. This had reached $3,400,000 by 1937 and stands now at a much higher figure. Ontario's federal taxpayers provide nearly half the dominion revenue out of which this gift to the bondholders would be provided." Toronto *Star*, Jan. 11, 1941.

> As a political observer I say that there is a fast developing body of opinion, not without cause, now promoting the idea that behind this untimely move, ostensibly as a war measure, is a well-cooked, nefarious deal to make good the losses in depreciation of certain bonds held largely by financial houses, to collect unpaid interest on Alberta bonds and to cause a sharp appreciation in bonds of certain provinces, which bonds were, because of circumstances beyond the control of the respective provincial treasurers, actually sold at much less than par, although the coupon rate was abnormally high. This possible huge capital appreciation is not even subject to federal income tax.

After continuing in this vein Mr. Hepburn added: "Is this the time to send a courier to bomb-torn London with a document in his hand and have him step into the Hall of Westminster and ask the British parliament to pause in its consideration of questions determining the very life of the British Empire in order to debate the question of a new constitution for Canada? To me it is unthinkable that we should be fiddling while London is burning." He concluded by saying that in his view the report was a peacetime document whose consideration should be postponed but that his government was willing to discuss any specific matters which might aid the common war effort.

This characteristic and singularly unconstructive speech did at least hold out the promise of discussion of such interim measures as could be described as relevant to the war. It was a bad, but not a hopeless beginning. As the premiers of the other provinces rose to express greater or less willingness to consider the report—ranging from the enthusiastic proselytizing of Mr. Bracken of Manitoba to the somewhat limp co-operation promised by Mr. MacMillan of Nova Scotia—the prospects of the conference brightened considerably. Mr. Pattullo of British Columbia, it is true, "reiterated that this is no time to make so radical a change as proposed by the commission. We do not know what conditions will be after the war. After the war we shall be in a much more favourable position to come to wise conclusions with much better knowledge of needs and requirements. I do not think that the provinces should be asked hurriedly to put their imprimatur upon this proposal."[39] But, as he said, British Columbia is in a category by itself, and his speech did not preclude the possibility of some constructive negotiations. He was followed by Mr. Campbell of Prince Edward Island and Mr. Patterson of Saskatchewan, both of whom spoke favourably of the recommendations contained in the report.

The last premier to speak was Mr. Aberhart. As far as the atmosphere of the conference was concerned his was the crucial speech.

[39]*Dominion-Provincial Conference*, p. 41.

Alberta was one of the provinces which stood to gain much by the recommendations, and whose adherence might well bring the other recalcitrant provinces into a more willing frame of mind. While the long and fruitless negotiations with Mr. Dunning over the Loan Council revealed the potential intransigence of the Social Crediters over the debt issue, in most of the earlier discussions with the Dominion and the bondholders the Alberta government had shown a willingness to negotiate even when it adopted a position which prevented the negotiations from reaching any conclusion.

His simple and characteristic introduction was not inauspicious. He felt, he said, like the old lady who was about to undergo her first operation. But the homely story was the old Aberhart trick of sweetening the pill. It became clearer, as his speech progressed and he returned periodically to the point, that he too would oppose discussion of the report. "I therefore submit," he said, "that we in Alberta are of the very definite opinion that this is a most inopportune time for the discussion of these highly controversial matters. With a struggle as great as the empire has upon its hands at the present time . . . it seems the greatest folly for us to engage in discussions of such contentious questions at the risk of dissension and misunderstanding." The full magnitude of the post-war problem was not yet visible. The present system would be unable to bear the load that was being placed upon it, and "a new organized economic and financial system must be set up." The provincial debt problem could wait, he thought, a little while longer, for the war would create such a vast problem of debt that the whole matter could be dealt with at one time after the war. The report represented a concerted and deliberate attempt of the money powers to increase the centralized control of the national life of Canada. The present system of finance could not be bolstered up. It was doomed. "We intend to preserve our constitution and our national unity and instead to overhaul the monetary system."[40] He concluded in the same vein that he had employed in terminating the Loan Council negotiations, by saying that Alberta stood ready to be the proving ground of the new order, and that all that was required was assistance from the federal government in refunding its maturities at a lower rate of interest.

His speech in effect killed the conference. The next day an attempt was made to proceed with the setting up of committees and the making of prepared statements by members of the government, but the intransigence of the three provinces closed off effective discussion.

[40]*Ibid.*, pp. 57–8, 60.

Twenty-four hours after Mr. Aberhart sat down Mr. King announced that there was no use in continuing the conference and events were concluded by the singing of the national anthem.

The persistent hostility of Alberta to the Commission from the beginning made Mr. Aberhart's attitude consistent and not unexpected at the conference. The terms offered by the Commission would have been such that the substance of the province's demands would have been met. All governments would have emerged better able to discharge their legitimate responsibilities. But the road to national power for the Social Credit party did not lie in bolstering the existing system of public finance.

CHAPTER EIGHT

# A Third Party in a Federal System

ON THE TWENTY-FOURTH of May, 1943, William Aberhart died in a Vancouver hospital at the age of 64. He had gone to the coast with his family for rest and recuperation. Then suddenly he was in hospital seriously ill, and within a few hours he was dead. The end was unexpected. The more intimate members of his cabinet, summoned to his bedside, were still on the train when he died.

He had been not only the leader of his party but its prophet. He had provided the imagery and the setting which made, for his followers in Alberta, an intellectual and emotional Exodus of Social Credit. He had spoken in prophetic language of the Promised Land and, like the Children of Israel, they had followed. To many of them it had been a great adventure of the spirit which he had summed up in 1936 in these apocalyptic terms: "The inevitable crisis is upon us. The rapture and the appearance of Christ is at hand. We will start a new social order."[1] Though his was not a movement which lived entirely in the person of one man, much of the heart of Social Credit in Canada died that day in Vancouver.

The death of the leader was a symbol and a symptom of the profound change which was taking place in the Social Credit party. It is difficult to say whether the course of the party's development would have been different had he lived, but the underlying conditions of violent protest began to change greatly after 1943. From that time the evangelical fervour of the party became less appropriate and harder to sustain, and it was only after a series of shocks and schisms that the party was able to readjust itself.

Political parties, particularly new parties, are unstable blends of three elements: leadership, ideology, and the interest groups upon which organization is based. A change in any one element is likely to affect a party's conception of its role and its ability to appeal successfully to the electorate. It is probable in any event that the economic and political changes brought about by the war would have made it necessary for the party to revise its strategy and its policy.

[1]*Winnipeg Free Press*, June 3, 1943.

Third parties, within the traditions of parliamentary and cabinet government which Canada has inherited, are almost as difficult to keep in being as they are to launch. The function of political parties in a democracy is twofold: to crystalize opinion around reasonable alternatives of policy, and to make stable government possible. The experience of parliamentary government in the British Commonwealth suggests that these two ends are best achieved if the number of political parties is two. On any single issue the only important groups are the "contents" and the "not contents" and stable majorities tend to bring about stable government. This is instinctively grasped by the electorate and voters are, as a consequence, mildly allergic to minority parties.

Nevertheless, minority parties continue to exist for they perform a necessary function in a democracy. Their task is to play the role of innovators in policy. Established parties are cautious of new ideas lest they offend their existing supporters. Substantial changes in the economic and social environment require new ideas and new policies which it is the business of political parties to lay before the public. The conservatism of established parties provides the organizers of third parties with their opportunities. It is therefore to be expected that violent social and economic disturbance will provide good soil for new parties. But when the troubles have been overcome the testing time comes. The struggle of the Social Credit party to adjust itself to the death of its founder and leader, as well as to the new economic and political conditions brought on by the war, provides useful evidence of the function and limitations of third parties within the Canadian federal system.

The fundamental conflict between debtor and creditor in a contracting economy, which the Social Credit party had exploited as a means of gaining and retaining power, was exorcized by the wartime recovery of the western economy. Good crops, combined with steadily rising prices, gradually pulled the wheat economy back on its feet; price control and other measures combined to improve the economic position of the western farmer both absolutely and relatively so that he was beginning to approach "parity" with other producers in the economy. Parity is a slippery concept, but, except perhaps in the matter of working hours, the farmer was pretty well off. Not only was old debt being liquidated out of the high earnings of the later war years but capital expansion and replacement tended to be financed out of current earnings rather than credit. By the end of the war western agriculture was on the threshold of economic stability—if not economic maturity. The dangerous experience of the depression, combined with the needs of wartime supply policy, led to greatly diversified cultivation. Capital, in the form of land and machinery, was largely free from fixed charges arising out of its acquisition. The conditions which had created the peculiar problem of western Canada in the depression had in the main been removed.

This change led to a shift in the emphasis in both propaganda and policy by the Social Credit government of Alberta. Prosperity, combined with the greatly enhanced wartime responsibilities of the federal government, reduced the provincial legislatures to the role of spectators in the business of wartime government, and this was reflected in the reduction both in the mass and the explosive content of Alberta's legislative programme. At the same time Social Credit propaganda turned into new channels. One aspect of this change is revealed in the annual reports of the Social Credit Board. Shorn of its administrative functions, the Board had become in these years the main propaganda agency of the government. The adjustment of the party to the altered political conditions of the war years led to a split within the party itself. Broadly speaking this split developed between the party leadership and those members of the party who still held rigidly to the objective of sweeping reform and of constant struggle with the financial powers.

On the one hand, the party leaders were faced with the responsibility of governing, the needs of normal administration, and the constant negotiation and accommodation by which a government must carry out its responsibilities. On the other hand, the more extreme members of the party were concerned not with the needs of the imperfect present but rather with the problem of adjusting their fundamental objectives to a greatly altered world situation. The events with which they were faced drove both groups to the right politically. The party leaders were driven into a conservative position while the extremest among their followers were driven into an irrational form of political reaction. The divergence between the two ultimately became so great that accommodation was impossible. The termination of this conflict was the triumph of the party leaders, the abolition of the Social Credit Board in 1948, and the sending of the extremists into the political wilderness.

The line taken by the Social Credit Board during the war years reveals the way in which this divergence took place and also shows the gradual movement of the party to the right. During the years of struggle with the Dominion the Board had concentrated on domestic constitutional issues raised by the Social Credit programme and an exposition of the achievements of the government in bringing in the new order. The 1942 report of the Board shows the new line assuming form and direction.

It begins with a warning of the dangers inherent in the then popularly discussed proposals for Federal Union, which it regarded as a sinister design by the forces of international finance to strengthen its control over the world. The remainder of the report is devoted to an assault on the Beveridge Report. After pointing out that Sir William Beveridge had been director of the London School of Economics and had received in 1930 the degree of D.Sc. in Economics, the Board added significantly that Sir William was generally considered to be a Fabian Socialist. "In 1932 he wrote 'Planning under Socialism,' the report asserted, "—a book, the title of which in itself reveals the nature of the philosophy to which he subscribes."[2] Sir William was also thought to be interested in the idea of Federal Union. For all these reasons it was indicated that he was a very sinister person indeed. The Beveridge Report advocated, it was alleged, "an anti-democratic philosophy based on the principles of national socialism."[3] The Board went on to denounce the Beveridge Report as a plan for the redistribution of poverty and to point out that the only true road to reconstruction lay in the programme of Social Credit.

In the following year the Board returned to the same theme, this time relating it to the Canadian scene and the Canadian federal system. Its 1943 report pointed out that the reconstruction programmes which were then being discussed laid the emphasis on national attacks on the problems of unemployment and insecurity. But this advocacy of a national programme was merely a device by the financial interests to solidify their power over the people by strengthening the central government at the expense of the provinces. While it was necessary in order to attain the objectives of the people to carry the aims of Social Credit into the national arena, it was necessary also to defend the provincial powers which were the citadel from which the sally must be made. The existing balance of the constitution was desirable and attempts to change it should be resisted. "Though the B.N.A. Act needs revision," the authors of the report wrote, "yet taken in conjunction with the Statute of Westminster, it constitutes our greatest safeguard against the establishment of a state dictatorship in Canada. Certain changes to the B.N.A. Act which are being suggested at the

[2] *Annual Report of the Social Credit Board, 1942* (Edmonton, 1943), p. 19.
[3] *Ibid.*

present time are of a nature that should arouse our gravest suspicions and should be considered with extreme caution. Social Security measures being formulated by the Dominion Government and the accompanying 'grants in aid' can easily accomplish the same undesirable results as the suggested changes in the constitution. They are to be viewed with alarm."[4] The wartime taxation policies and the creation of the "colossal" wartime debt were certain to bring the country to the brink of economic disaster. The fate of Alberta, the report added, would in the post-war period be "closely linked to that of Canada." The only way to avoid this disaster would be by the establishment of "an economic front on a national scale and cutting across traditional political party lines, thus uniting all people with a common aim against a common enemy."[5]

This report was published in 1944, and the attack on the reconstruction programme must be considered part of the election propaganda of the Social Credit party in the Dominion election which was then imminent. The tactical emphasis was clear. The provincial sphere of action must be magnified both to limit the scope of Dominion action—where control by "international finance" was already patent—and to enlarge the provincial bridgeheads for a Social Credit programme. At the same time ultimate success would be possible only by an increase of electoral strength in the national field.

Socialism, as well as centralization, was an issue in the election. The Board turned to the Report on Social Security which had been prepared for the National Advisory Committee on Reconstruction by Dr. Leonard Marsh. It was found to aim at the same sinister designs as the Beveridge Report with which the Board had dealt previously. It contained palliative measures and failed to seek out the root cause of economic insecurity. At the same time it was a scheme of socialistic regimentation. "The compulsory contributory form of social insurance is favoured by the Marsh Report. It would certainly provide a most effective means of reducing individuals with names, to robots with numbers, in a vast state-controlled machine. This form of society seems highly acceptable to all planners of the socialistic school of thought."[6] These conclusions were to be expected from Dr. Marsh, it was argued, since he was known to be "an avowed socialist." A large part of the report was then devoted to an attack on socialism as a form of regimented tyranny. It would involve a further centralization

[4]*Annual Report of the Alberta Social Credit Board, 1943* (Edmonton, 1944), p. 7.

[5]*Ibid.*

[6]*Ibid.*, p. 13.

of power in Ottawa, a continuation of government by order-in-council; "The trend of the modern financial system and that of socialism lead to the same ultimate objective—the creation of a world slave state."[7] Numerous quotations were adduced to prove that socialism was anti-Christian.

The Board reached the conclusion that socialism and international finance were one and the same thing, and that the dark powers of financial interest promoted socialism for their own sinister ends.

> If international finance and socialism are travelling in the same direction is it possible that socialism is promoted by the money power to hasten the completion of their plot for world domination? Not only is it possible but there is a fund of evidence which leads to the inevitable conclusion that there is a plot, world wide in scope, deliberately engineered by a small number of ruthless international financiers, to accomplish their objective. Their chief weapons are the power of money and the promotion of socialistic doctrines. However innocent many socialists may be of any intention of playing any part in so evil a plot, they are nevertheless the unwitting tools of that financial dynasty whose lust for power has caused untold human misery. The evidence which links socialist doctrine to the money power is so overwhelming that it can no longer be denied.[8]

The "evidence" adduced for this discovery is even more improbable than the discovery itself. Sir William Beveridge, the Board believed, was a socialist; he had been for some years director of the London School of Economics (the latter statement was at least true); and the Beveridge plan had "been acclaimed by that section of the press most closely linked with the financial interests." Dr. Leonard Marsh, moreover, was not only an "avowed socialist," but "a product of the London School of Economics." The London School of Economics had been "founded and richly endowed by Sir Ernest Cassell, a great power in the financial world."[9] Since both socialists and persons associated with financial circles advocated some form of world government their purpose and inspiration must be the same.

In Canada the two groups were found to be advocating further centralization of power in Ottawa in peacetime by the advocacy of extended schemes of social security. The Board supported this argument by quoting from an attack on health insurance by the Research Bureau of the Canadian Pharmaceutical Manufacturers' Association. Health insurance financed by federal grants in aid, the Pharmaceutical Manufacturers suggested, was a method by which the Dominion

[7] *Ibid.*, p. 30.
[8] *Ibid.*, p. 32.
[9] *Ibid.*, p. 33.

was "usurping the power to which it has no right." "Is it not by this indirect procedure," the Association asked, "interfering with the autonomy of the provinces, by encroaching upon the right given them under the B.N.A. Act to legislate as they see fit on matters of health? And if allowed to go unchallenged in taking that step, may it not later and with equal impunity find ways for invading the autonomy of the provinces in fields other than health, such as education?"[10]

Centralization in Canada was a necessary first step to world government, the Social Credit Board pointed out, because "obviously the national government cannot surrender a sovereignty it does not possess."[11] Only when all sovereignty was drawn into the hands of the federal government would the conditions be created by which the enemies of the people could give up their sovereignty to a world government. The evidence was found in a quotation from Dr. Ludwig Mises, whom the Board described, quite wrongly, as a "Socialist professor of Economics." Dr. Mises had been expressing his "socialistic" views in *The Voice of Austria*, a New York publication of extremely reactionary views:

> The history of international financial relations has, in the past 20 years, been one of continual embezzlement. The governments of the debtor countries have behaved like swindlers for the benefit of their own people. The new covenant of the League of Nations will therefore have to include a rigid limitation of sovereign rights of every country. Measures which affect debts, the money systems, taxation and other important matters have to be administered by international tribunals, and without an international police force such a plan could not be carried out. Force must be used to make debtors pay.[12]

How the Board could regard the author of these views as a socialist is difficult to understand. It is true that in its 1942 report the Board had noticed that Mises was the author of *Socialism—an Economic Analysis*. From this they must have reached the hurried conclusion that he was a socialist, obviously without reading the book.

At any rate, the Board was convinced of a sinister design which was being plotted in the secret places of international finance and international socialism: "An international government, controlling money, a world police force, and taxation,—a world in which Christianity and democracy have been completely destroyed,—this is the New Order being planned for all people by socialist and international finance alike."[13]

[10] *Ibid.*, p. 35.
[11] *Ibid.*
[12] *Ibid.*, p. 36.
[13] *Ibid.*

This was also the theme of the Board's report for 1944. The proposals for a world security organization drafted at Dumbarton Oaks "could easily be used" to further the international conspiracy to create a world state. "It is quite apparent," the Board said, "that the International Stabilization Fund and the International Bank, agreed upon at the Bretton Woods Conference, are an important part of the world plan. Perhaps they constitute the most important part of the world plan. Perhaps they constitute the most important cogs in the proposed international machine. That is to be expected, because where other methods fail the use of the power of money to enslave individuals and nations rarely does."[14]

The Fund, by tying national currencies together at a stable rate, would in no way correct the defects of the present monetary system. On the other hand it would deny to any nation "even the temporary relief of a period of false prosperity generated by a mild controlled inflation. The chronic shortage of purchasing power inherent in the existing system which is the cause of poverty in the midst of plenty, mass unemployment, restricted production, savage competition and eventually wars, would be in no way corrected but rather aggravated by the imposition of the proposed scheme."[15] The Fund would be controlled by the financiers who would thus strengthen their hold on the people.

Similarly the Bank, by saddling the nations with debt, would contribute to their enslavement to international finance. For "one of the most effective means of controlling the individual and eventually divesting him of his property and freedom is first to saddle him with debt. Nations can likewise be controlled and forced to surrender their sovereignty. The proposed bank is designed to lend to war-impoverished countries, presumably to help them in their work of reconstruction. In actual practice, however, the scheme would prove to be just another link in the chain of international agencies forged to shackle the nations of the world."

Even UNRRA was part of the grand conspiracy, though its role was "somewhat obscured by the emotional appeal of its highly humanitarian purpose."[16] ". . . If [it] were brought under the control of the international planners, and there are already indications that it has been, then it will prove to be one more effective means of controlling nations by the simple expedient of agreeing or refusing to provide them with

[14]*Annual Report of the Alberta Social Credit Board, 1944*, p. 12.
[15]*Ibid.*, p. 15.
[16]*Ibid.*, pp. 17–18.

the goods which they must have in order to survive. Just as the rationing of goods on a national scheme has proven to be an effective method of gradually conditioning the people to a docile acceptance of bureaucracy and regimentation, so may UNRRA carry out a similar policy on a world scale."[17]

These foolish and ill-informed broadsides reflect a change which was taking place in the position of the Social Credit party. The propaganda line which they represented had several important characteristics. The emphasis on things far away and not immediately relevant to Alberta, such as the assaults on Sir William Beveridge and the imputation of sinister motives to protagonists of international organization, reflected the decreasing importance of the government's legislative programme as a means of gaining support. The war and the wartime recovery had reduced the battle with the "interests" to a shadow war and a new enemy had to be found for the party to denounce. The movement, too, was becoming increasingly conservative. A combination of a long run of power and local prosperity had killed much of the enthusiasm for reform and change which had been the animating spirit of the movement in its early days. Consequently the attack was now levelled not so much at the local financial interests as at the centralizers, the socialists, and the planners. The purpose of these tactics was to make political capital out of a combination of weariness with wartime controls and the natural xenophobia of a remote and landlocked area.

It must not be thought that this propaganda was fully representative of the policy of the Alberta government, though it appeared frequently enough in the speeches of Social Credit M.L.A.'s and M.P.'s. Indeed, certain of its elements, particularly the thinly veiled isolationism and anti-semitism, were politically embarrassing. Nevertheless the same influences which had driven the intransigent revolutionaries in the party into reaction were forcing the party itself away from its earlier position of radical reform. While the Social Crediters had been the residuary legatees of the Progressives in Alberta, the movement's legitimate heirs were elsewhere. The U.F.A. had been one of the constituent elements in the Co-operative Commonwealth Federation and had fought in Alberta politics as the political arm of the C.C.F. When the U.F.A. passed from the political stage its role in Alberta descended on the C.C.F itself. While the C.C.F. had failed in Alberta to recapture the old U.F.A. support, its relative success in the rest of western Canada had been at the expense of the Social Credit party. It was the

[17]*Ibid.*, p. 19.

rise of the C.C.F. which had prevented the Social Crediters from making a strong bid for power elsewhere in the West.

The strength of the C.C.F. outside Alberta and the threat that it might in its turn inherit the mass following of the Children of Aberhart, made it, in a party sense, the natural enemy of Social Credit. This threat undoubtedly hastened the process by which the Social Credit leadership quietly made its peace with its ancient enemies and continued to thrive in Alberta as the main bulwark against the C.C.F. With the liquidation of the private debt problem as a result of wartime prosperity the only issue between the Social Credit government and the eastern financial interests was the settlement of the outstanding payments on the public debt of the province. This matter was settled amicably in 1945 by a Debt Reorganization Programme agreed to by the government and the Alberta Bondholders' Committee. Under this arrangement the holders of matured securities—those which had matured on or prior to June 15, 1945—were offered the principal amount in cash, together with a cash adjustment in respect of interest unpaid in the nine years from June 1, 1936. Holders of unmatured securities were offered in exchange new serial 3½ per cent securities of an equal principal amount, dated June 1, 1945, and maturing from 1961 to 1980, together with an adjustment in respect of the higher contract interest rates to the original maturity or call dates. Approximately 50 per cent of this adjustment was paid in cash, and the balance in five equal annual instalments. Altogether outstanding debts of $113,253,109 (of which $33,360,201 were matured securities) were met in this way. This refinancing was covered chiefly by issue of new securities.[18]

With the settlement of this prolonged dispute there remained no fundamental conflict between the Social Crediters and the eastern financial interests which had been denounced from one end of Alberta to the other in the good old days. The new alliance was welcomed on both sides with appropriate expressions of mutual respect.[19]

[18]The details are contained in a Prospectus issued October 24, 1945, in connection with the issue of $26,093,000 in serial debentures.

[19]The Montreal *Gazette*, Nov. 15, 1946, reported the opinion of Mr. Henri Renaud, the president of the Canadian Retail Merchants' Association:

"Viewing the political situation in Western Canada, Mr. Renaud claimed he could not help contrasting the discriminatory policies of the C.C.F. government in Saskatchewan with the 'highly constructive programme of the Social Credit Government in Alberta.'

"He met ministers of the Alberta cabinet and was impressed with their plans to aid business in that province.

" 'They opened our eyes,' he said. . . . 'They have a sound viewpoint regarding business, asking only for monetary reform.' "

The changed attitude was not unconnected with the need for capital to develop newly discovered resources in the province, particularly oil, and with the policy of the government in encouraging the large oil companies to bear the cost and risk of development. This enthusiasm for private capitalist interests reached an extreme point in the 1948 election. In response to considerable agitation for an extension of electric power development by the province the government called a plebiscite—held concurrently with the election—on whether electric power development should be undertaken by the province or be left to the private power companies. During the course of the campaign Premier Manning is reported to have said that he felt that the private power companies had done a good job and expressed doubts as to the desirability of the province going into the power business.[20] The result of the plebiscite was to confirm Mr. Manning's judgment by a fairly narrow margin, though a majority of voters in rural areas expressed a preference for public power. Thus Alberta and the Social Credit party turned against a trend which for over forty years has led most Canadian provinces into the ownership and operation of hydro-electric power facilities.

The Social Credit party, in order to retain its control of Alberta, and to retain its place on the national scene, had altered both its ideology and its tactics to meet the challenge of its changed environment. Two of the causes of the change were the steady prosperity of the war years and the change in the state of political parties in the West. Equally important was an alteration in the character of the federal system. The anaemic federal government of the inter-war years was the result of a paralysing lack of self-confidence among Canadians, frightened by strange economic maladies, and hampered in economic policy by the superstitions of the past. The war, by restoring national self-confidence, gave body to the national purpose and called into being a central government big with authority and responsibility.

With the Liberals and the C.C.F., for different reasons, occupying the "national" pole in Canadian party life, it was only natural that a party opposed to them should be driven to the opposite, or "provincial" pole. Such a position, in any event, suited the needs of the Social Credit party. Confined to a single province, anxious to strengthen its powers and position in its only citadel, and driven by its unique theory of history to regard the centralization of power as the hallmark of its enemies, it came inevitably to be the party of provincial

[20]*Montreal Star*, Aug. 17, 1948.

rights, the opponent both of enhanced central government and of increasing collectivism.

The life-history of the Social Credit party illustrates the role of new parties in Canadian politics. It reveals the structural and ideological modifications which are required of third parties in an environment both parliamentary and federal. For, if political parties are the flesh of the body politic, the more formal constitutional structures such as parliaments, the courts, and a federal division of the powers of government are its bones. The most essential of democratic political institutions, parties tend also to be the most mortal. Party warfare is ruthlessly competitive, and political parties survive by their ability to adapt themselves to the changing moods of the electorate. They reflect subtle changes in the body politic with accuracy and rapidity. Political parties, and third parties in particular, are thus important elements in constitutional change. Third parties come into being when there is widespread desire to modify the common purposes which the state is constructed to foster. These common purposes are comprehended in the national interest.

In the Canadian constitution the assertion of the national interest is the business of the federal government, while the provincial governments are expected to deal with those matters in which no significant national interest exists. In a perfectly static situation this division of labour would work without friction because the particular form which the national interest would take would always be the same. But this situation does not exist. If there is an equilibrium within the Canadian federal system it is a dynamic equilibrium in which those common purposes which are the proper concern of the federal government are in constant mutation. The national interest expands and contracts; it is ever shifting its ground.

It has been quite impossible to contain this elusive concept within the angular Victorian frame of the British North America Act. It would be unrealistic to suppose that the division of legislative power in the constitution created entirely water-tight compartments of action for the Dominion and the provinces. It could not. There is a very large range of government activity which quite evidently may be the preserve either of Parliament or of the provincial legislatures, or, in fact, of both. Much of the difficulty which was created by the judicial interpretation of the constitution between the nineties and the nineteen-thirties flowed from an attempt to make the enumerated heads of section 91 and 92 represent fields of exclusive legislative power. The only way in which this could be done was by interpreting away the meaning of several heads of section 91 in order to preserve some meaning for section 92. This search for water-tight compartments was unnecessary and contributed to the unsatisfactory court decisions of those years.[21] One result was that before 1939 the effective range of activity of Canadian governments—dominion *and* provincial—was restricted to such functions as would commend themselves to a Victorian liberal.

Between 1867 and 1920, in the great era of development, these limitations did not seriously hamper government activity. The common national interest was comprehended by the basic policies which brought a rapid inflow of population and investment. The programme of expansion was impelled onward by the tariff, by railway construction, and by a national fiscal policy which threw the financial resources of the government behind the movement. The simple east-west economy which resulted spread its benefits across the country with a fairly even hand. The National Policy was a rough but acceptable basis for the national interest. But the content of an acceptable national policy is in constant flux as a result of economic progress and decay. After the First World War the simple east-west relationships were complicated by the emergence of new north-south relationships with the development of non-ferrous metal mining and the pulp and paper industry in British Columbia, Ontario, and Quebec. One of the effects of this proliferation was to make it more difficult to achieve a balanced economy and a national policy on the old model which was mutually acceptable to all regions.

For these new industries the developmental functions were assumed not by the Dominion, but by the provinces, through the construction of highways, railways, and hydro-electric power undertakings. Thus for a time the centre of gravity in economic policy shifted from the Dominion to the provinces. On the one hand the balance of power in the Canadian federal system had shifted in favour of the provinces, and on the other the policy which would express the national interest was in the process of re-definition. The limits imposed by judicial interpretation made the process of re-discovering the objectives of national policy slower and more difficult.

The normal give-and-take between groups in the dynamic equilibrium of a constitutional state takes place through the party system. In Canada the federal character of the constitution gives this interplay of parties a special form. Besides the interaction of government

[21]See F. R. Scott, "The Special Nature of Canadian Federalism," *Canadian Journal of Economics and Political Science*, XIII (1947), p. 13.

and opposition in and out of Parliament and on the provincial plane, there is also a clash between the Dominion and the provinces. Dominion-provincial relations are a part of normal party strife and shifts in the balance of power between the Dominion and the provinces reflect the manœuvring of groups to secure the initiative in advancing their interest. Where the federal and provincial parties are the same, having not only the same names but the same organization, this may not be of great significance. But where the political parties are different on the two planes they are bound to make Dominion-provincial contacts a part of party warfare. In this case the change in texture and colour of the parties on the provincial scene will have considerable national significance. In extreme cases parliamentary opposition may be reduced to an impotent shadow with the real opposition to the national government located in provincial capitals. Such a state of affairs is evidence that local and particular issues loom large and the area of common interest is small.

The old two-party system lost, in the inter-war years, a great deal of its coherence and its vitality. The shifts in power from Conservatives to Laurier Liberals to Borden Conservatives had been accomplished smoothly because each of the two old-line parties accepted the same ends of policy, and were able to draw support from all sections of the country.

> The essence of a national political party which is capable of government in Canada [says Professor Underhill] is that it should have a substantial following from all the main groups and sections of the country—geographical, racial, religious, and economic—and especially that it should unite enough of the French and English within its ranks to make possible a stable and continuous administration of the country for a decade or a generation. In the past it has always had an opposition party striving with it which was also potentially national in the comprehensiveness of its appeal and which was always threatening to win away from the governing party a sufficient number of interest-groups to supplant it in office.[22]

The influence and location of interest groups change as investment follows new discoveries and inventions. At the same time the programmes of political parties will reflect this change in the equilibrium of the economy and, if the change is of sufficient magnitude, the balance between the parties will be materially affected. Professor Fowke has shown how the policy of western development had the primary aim of benefiting the financial and commercial community. The development of western agriculture was, in a sense, a by-product of the

[22]Frank H. Underhill, "The End of the King Era," *Canadian Forum* (Sept., 1948), p. 121.

cultivation of what was primarily a field of investment and a market for durable goods.[23] When investment and settlement had built up the wheat economy of the West, Canadians found themselves without a common economic objective around which a national policy could be constructed. The growth of new parties was part of a market process by which groups attempted to build majority support for a nationally accepted policy. In essence the Progressive movement was a search for a new set of national aims.

In Canada the great source of vital growth for a party is power in a province. But this is not an end in itself. The range of activity of a provincial government is too limited to satisfy the aspirations of the supporters. The capture of a province is merely the necessary means to enduring success. It gives the organizational strength, the patronage, and the administrative experience which are needed to attain and make effective use of power on a national scale. Parties which fail to achieve office die almost unborn; a party which achieves provincial power has achieved the conditions of success. But if the solid objectives of party policy are to be gained the party must go on to the national scene. It was the failure to do this successfully which destroyed the Progressives, and left them to wither away ingloriously on the less influential side of the Great Lakes.[24]

The Social Credit party was flung into power in Alberta almost by accident. But the very conditions of its victory impelled it to go on. The leaders were shrewd enough to see that it was impossible to make Alberta a self-contained social credit state. The tactics and programme of the first two years make plain their doubts and hesitations. But no such misgivings animated the rank and file, and the great problem for the leaders of the movement was to pursue the appropriate tactics without sacrificing the enthusiastic support of the ordinary voter and member. The desperate attempts to organize Social Credit parties as going concerns in other provinces, particularly Saskatchewan and British Columbia, continued. For fifteen years they trumpeted in vain about the walls of the neighbouring citadels. Alberta, though it abounded in the physical wealth of the last frontier, was insufficiently populous to be other than a political wilderness in which the Social Credit party remained in virtual exile, hopelessly far from the Promised Land of Ottawa. Though all else failed, the disintegration of the Liberal-Conservative coalition in British Columbia

[23]V. C. Fowke, *Canadian Agricultural Policy: The Historical Pattern* (Toronto, 1946), *passim.*

[24]W. L. Morton, "The Western Progressive Movement," *Canadian Historical Association Annual Report* (1946), p. 41.

brought a totally unexpected consequence of the newly introduced single alternative ballot. The general election of 1952 gave British Columbia a Social Credit government which, in a general election of 1953, was able to gain a clear mandate with a majority.

The lack of Social Credit gains in the federal election of 1953 showed that, while the party possessed the means of survival, it still lacked appeal as a national party. Whether it can go further, either alone or in coalition, remains to be seen. Time does not, as a rule, deal kindly with parties addicted to specific and eccentric dogmas. Political programmes, like other consumer goods in the twentieth century, reach obsolescence quickly. The fortunate parties are those whose names no longer carry meaning to the electorate. Nevertheless, whatever its future, the Social Credit movement has been a significant part of Canadian political development. It grew up as part of a process of secular change in which the old common policies which went to make up the national interest were being rejected piecemeal in the areas where they no longer conferred visible benefits. At the same time policies were gradually taking shape which might be a new basis of common action by a national government. Social Credit in Alberta was more than a local aberration to be explained in terms of dust, altitude, racial composition, or ideological allergy. It was a significant symptom of a mutation of continental magnitude.

CHAPTER NINE

# Disallowance and the National Interest

DISALLOWANCE is one of several constitutional methods of defending the central citadel of federal power against invasion by provincial governments. These assaults have taken place when provinces have been captured by interest groups on whom the effect of the national policy is so adverse that they must insulate themselves against it. The instances of disallowance reveal the vital interests which the federal government has felt it necessary to protect against local particularism at all costs.

One of the most significant facts which emerges from a study of disallowance is that the power has been used primarily against the West. These disallowances fall into two distinct groups. In some instances, disallowance was the result of the unflagging attempt, in the defence of imperial interests and imperial treaty obligations, to minimize the attempts of British Columbians to reduce their Asiatic fellow-citizens to the status of helots in their modern Athens. The remainder of the western disallowances were defensive measures to protect the commercial and financial interests from attack in the western provinces.

The West was, after all, Canada's empire. The expansion of the West provided the life-blood of eastern Canadian commerce, finance, manufacturing, and transportation. It furnished the market for the goods and services which, by permitting the economies of large-scale operations, made eastern undertakings successful. To put it crudely, as Macdonald did, the Dominion had purchased the West and was entitled to the profits of its exploitation. For its part, the West had desired to gather the fruits of several centuries of economic history in a generation. The price demanded was not steep, but it was a form of mortgage which was a heavy burden when times were bad. The conditions of the agreement were in the best tradition of hard-fisted mortgage lending. The public lands of the West were alienated to create the working capital for expansion, the railway was fortified by an irritating monopoly against competition, and the profits of development built gilded-age residences along Sherbrooke Street and vast, gloomy, and incredibly ugly temples on Bay and St. James streets.

Whichever way the farmer turned to break the stranglehold of monopoly he met an impenetrable barrier of constitutional remedy or of influence. The legal and financial resources of the grain trade were deployed for a generation to prevent the wheat pools from marketing grain. The province of Manitoba, thwarted in its attempts to modify the monopoly hold of the Canadian Pacific when it tried to finance its own development, found that the agents of Macdonald had preceded it into the money markets of the world. When times were hard and equity demanded some adjustment, legislation to modify the legal rights of creditors met with disallowance and opposition in the courts.

In Alberta, the newest section of the new West, the struggle between eastern financial interests and agricultural producers has a long history. Investment and settlement were complementary. They were the two facets of the process by which the province was to approach economic maturity in a generation. But while settlement and investment were complementary and mutually dependent they were also competitive since they had to bargain for the division of the fruits of development. The price of rapid investment had been the alienation of large parts of the public domain to railroads, land companies, and other organizations which developed it as a source of cash for working capital. The price was also implicit in a system of legal relations which both protected the principal and guaranteed the income of the investor and left the nominal owner to bear the full burden of fluctuations in the regional income.

The favourable bargaining position of the capitalist interests was the result of the total political and constitutional environment. It followed therefore that the only way in which the balance could be redressed was by a modification of this environment by political action. This explains why agricultural organizations were driven into political action and explains also the nature of the legislative actions which they undertook. But these actions were limited to the provincial plane and even there they were hedged in by the constitution. The narrowness of provincial authority in economic matters and the use of the reserve powers of the federal government to protect the dominant national interest are illustrated by one of the few disallowances in the nineteen-twenties.

The Alberta Mineral Taxation Act of 1923 was an attempt to use the tax weapon to hasten the exploration and development of the large land holdings of several corporate holders including the Canadian Pacific Railway and the Hudson's Bay Company.[1] These lands

[1]Disallowed by Order-in-Council P.C. 702 of April 29, 1924.

had been secured mainly by Dominion grant and were being held in idleness until their potential wealth might choose to reveal itself. To point up the contrast it should be remembered that most of the eastern provinces had retained at least some of the undeveloped land within their boundaries and were able to grant it under leases which left them not only control of development but also with a significant source of revenue. The bulk of the public lands of the western provinces had been retained by the Dominion and a large part of these had been alienated to encourage participation in development by railway and other companies.

It was alleged against the Act that it was "discriminatory, oppressive and unjust," that it damaged the security of mortgagees and others, and that in general it would inhibit the inflow of capital which should be the paramount public interest in the province. These reasons were apparently acceptable to the Dominion government for Mr. Lapointe's memorandum was very strongly worded indeed.

The strongest motive for the agricultural economy to redress its bargaining position arose in a period of falling prices when both the cost of meeting its obligations in real terms had risen sharply, and its ability to meet them had declined. The existing system of legal relations not only rendered the creditor group practically immune from the burdens of the adverse price change, it provided them with a windfall advantage in that their debtors were forced to repay them in money which was worth a great deal more in terms of goods than it had been when it had been placed at the disposal of the debtor.

Though a part of the Social Credit programme attempted to redress the balance in a somewhat unusual way, it was directed towards the same objective as the legislative programmes of other protesting agrarian interests, that of shifting the burden of a fall in the value of the farmer's product. And, like these other legislative programmes, it was resisted by the creditor interests with whatever constitutional remedies came to hand. The struggle was one for which historical parallels already existed both in the United States and in Canada.

By the end of the first quarter of the twentieth century a good many of the battles had been won. The monopoly power of the railways had been reduced by modifications in the national transportation policy, and the grain trade no longer deprived the producer of the major part of the return for his product. But many of the difficulties remained. The chief one on the newest agricultural frontier was that the necessary period of undisturbed profitable production to amortize the original debt had not elapsed and all the evils of deflation had fallen on the exposed debtor section of western agriculture. On the one hand income could not be expanded to meet inflexible costs, and on the other within the cost aggregate only the producer's standard of living seemed capable of contraction.

When, driven by his privation, the farmer reacted politically to protect himself, he reacted according to the intellectual heritage of the radical agrarianism of the western North American plains. Thus his identification of his enemies, his concept of the nature of historical causation, and his notion of remedies, sprang chiefly from the experience of the past. But in Alberta new active elements were leavening the lump of revolt. To some extent the old agrarian leadership had been discredited and the new combination of religious zeal and monetary reform dominated the revolt.

It was not unnatural that the Social Credit party should attempt monetary reform before falling back on the traditional debt adjustment remedies. The two years between 1935 and 1937 cover the period when the power and authority of the federal government was at its lowest ebb, partly as a result of constitutional evolution and partly because of the limited view which Parliament had come to take of its responsibilities. It is not surprising, therefore, that it had come to be widely believed that the right of the Dominion government to protect its sphere of power by overriding provincial legislation by disallowance was obsolete and no longer valid. Nor is it surprising that a provincial legislature should push its powers as far into the realm of federal jurisdiction as it chose without much fear of opposition.

The revival of disallowance against the purely monetary reform legislation of Alberta revealed that the hard core of national interest which the federal government was prepared to defend included at least the most important of the enumerated heads of section 91. The basic grounds for disallowance were much the same as they had been in 1868 though the conditions under which the power might be invoked had been somewhat modified and considerably clarified.

Of the four grounds which had been worked out before the turn of the century, two had been materially affected by changes in other parts of the constitution. Thus it had come about that the growth of the external aspects of the autonomy of the Dominion had made obsolete altogether the first ground for federal interference in provincial legislation. After imperial treaties ceased to apply to Canada, and Canada began to make treaties in her own right, there was no longer any need to enforce the observance of imperial treaty obligations. The last occasion for the use of this power was its employment to curb British Columbia legislation against orientals.

The growing importance of judicial review provided a method by which *ultra vires* legislation could be disposed of without political repercussions on the federal government. Thus Mr. Lapointe, in distinguishing between the Alberta acts which had been disallowed in 1937 and the Ontario power contract cancellations which he had refused to disallow, said that it was no longer appropriate to disallow an act merely because it was *ultra vires*. In this case the remedy could safely be left to the courts, as in the power contract cancellations.[2]

The power was still used, however, to protect Dominion interests or policies, and to protect private interests which had no effective constitutional remedy at the polls. The sharp decline in the use of disallowance after 1896 does not reveal any retreat from those grounds. The decline is accounted for rather by a change in circumstances which, while it did not diminish the influence of the Dominion, tended to reduce the occasions on which open coercion by disallowance became necessary. The change in the economic circumstances of the country on the one hand made the national interest less intimately dependent on the absolute goodwill of the overseas or foreign investor and on the other reduced the number of attacks by provincial legislatures on vested creditor interests. Thus while the Duchess of Marlborough's agent might threaten to withdraw the fortunes of the British aristocracy from Canada if the Ontario Power Commission Act of 1909 were not disallowed,[3] it was obvious that if the Duchess and her friends would not invest in Canadian enterprises there were other people who would.

At the same time, as the party system became more closely knit, the use of such openly coercive measures as disallowance might prove politically costly. It would be very difficult for a Dominion government to interfere with a provincial government of the same party without the prospect of serious trouble. On the other hand the use of disallowance against a province which was in the hands of the opposition might lend so much ammunition to the enemy that it could be equally disastrous. Disallowance could be kept in the background as a potential threat but the objectives sought could very often be gained by more diplomatic means.

Why, then, was the power of disallowance used belatedly in 1937 after the Alberta government had been left undisturbed for two years?

[2]*Canada, House of Commons Debates*, 1938, p. 177.
[3]W. R. Plewman, *Adam Beck and the Ontario Hydro* (Toronto, 1947), p. 90.

One reason was that diplomacy had failed and in a sense the bluff of the Dominion had been called. Aberhart would not refer his legislation to the Supreme Court, he would not delay its proclamation, and he would not delay the appointment of his bank directors. The disallowance came so swiftly that there was in fact no formal petition for it. There can be no doubt, however, that the fears of the banks were laid before the Dominion government. The plea of the banks that speedy action must be taken to prevent irreparable harm to their interest and to Dominion jurisdiction over the field of banking was heeded.

The second reason is equally important. It was all very well to say that the banks had a constitutional remedy in the courts and at the ballot box. But in fact the former had been denied to them by the legislation and the latter was unlikely, in the conditions of the time, to be effective. The Aberhart government was not likely to suffer because the banks and the eastern press were convinced that its programme was folly and doomed to fail. It was perfectly evident that Mr. Aberhart's prestige had suffered only when he had gone too slowly. The Liberals at Ottawa had nothing to lose by disallowing the legislation since the loss of support in Alberta was negligible set against the loss of prestige and eastern support by a refusal to disallow. Those who were adversely affected by the Alberta legislation could vote or influence votes mainly outside of Alberta. It could not be said that disallowing the Aberhart legislation would save the Social Creditors from the consequences of their own folly. The conditions in Alberta at the time were such that to let their programme go without challenge would have strengthened rather than weakened the cause of social credit.

The disallowances of the banking legislation do not of themselves add much to our knowledge of the disallowance power. The legislation fell so clearly across the federal jurisdiction and the national interest that the disallowance was almost inevitable. This, coupled with the fact that the differences between the two governments could not be muffled and diffused by settlement within the party system, made the whole affair a clear-cut situation in which there was no alternative to disallowance. It was useful to have such a forthright declaration from the Supreme Court though there was nothing in the precedents which suggested that any other decision could have been reached. The constitutional writers who had concluded otherwise were generalizing from an imperfectly understood particular instance. It is possible, however, that only a provincial government marching under such a strange device could have provoked such a forthright attitude on the part of the courts and the Minister of Justice.

The later disallowances of moratory and debt adjustment legislation are more illuminating. The attempt to bring bank credit instruments under section 92, on the ground that title to them constituted a civil right on the part of the holder and the granter, was defeated rather easily since it was not difficult to demonstrate that bank credit is both currency and of the essence of banking, which are subjects of exclusive federal jurisdiction. With the moratory legislation the matter is more complex. The courts found no difficulty in accepting the proposition that an alteration of the terms of a contract of public bonded indebtedness was essentially legislation concerning interest, on the ground that the subject of the contract was the payment of interest. It is doubtful if such a sweeping prohibition of provincial legislation concerning interest had in fact been intended by the constitution, though doubtless a good many of the Fathers would, under the circumstances, have endorsed such an interpretation. The courts, however, had doubled in their own tracks when they ruled that legislative bodies possessing wide sovereign attributes "within their own sphere" could not even exercise one of the basic characteristics of sovereignty, which is to default without penalty.

This sacred fence around "interest" was useful in the disallowance of legislation dealing with private debts, and soon drove the provincial legislature to roundabout attempts to reduce the principal without violating the interest—a strange perversion of social credit values. The disallowance of most private debt legislation was in fact on the old ground that it was "confiscatory" though considerable ingenuity was displayed in finding such statutes *ultra vires*, at least in part. This, however, was legislation which clearly dealt with property and civil rights and far less definitely with any enumerated field of Dominion jurisdiction. The Minister came to rely largely on an argument based on probable consequences, of which the best examples are the disallowances of June 15, 1938, when Mr. Lapointe leant heavily in his memorandum on the report of the Superintendent of Insurance.

It is clear that, at least as far as disallowance is concerned, provincial legislation on the subject of property and civil rights has very definite limits. Where the property and civil rights are those of persons and corporate persons doing business under federal jurisdiction and doing business which is national in scope the federal government would seem to be prepared to resist any attempt by a provincial legislature to impair seriously such rights.

Where the property and civil rights are less valuable in monetary terms and the civil rights involved are merely the innocent use of property the case may be somewhat different. Thus the Padlock Act failed signally to arouse the Department of Justice to the pitch of indignation it might have reached if the property padlocked had been a branch of a chartered bank. Mr. Lapointe's refusal to disallow the Padlock Act stressed this point by implication. Disallowance was not lightly to be used where other legal remedies existed, and the Minister did not seem to think that all avenues of legal redress had been explored. If the complainants lacked the determination to exhaust all possible remedies, that would suggest, it was implied, that the injury was not as serious as was alleged. If they did not consider the issue at stake sufficiently important to finance exhaustive litigation, then the rights alleged to be attacked could not possess great value. In Dr. Forsey's words, "he would be rash indeed who would now venture to suggest that the power of disallowance is any safeguard except for the liberties of those who are as a rule well able to look after themselves. The Dominion Government will be on the side of the big battalions. The revival of dominion control over the provinces is really the revival of dominion control over such provinces as try to do things which the dominant economic interests of Canada dislike."[4]

This suggests, as has in fact been the case, that in recent years the disallowance power has been used principally against those provinces which have sought to attack vested rights and interests lying close to the heart of the commercial and financial system of Canada. The special position of Ontario and Quebec in Canadian federalism is the result of both political and economic factors. Politically each is strong enough to be the majority within a national majority or the power centre of a national opposition so that in a party sense their bargaining position is strong against a federal cabinet. In addition, between them, they are the commercial, financial, and manufacturing centres to which the rest of the country is tributary and so far these interests have contrived to hold power—or reach a *modus vivendi* with the group holding power—in both provinces.

These circumstances have tended to make of the disallowance

[4]Eugene Forsey, "Canada and Alberta: The Revival of Dominion Control over the Provinces," *Politica*, IV, no. 16 (June, 1939), p. 95. The quotation is the concluding paragraph at p. 123.

power an imperial device for holding other provinces under the sway of the predominant economic interest of the central provinces. The outlying provinces are still Canada's empire and Canada is still, for many purposes, little more than the original area which it encompassed at Confederation. The inequalities in size and population of the provinces of Canada have been recognized tacitly in a constitution which to a large extent embraces two levels of federalism. The superior size and bargaining position of Ontario and Quebec give them a status and an autonomy which are different in kind to those of the rest of the provinces. The other provinces are subject to a much greater degree to a large reserve of central power which limits their autonomy even within the provincial sphere of action. The Canadian constitution thus recognizes what have been, so far, the economic realities of the country.

When one comes to define the scope of the disallowance power in Canada there are three distinct criteria which have to be applied simultaneously in each case. These three criteria are the position of disallowance in the law of the constitution, the policy principles which have been evolved governing its use, and the objective conditions which will make the application of these policy rules appropriate or not.

The law on the subject is perfectly clear. "It is undisputable," said Sir Lyman Duff, quoting an earlier judgment of his own, "that in point of law the authority is unrestricted."[5] The power of the Dominion to disallow legislation extends to any act of a provincial legislature whatsoever. Moreover, this unrestricted power does not seem capable of destruction by adverse convention. It could only be limited by constitutional amendment.

But though the power of disallowance is unrestricted, the policy regarding its use, enunciated from the earliest times, has in fact left a wide sphere of provincial autonomy in which the federal government was not disposed to interfere. The first rules were laid down by Macdonald in 1868 and subsequent modification of the policy has been the result of the growth and acceptance of two other methods of controlling the freedom of action of a provincial legislature. Particularly since the creation of the Supreme Court of Canada by the Act of 1875, judicial review has come to play, as we have seen, a major role in keeping the provinces and the Dominion within their proper

[5]*Reference re the Power of the Governor General in Council to Disallow Provincial Legislation and the Power of Reservation of a Lieutenant Governor of a Province*, [1938] S.C.R. 78.

sphere of action. Thus it is now highly unlikely that provincial acts which are *ultra vires* will be disallowed on that ground alone. In such cases judicial review is generally accepted as preferable not only because it subjects the delimitation of provincial power to objective rules, but because it achieves its object without generating Dominion-provincial discord.

In a second way also Macdonald's position has been modified by the passage of time. With the increasing respectability of democracy and the growing political maturity of the country, it is now assumed that a government which passes unfair or foolish legislation will suffer a loss of support at the polls. There is not much evidence in Canadian provincial politics to justify the belief that truth and good sense will eventually overcome folly and rascality but it is to the credit of the Canadian people that such a belief is still accepted. Accordingly it is now unlikely, though not impossible, that provincial legislation which is merely discriminatory, vindictive, or foolish will be disallowed if some other effective constitutional remedy exists.

In summary, then, the policy rules regarding disallowance are now something as follows: Provincial legislation may be disallowed (1) where it invades the constitutional power of the Dominion or impairs seriously some vital national interest; (2) where it is *ultra vires*, and no other effective constitutional remedy exists; (3) where it is unreasonable, discriminatory, or contrary to the principles of good government and no other effective constitutional remedy exists.

Whether in fact these rules will be applied and provincial legislation disallowed depends on the third set of conditions mentioned above. In each case we must examine the total situation. The disallowance power is coercive and politically costly to the ministry which employs it. Canadians possess a pride of locality which makes it dangerous to ride roughshod over local actions. Inevitably a government will spend anxious days in the cheerless political manœuvre known as exploring every avenue and leaving no stone unturned before embarking on disallowance. It is quite possible that an examination of the petitions for disallowance which went unheeded would be more illuminating than a consideration of those that were acted upon.

That is why the rules enunciated by successive ministers—and the apparent inconsistency of some individual ministers—seem to make so little sense. The considerations which will lead to the invocation of the power are in the main pragmatic. Very often the objective of disallowance can be, and is, secured more cheaply by other means, such as judicial review or changing local public opinion. Sometimes the very threat of disallowance or even the fact that it has been requested will bring home to an erring provincial government the character of the opposition which it has aroused.

The Prince Edward Island Trade Union Act of 1948 is a case in point. This extraordinary statute made it illegal for a resident of Prince Edward Island to be a member of any national or international union, excepting railway unions, outlawed the closed shop in labour contracts, and generally attacked the accepted machinery and procedures of collective bargaining in Canada. If ever a provincial statute deserved prompt disallowance it was this hasty, contradictory, repressive, and unreasonable piece of legislation. Both the Trades and Labour Congress of Canada and the Canadian Congress of Labour petitioned for its disallowance. There was, however, little reason to believe that it would be disallowed since the ultimate criterion was not met. The Prince Edward Island government was Liberal and failure to act would probably not materially affect the labour support of the federal Liberal party.

And yet the very existence of the power of disallowance and the appeal for its use in this case was a sufficient remedy. The next session of the Island legislature passed a much modified statute which removed most of the clauses to which the trade union organizations had objected. There can be little doubt that the ultimate possibility of disallowance was decisive in bringing about a change of heart on the part of the provincial legislature. As long as the power of disallowance remains it acts as a mental hazard which prevents provincial legislatures from straying too far from the general current of opinion in the country. In that sense it is an integrating, unifying, and conservative force.

A study of disallowance reveals the persistent pattern of national interest which successive federal governments have been prepared to defend. While the emphasis has differed the central pattern has remained the same. Despite the change and decay which flow from economic development, the interest has been that of the dominant commercial, financial, and manufacturing activity, mainly centred at the pressure points on the St. Lawrence system, which functions on a national scale. Whatever changes have taken place in the Canadian constitution and in the relative balance between the Dominion and the provinces, they have not yet materially limited the manœuvrability of dominant economic interests similar to those which were at once the strongest advocates and the greatest beneficiaries of Confederation. It becomes clear how Hamiltonian, not only in conception, but in execution, the Canadian constitution is. The facts of geography and economic power have made it so.

This need not always be. The facts may change. Changes in electoral strength which reflect changes in the location of economic and political power will alter the balance both between the Dominion and the provinces and between the Dominion and particular provinces. But the Canadian constitution contains machinery which, given basic incentives to unity, may act as a conservative and conserving force, holding the country reasonably together and keeping the rate of change slow enough to prevent the appearances of yawning cleavages.

There are those who regard it as a happy feature of Canadian federalism that the provinces are laboratories of social experiment in which a part of the Canadian people are free to explore novel avenues of public policy. Laboratories in unskilled hands may lead to unheralded explosions. The power of disallowance, in conjunction with other conservative forces in the constitution, minimizes the possibility of such disasters. In liberal theory the desirability of a variety of human experience may be a self-evident proposition, but the laboratory technicians in such experiments are too often cast in the image of William Aberhart.

CHAPTER TEN

# Adjustment of Constitutional Law to the New Equilibrium

BECAUSE much of the battle between the Social Credit party and the interests which it from time to time opposed was fought in the courts, the cases are sufficiently numerous to merit examination for evidence of alterations in the content of legal doctrine. The decade between 1937 and 1947 spanned as vast a change in the political and economic position of Canada as any in Canadian history, and compressed into a shorter period progress as striking as that which took place in the twenty-five years between 1896 and 1921. It would be surprising if these events did not cause a disturbance in the balance of the federal constitution. The dynamic system of relationships in the constitution is difficult to define and describe because its several parts are constantly changing in relation to one another. Every now and then, however, we get an instantaneous picture of some parts of the system, which represents actuality in much the same way as a two-dimensional still photograph represents the actuality of the planets. As a series of such stills reveals the outline of the solar system in motion, so also judicial decisions give a three-dimensional picture of the constitution. They set down for all time a record of how a complex arrangement of bodies in space looks from one particular point within it. As in the photograph, some of the facts are foreshortened and some are blurred but it is the foreshortening and the blurring which suggest the absent dimension of the picture.

A particular judicial decision in a particular case, or even a body of case-law made up of a series of decisions, does not take place in a vacuum in which the result is a simple arithmetical conclusion from purely abstract data. Three factors determine the responses which the courts will make in applying the body of law to the tangle of fact. The first of these are the ideas of the common law which reflects a long-run bias in favour of a particular social interest. The individualism of the common law in the nineteenth century is the obvious example. The second factor, which cannot be left out, is the amount of tension in the community, the presence or remoteness of danger from either external aggression or internal disorder, which dictates the degree of flexibility and variety which the community can tolerate in its institutions. The third factor is the nature of the dominant interests in the community and of the interests which oppose them. In a constitutional state with some degree of separation of powers it may happen that a particular vested interest will capture control of one branch of the government but not another. With control of the legislature but without control of the courts or the administration a particular class or interest is limited in the extent to which it can impose its will on the community. In this case the process of judicial review and interpretation of executive or legislative acts may become the battle-ground of competing interests, and judicial decisions something more than the objective precipitation of legal principles.

For the courts are not only the agency for interpreting the law in a constitutional parliamentary state. They are also a checking mechanism whose function is to keep the particular acts of executive and legislature in harmony with the accepted ends of government. If the legislature fails to legislate according to what Burke called the grain of society, at least its acts are interpreted according to the grain of society as the courts understand it.

The modern constitutional state is a partnership of the past, the present, and the future, and its political institutions more or less deliberately foster this continuity. Only the patricide of revolutionary crisis can destroy the orderly organic change of constitutional development. Political change must take place by a readjustment through time from one equilibrium position to another. In the period of adjustment, of a change in ideas and in interests, the branches of government will fall one by one to the newly emergent dominant interest. In the process different institutions in the state become the outposts of competing interests. Of these institutions the courts are by nature and by constitution designed to hold a watching brief for the past. The high average age, the method of selection, and the security of tenure of judges free them from the pressure of present controversy. The fact that their outlook has been shaped by the dominant issues of thirty years ago creates an intellectual time-lag in their approach to events. New ideas and new interests may capture the legislature and the executive branch of a constitutional state by political action. But they capture the courts only by the ripening of a generation of human minds.

The judge is aware that the law in his hands is a leavening lump and that he is the custodian of the process.

It has often seemed to me [wrote Sir Edward Fry] that the army of those who work for righteousness is divided into two corps: those who strive to maintain and to protect the precious results of the past life of the race—the spoils of the ages; and those who skirmish in front and help to lead on to new victories; and I think that neither body should think lightly of the other, though too often in fact they are apt to despise one another. The functions of the law, of the Established Church, of Universities, are all, if they be rightly discharged, primarily of the conservative kind; it is for them to protect and to hand on the inheritance of the ages: it is their duty to improve and to add to this treasure if they can; but if they preserve it and no more, they yet do something. This primary duty of preserving and not losing what has been won imposes upon them obligation to care and caution, lest they should by one false action imperil that of which they are the custodians, an obligation which exists in a much lesser degree on those who seek to make advance, and who, if they fail in one direction, can yet try in another. The one are to guard the stuff, the others are free to skirmish.[1]

The general election of 1935 in Alberta gave power to the Social Credit party, a party whose support came from agrarian and lower middle-class sources, and whose intellectual basis was hostility to financial institutions and creditor interests generally. The nature of cabinet government gave them control of the legislative and executive branches of government. They could by legislation change the law to meet their own sense of urgent social need and they could carry out the law. But the third branch of the government was beyond their control, deliberately freed from dependence on the majority of the day. Appointment to judicial posts is a federal matter, and judges enjoy both a security of tenure and an ultimate responsibility only to the Parliament of Canada.

There was therefore one place where Social Credit appointees could not assume office and one place where social credit ideas had no influence. Even in the absence of a federal constitution which denied to the provincial legislatures authority to legislate on the subjects of banking, interest, and bankruptcy there would have been conflict in the courts with the creditor interests. The creditor interests, relying only on the bias of the common law (imposed by the needs of the nineteenth century) in favour of the sanctity of contracts and of the protection of creditors generally as a preferred class, could have had good grounds for legal obstruction to much of the Social Credit legislation. The division of powers in a federal constitution, however, loaded the scales in their favour by giving them a strategic initiative in choosing the ground on which to resist.

[1]Agnes Fry, *A Memoir of the Right Honourable Sir Edward Fry, G.C.B.* (London, 1921), pp. 51–2.

To many members of the creditor group, and indeed to many judges, much of the Social Credit legislation offended in two main ways against the common law and the concepts of constitutionalism which it had developed: it represented a collectivist attack on the individualist principles of the law, and it contained in its administration an attack on the courts and on the procedures summed up in the concept of the rule of law.

With regard to the first of these objections against parts of the Social Credit programme, evidence has been adduced above that the legislation was regarded as collectivist in character in that it attempted to solve problems by strengthening the hands of debtors as a class at the expense of creditors as a class. It ignored the social value hitherto attached to the individual's assuming responsibility for the consequences of his own mistakes, and it prevented or limited settlements based either on individual bargaining or on considerations of individual worth. The creditor interests attacked the debt adjustment legislation as socially bad because it prevented them from encouraging the energetic and deserving debtor, a course which they insisted they were prepared to follow. It forced them to extend clemency to the shiftless debtor who would never pay unless compelled to do so and who might better be off the land altogether. Human nature being what it is, they were able to cite a large number of individual cases which supported their point of view.

A particular objection to the Social Credit legislation, both in the debt adjustment field and in relation to the public debt, was that it seemed to set at naught the conception of the sanctity of contract. Not only was the provincial government encouraging individuals not to pay obligations which they had assumed, it was setting an example of bad commercial morality by trying to avoid paying its own obligations.

It must be remembered that to many men the experience of the nineteen-thirties was a disquieting one. They lived, it seemed, on the brink of social chaos. A widespread loss of faith in the old social procedures and the old virtues was weakening the sanctions of their society. One by one the bases of the world of their youth were slipping away. Every attack on the concepts of their world was a revolutionary challenge which must be opposed, not by the cold and rational principles of sound stewardship, but in the heat of constitutional principle. In a period of marked social tension the variety and flexibility which a society can permit are curtailed. The calm sense of security which nurtures a free market in ideas is succeeded by a time when every doubt becomes a clear and present danger to peace of mind.

The fears and tensions of a period of uncertainty force vested interests into identifying the preservation of their own rights and privileges with the preservation of the constitution itself. The threat to the social fabric implied in such tensions makes judges more conservative and more rigid in their opposition to novelty. Thus the Social Crediters found ranged against them not only the vested interests whose property they attacked, but the judges and the very principles of the law. Out of this struggle must come one of three solutions. There might be a resounding triumph of the old conceptions of law and property and a discrediting of the men and the principles which attacked them. There might instead be a social revolution in which the Social Credit party would, by gaining substantial political power on the national plane, change the law and the constitution according to the dispensation of Major Douglas. Or, thirdly, the conflict might be caught up in some long wave of change in which the protagonists achieved a new basis for mutual amity and harmony of interests from a synthesis and sublimation of their conflict.

The second important aspect of Social Credit legislation, which in part explains its hostile reception in the courts, is that it became involved in a conflict of constitutional principle of which its authors were almost certainly unaware. This unconscious conflict with the constitutional principles governing the discretionary power of the executive arose to a certain extent out of the nature of the Social Credit movement. It is a movement which appeals primarily to those people whose intellectual life is spent with determinate problems. It is significant that Major Douglas himself was an engineer and that many of the leaders of the movement were accountants, school teachers, and others of similar occupation. On the other hand the movement possessed a marked distrust of lawyers and experienced politicians, who are precisely the members of the community most likely to distrust experts and to venerate compromise.

The type of person attracted by Social Credit was likely to have both a distrust of, and a faith in, experts and expert knowledge. The Social Crediters attacked the bankers and the financiers for devilishly efficient exploitation of special knowledge, but they believed in remedies of equally superhuman simplicity and efficiency. The translation of their ideas into policy involved the expert. A typical statute of the Alberta legislature in those years occupied but a page or two of the statute book. The statute would express in the most general terms the intention of the legislature, and would then delegate to the Lieutenant-Governor-in-Council, or to some other statutory authority, wide powers to declare the law in more precise terms. Three examples of this will suffice.

The Credit of Alberta Regulation Act, 1937, gave to the Social Credit Board the power to license all banks and bank officials in the province, together with the power to make regulations for controlling the credit policy of the banks in Alberta. This Act, surely one of the shortest on record, is about as meaningful as a preamble. It did not prescribe the objectives of regulation, nor the limitations on it; it was vague on the techniques of regulation. It left a vast amount of unspecified and unlimited power in the Social Credit Board to prescribe its objectives and its means of attaining them.[2] An earlier Act contained a less spectacular, but nevertheless striking example of delegation. Section 31 of the Alberta Credit House Act, 1936, had empowered the government, by order-in-council, to "vary, add to, or supplement with new provisions, any of the provisions of this Act." Another example of substantial delegation of legislative power is contained in the Reduction and Settlement of Land Debts Act, 1936. This Act had given to the Lieutenant-Governor-in-Council the power to exclude certain debts from the operation of the Act itself.

All three of these statutes conferred the power of substantive legislation on some delegated authority, giving to that authority the power to change materially the operation of the law as it appeared in the act. As far as Alberta was concerned this was probably done in all innocence and was perfectly in accord with the psychology of the Social Credit movement. What no doubt the authors of this legislation did not realize was that they were involving themselves in one of the major debates of parliamentary constitutionalism of the day. The origins of this controversy lay in Great Britain.

Since 1850 there has been a growth in England of the practice of delegating minor legislative power to the executive. The new purposes of state action accepted after the middle of the nineteenth century imposed on Parliament a tremendous burden in the passing of de-

[2]This Act was evidently drafted by the Social Credit Board and not by the regular draftsmen, which may explain its rather unconventional structure. Evidence in support of this hypothesis is patent in the authentic copy of the Act transmitted to Ottawa. This copy is a proof of the original text of the bill with certain alterations in ink. For example section 2(b) originally read: "'Business of Banking' means 'the receipt of money on current or deposit account.'" Inserted in ink after "deposit" (the English term for a savings account) is the phrase "or savings." This and one or two other changes suggest that the Act had been drawn up by someone unfamiliar with Canadian banking terminology, and that the change had been made at the last minute to make the intention of the Act clear in terms of Canadian usage. Both Powell and Byrne, the Social Credit "experts," were recent arrivals from England, and they, presumably, drafted the Act themselves.

tailed and highly technical legislation which required frequent amendment to take account of technological change, invention, and the ingenuity of the public in evasion. To meet this difficulty the practice grew up of drafting statutes in general terms and allowing their details to be filled in by ministerial order. The growth of delegation after 1850 had been a silent revolution during which no one had realized that a new technique had been adopted. Dicey's belated discovery in 1915 that there was an administrative law in England was almost the first awareness that the extent of this delegation posed a constitutional problem. The courts had been unmoved by the growth of delegated legislation itself—after all they themselves were repositories of wide powers of delegated legislation over the rules and constitution of the courts of justice. Similarly railway companies and local authorities had gained wide powers of delegated legislation without any constitutional feathers being ruffled. It was not until the departments of state became entrusted with decisions which closely touched the liberty of the subject in the disposal of his property that the judges awoke to the situation.

Attacks on delegated legislation and on the alleged abuses of delegated legislative power came to be a common method of discrediting those collective objectives of state policy which were least pleasing to propertied interests. In time these attacks came to be clothed in a reasonably coherent mantle of principle in which it was alleged that the royal prerogative was abroad in the land, intent on restoring the executive absolutism of the Stuarts to the hands of a ruthless and lawless bureaucracy.

Perhaps the most striking attack on the evils of delegated legislation was Lord Chief Justice Hewart's *The New Despotism.* This little book, which Felix Frankfurter dismissed as "a piece of lurid journalism,"[3] was something of a best-seller in the nineteen-thirties and became the handbook of those whose quarrel with much of modern legislation is not really with its means but rather with the ends which it seeks to serve. It is not, however, politically decent to attack the popular will which has ordained the legislative means to a more collectivist society. Obstruction has had to take the form of indirect attack. The dangers of delegated legislation were therefore a godsend for those groups who were conservative because they stood to gain by

[3]Quoted in C. J. Friedrich, *Constitutional Government and Democracy* (Boston, 1941), p. 112. Lord Hewart's accusations were not substantiated by the Committee on Ministers' Powers (Cmd. 4060/1932), and were effectively refuted in a masterly analysis of the problem in John Willis's *Parliamentary Powers of the English Government Departments* (Cambridge, Mass.), 1933.

the status quo. A constitutional issue of great historical significance could be raised on behalf of things as they were. As a means of obstruction in the courts the cry of bureaucratic despotism was both a constitutional argument, which might even upon occasion be relevant, and an image designed to inflame the mind of the court against the statute before it.

In all innocence the Alberta legislators enacted most provocative statutes, which in some cases must have influenced the courts against the legislation, and in others became a valid reason for a finding of *ultra vires*. This was true, for example, in *Credit Foncier* v. *Ross et al.*[4] In that case, as noted above, one of the specific grounds on which the Reduction and Settlement of Land Debts Act was rejected by the courts was that it conferred a degree of delegated legislative power which was inconsistent with the terms of the British North America Act.

These currents of legal and constitutional opinion have always been a significant element in determining the centre of gravity of the Canadian constitution. A pronounced suspicion of collectivism, together with an elaborate attempt to square the law with the maxims of *laissez-faire* individualism, probably curtailed the expansion of provincial legislative functions in the pre-1914 period. The crisis of the inter-war period, by enlarging the area of legitimate interest of the federal government, generated a new conflict, in which the sympathies of the courts and the individualistic doctrines of the common law were enlisted in the struggle to thwart an extension of the federal power.

By the nineteen-thirties, however, the tide was on the turn. In the *Aeronautics* and *Radio* references the courts admitted for the first time an enlargement of federal responsibility beyond the explicit terms of section 91. The needs of the depression, moreover, forced the Dominion government into positive measures of statutory regulation which, to some extent, abandoned the assumptions of the free market. But it was one thing for the courts to admit a general proposition that the Dominion should have jurisdiction over the field of aeronautics. It was, apparently, quite another to admit the constitutional validity of a statute like the Natural Products Marketing Act.

The action of the courts in finding unconstitutional the New Deal legislation of Mr. Bennett created a serious constitutional crisis in Canada which might have had very grave consequences if events had turned out otherwise. These decisions revealed a dangerous and

[4][1937] 3 W.W.R. 273.

absurd disparity between what seemed to most Canadians to be perfectly proper ends of government and the constitutional means which would be acceptable to the courts.

At the same time they saved the Liberal government from the embarrassment of having to enforce these or similar measures to mitigate the depression. To some extent courts were blamed for a fault which lay elsewhere. Whether by good luck or by clever manœuvring, Mr. King had made it appear that he and his government were prevented by the courts from taking the measures which they would like to take to deal with the depression. Actually the nature of Mr. King's majority was such that it is doubtful if his party would have supported such measures. Both the Liberals and the Conservatives were deeply divided at that time over conflicting policy recommendations. Each party represented a babel of mutually contradictory vested interests and there was no coherent body of doctrine which could be an agreed basis of policy in either party. Events had demonstrated the utter wrongness of the orthodox deflationary approach to the depression long before even a minority of economists were able to provide the intellectual basis for an alternative policy. The constitutional stalemate in Canada represented an intellectual stalemate in the minds of the Canadian people.

It is at this point that the rise of the Social Credit movement in Alberta is relevant to the solution to this constitutional impasse. The emasculation of the Dominion left the provinces as the only available agencies for the formulation and application of remedial measures to relieve the strangulation of the economy. The resistance to these measures put up by conservative forces had the effect, in so far as it was successful, of circumscribing the legislative power of the provinces, and, by inference, widening the acknowledged legislative territory of the Dominion. The Social Credit party in Alberta not only helped to shift the weight of legal pressure against the provinces, but also ensured the success of that pressure by the nature of its programme. The Aberhart programme provided the *reductio ad absurdum* which was required to demonstrate the unsuitability of the provinces as agencies of major fiscal and economic policy.

But the Social Credit movement was not the sole cause of the shift in the centre of gravity of the constitution in the direction of the central government. Two other factors combined with it to strengthen the trend. One of these was the waning of the belief in *laissez-faire* and the consequent erosion of many legal principles derived from it. The other was the change in the world situation after 1939.

The excessively individualist character of the law was waning before a change in opinion. As the number of people diminished who could remember a set of facts which corresponded to the assumptions of the *laissez-faire* individualist society of the nineteenth century, the influence of that school of thought diminished. Big corporations and big powers, general strikes and world wars, famines, depressions, and civil disorders had combined to narrow considerably the area of free decision in human life. It was no longer obvious that thrift, honesty, and industry led inevitably to wealth, power, and social recognition. Nor was misfortune in any way closely related to the absence of virtue. Thus the great inhibition about state action was removed. No longer, if the state provided collectively those services which might perhaps have been provided privately at greater cost, was it pertinent to pause to inquire whether such action was interfering with the natural process by which, in one single sorting motion, the good and the efficient were singled out from the wicked and inefficient.

In time the law came to discard a doctrine which no longer commanded social acceptance. Once people no longer thought that the public interest lay pre-eminently in the preservation of a *laissez-faire* society the rules of law which fostered that public interest suffered modifications. There are a few leading cases in recent years which suggest that this is the case.

During the war years there were attempts to upset the constitutionality of the wide wartime powers of the federal government but it is significant that such attempts were completely abortive. The two main legal devices used were either to attack the delegated legislative or executive power of the minister, or to challenge the power of Parliament to legislate in the field at all. The wide power of the Dominion to legislate for peace, order, and good government in wartime was sufficiently sweeping to make the latter expedient a very doubtful one. Consequently most attempts to limit the application of the federal power during wartime were based on the more sophisticated ground of abuse of delegated power. They were not conspicuously successful. In the most important case on the wartime powers of the federal government where this legal issue was before the court, the Supreme Court of Canada upheld the right of the Minister to exercise wide powers of delegated legislation.[5] Even in taxation cases, where there is a considerable body of English and Canadian case-law which reveals exceptional judicial scrutiny of ministerial power, a

[5]*Reference as to the Validity of the Regulations in Relation to Chemicals*, [1943] S.C.R. 1.

Canadian court has in at least one important case shown itself unwilling to upset very wide discretionary powers of the Minister.[6]

Such a trend may indicate a waning in the minds of the judges of that blind hostility to the growth of centralized executive power which animated Lord Hewart's *New Despotism* and which was a decisive factor in the decision of many British and Canadian cases in the inter-war period. It is, of course, possible to dismiss these cases on the ground that the war situation was abnormal and that it created, even in the minds of judges, an unusually accommodating spirit to the ends of state action. In times of serious emergency judges are inclined, like other citizens, to give the government the benefit of the doubt. One cannot, in the midst of a deluge, stand too much on ceremony. This, no doubt, explains the decision of the majority of the House of Lords in the English case of *Liversidge* v. *Anderson.*[7]

However, cases dealing with the constitutional issues created by the problem of controlling executive power have not been too important in Canada. The whole issue of the delegated power of the administration has not been thrashed out in the courts in Canada with anything like the thoroughness it has in the United States or the United Kingdom. The issue has intruded itself almost unbidden into several important cases, notably the *Board of Commerce* case, but it has not been skilfully handled by either Canadian lawyers or Canadian judges. Because Canada is a federal country most of these cases have been made to turn on the question of the division of legislative power—a well-fought ground on which Canadian lawyers can manœuvre with subtlety and skill. It is to this class of case that we must turn to see what kind of constitution the judges are dealing in today. Here there is evidence of a change in the line of interpretation, a change at first hesitant and uncertain, but now clear and unmistakable.

The most interesting case to be decided in the decade of the nineteen-forties was undoubtedly *Attorney-General for Ontario* v. *Canada Temperance Federation.* This case takes us back again to the Canada Temperance Act and the famous case which dealt with it. For over fifty years the spectre of *Russell* v. *the Queen* had haunted the Canadian constitution. Many judges had wrestled with the implications of this case, but none more skilfully than Lord Haldane, who finally succeeded in explaining it away in the *Snider* case.

The wording of the judgment in the *Russell* case had suggested a flexible concise definition of the federal power which judges from

[6]*Pure Spring Co.* v. *Minister of National Revenue*, [1946] Ex. C.R. 471.
[7][1942] A.C. 206.

Lord Watson to Lord Haldane have evaded. In essence the Board had laid down in the *Russell* case that the division between federal and provincial spheres of power was not one between mutually exclusive assigned fields, but rather between matters which were properly of national concern and matters which were in their essence of local concern only.

For reasons which have been discussed above, the courts had sought for many years to confine the jurisdiction of Parliament to certain narrowly defined fields. This narrow construction created a rather loose but harmonious federalism which worked passably well in the era of expansion but was clearly impossible in the period of a major war. The courts therefore invented an overriding power which could be used in wartime but which was still subject to judicial review. This ingenious solution was the only one which permitted the legitimate needs of wartime government to be met without any sacrifice of the underlying assumptions of *laissez-faire* constitutionalism. But the assumptions on which this elaborate and fanciful structure rested were completely abandoned in the *Temperance Federation* case. In a terse and pointed judgment Lord Simon said:

The first observation which their Lordships would make on this explanation of *Russell's* case is that the *B.N.A. Act* nowhere gives power to the Dominion Parliament to legislate in matters which are properly to be regarded as exclusively within the competence of the Provincial Legislatures, merely because of the existence of an emergency. Secondly, they can find nothing in the judgment of the Board in 1882 which suggests that it proceeded on the ground of emergency: there was certainly no evidence before the Board that one existed. The Act of 1878 was a permanent, not a temporary, Act and no objection was raised to it on that account. In their Lordships' opinion, the true test must be found in the real subject matter of the legislation: if it is such that it goes beyond local or provincial concern or interests and must from its inherent nature be the concern of the Dominion as a whole (as for example in the *Aeronautics Case* . . . and the *Radio Case* . . .) then it will fall within the competence of the Dominion Parliament as a matter affecting the peace, order and good government of Canada, though it may in another aspect touch upon matters specially reserved to the Provincial Legislatures. War and pestilence, no doubt, are instances; so too may be the drink or drug traffic, or the carrying of arms. In *Russell* v. *the Queen*, Sir Montague Smith gave as an instance of valid Dominion legislation a law which prohibited or restricted the sale or exposure of cattle having a contagious disease. Nor is the validity of the legislation, when due to its inherent nature, affected because there may still be room for enactments by a Provincial Legislature dealing with an aspect of the same subject in so far as it specially affects the Province.

It is to be noticed that the Board in *Snider's* case nowhere said that

*Russell* v. *the Queen* was wrongly decided. What it did was to put forward an explanatior of what it considered was the ground of the decision, but in their Lordships' opinion the explanation is too narrowly expressed. True it is that an emergency may be the occasion which calls for the legislation, but it is the nature of the legislation itself, and not the existence of the emergency, that must determine whether it is valid or not.[8]

This judgment of Lord Simon's sweeps away in a single paragraph an elaborate tissue of abstraction which has befogged the judicial interpretation of the Canadian constitution for half a century. It has been suggested above that the great judges in whose hands the Canadian constitution took shape—from Lord Watson to Lord Haldane—were confronted by a mounting flood of new government activity which they fitted with difficulty and much misgiving into the categories of Canadian federalism. They shared the preoccupation of their generation with the challenge which the widening area of state responsibility presented to constitutional government. This intellectual disturbance made their reasoning unnecessarily elaborate and often artificial.

Subsequent cases suggest that Lord Simon's judgment was a premature attempt to resolve this serious problem. These later cases have succeeded in reaching an accommodation between the needs of big government in a crisis and the multiple sovereignties of Lord Watson. However, this accommodation has been by a different, and somewhat less clear-cut, route. A year after the *Canada Temperance Federation* decision the Privy Council returned, in the *Japanese-Canadians* case, to the emergency doctrine as a justification for the expanding powers of the federal government. The editors of the Dominion Law Reports, in an acid note attached to this case, expressed concern at this "inexplicable relapse into the 'emergency' language of the *Fort Frances* and *Snider* cases after [the Privy Council's] rather startling *volte face* on emergency in the *Canada Temperance Federation* case."

Such vacillation, without explanation, in a court having ultimate power to define the limits of legislative authority in a federal state, indicates a want of appreciation of the important stake that Canadians have in understanding what scope for legislation resides in the central and local legislatures respectively. It reflects a casualness about constitutional power in Canada that is the more irritating because exhibited by a tribunal, the membership of which, generally speaking, does not have to live with the results of its own pronouncements.

In reverting to the "emergency" doctrine as of old the Judicial Committee has added something which appears to be new. It speaks of requiring "very

[8][1946] 2 D.L.R. 1, *per* Lord Simon at p. 5.

clear evidence that an emergency has *not* arisen . . . to justify . . . over-ruling the decision of the Parliament of the Dominion that exceptional measures were required." Shades of the Board of Commerce Case! It may be too much to hope, however that this self-denying attitude to "emergency" legislation carries with it any promise of enlargement of the categories of emergency beyond the single instance of war.[9]

This testy outburst may have been unfair to a tribunal which "does not have to live with the results of its own pronouncements," and whose jurisdiction over Canadian cases ceased with the Supreme Court Act of 1949. For the fact is that it is precisely the elaboration of the emergency doctrine which seems to have commended itself to the Supreme Court of Canada. This emergency doctrine has been adapted to the conditions of a world even more preplexing than that which troubled Lord Haldane in the twenties. Lord Wright, for the Privy Council, defined the emergency jurisdiction with much less caution than Lord Haldane had done in the *Board of Commerce* case:

Under the *B.N.A. Act* property and civil rights in the several Provinces are committed to the provincial legislatures, but the Parliament of the Dominion in a sufficiently great emergency such as that arising out of war has power to deal adequately with that emergency for the safety of the Dominion as a whole. The interests of the Dominion are to be protected and it rests with the Parliament of the Dominion to protect them. What these interests are the Parliament of the Dominion must be left with considerable freedom to judge.[10]

The decision of the Supreme Court of Canada in the *Margarine*[11] case is quite consistent with this tendency to use the emergency doctrine as a new philosopher's stone in the constitution. It is hard to see what a section of a very old statute, the Dairy Industry Act, which prohibited the manufacture and distribution of margarine, has to do with national emergencies, and yet one of the grounds for finding that section *ultra vires* was the inability of the Court to perceive the emergency with which such a prohibition might deal. The confusion created by this decision has been somewhat cleared up in the *Rentals* reference,[12] which not only provides a clear statement of the new emergency doctrine, but also attempts to fit the *Temperance Federation* case and the *Margarine* decision into the conception of the constitution which the Court has now evolved.

[9]*Co-Operative Committee on Japanese-Canadians* v. *Attorney General for Canada*, [1947] 1 D.L.R. 577.

[10]*Ibid.*, p. 585.

[11][1949] 1 D.L.R. 433.

[12][1950] S.C.R. 124.

It is now clear that the Parliament of the Dominion has the power to enact legislation which is otherwise beyond the normal scope of its activities, not only during war, but also for whatever period seems necessary to secure an orderly return to the conditions of a peacetime economy. This was stated emphatically by Chief Justice Rinfret:

There is no doubt that under normal conditions the subject-matter of rents belongs to the provincial jurisdiction. . . . There is equally no doubt that under abnormal conditions, such as the existence of war, Parliament may competently assume jurisdiction over rents. The *Fort Frances* case, *supra,* is authority for the proposition that, notwithstanding the cessation of hostilities, Parliament is empowered to continue the control of rents for the purpose of concluding matters then pending, and of its discontinuance in an orderly manner, as the emergency permits, of measures adopted during and by reason of the emergency.[13]

The implications of this position in relation to the preceding cases was made clear by Mr. Justice Taschereau:

The case of *Russell* v. *the Queen* has been referred to during the argument. This case which is very frequently cited has no application. Moreover, it has not the meaning that has been attributed to it, as a result of the dictum of Viscount Haldane in *Toronto Electric Commissioners* v. *Snider.* In *Attorney General for Ontario* v. *Canada Temperance Federation,* Viscount Simon has definitely settled the matter and removed all possible doubts. Speaking for the Judicial Committee, he held that the *Scott Act* was a permanent law and not a law, the validity of which was justified by an emergency. It is not the existence of abnormal and transitory conditions that justified its validity.

The present case must also be distinguished from the Reference submitted to this Court as to the validity of the *Dairy Industry Act.* . . . In that case, among other submissions, it was contended that there was an emergency that justified the Parliament of Canada under the "Peace, Order and good Government" clause of section 91 of the *B.N.A. Act* to enact the legislation, but this Court held that an emergency did not exist, particularly in view of the allegation in the Order in Council, that margarine was not obnoxious to health, and that therefore the matter was of provincial concern.[14]

What is it that the Supreme Court has done? Instead of allowing Lord Simon's judgment to be used as a means of returning to an earlier functional approach to the constitution, they have used it as a means of returning the *Russell* case to its grave. Lord Simon's decision would have given the courts a means of reconciling certainty with flexibility in interpreting the constitution. It would have been only necessary to ask in most cases what is the inherent nature of the

[13] *Ibid.*, p. 130.
[14] *Ibid.*, p. 142.

legislation before the court. If it concerned the peace, order, and good government of Canada as a whole, then it would clearly lie within the power of Parliament to legislate about it. To have adopted such a course would have meant the abandoning of the fixed areas of sovereignty which have enabled provincial politicians to drive desperately hard bargains with a federal government charged with the survival of the nation as a whole. And yet events have moved to a point where the requirements of national security will not leave the constitution alone. The rights of the first-class promenade deck have become submerged in the obligations of the life boat.

The courts have reconciled tradition with necessity by this refurbished version of the emergency doctrine. In this way they can admit as legitimate every inroad by the state on the free market, meanwhile consoling themselves by fixing their eyes on the vision of some future normalcy, when the emergency will cease to be normal, and the Road to Serfdom will have been blocked by a washout. The emergency doctrine has enabled the courts to postpone recognition of the fact that the growing collectivist responsibilities of the state have knocked the federal system off balance. But even the postponement of its recognition is acquiescence in the *de facto* existence of a much more centralized state than has existed since the advent of Lord Watson.

Some kind of synthesis has taken place in which the underlying principles of the law no longer operate to frustrate governments in the pursuit of objects which seem to the majority of their electorates to be appropriate. The obstacles which prevented, in the inter-war period, the general acceptance of a broadly conceived national policy in Canada have been overcome. Political society in Canada is once more in a state of equilibrium. That is to say there is now an underlying harmony between the ideas and assumptions of political life on the one hand and our political institutions on the other. This state of harmony or equilibrium does not always exist. Political objectives, and the political theories which seek to give them universality, change in response to the most deeply felt needs of succeeding generations of men. But political institutions, including the framework of law by which men realize their social needs, are slow to change. The law is a conspicuous laggard in this respect and it is the existence of this lag which causes a political disequilibrium such as that which existed in Canada in the inter-war period. When the lag is minimized, equilibrium has returned. We are now settling into an equilibrium position in which the federal government has greatly increased in responsibility and power in Canada. To this position the courts have now given (somewhat equivocally) their blessing, for the law cannot allow itself to become too much at variance with the facts. Burke's warning that it is essential to legislate according to the grain of society applies as much to the courts as to Parliament.

Three factors have contributed to bring about this new balance in the Canadian federal system. The first factor is greater readiness on the part of the courts and the public to tolerate collectivism *per se*. Almost any activity of governments is now *prima facie* legitimate and the task of the elector and of the judge has become merely one of deciding whether it is an activity appropriate to the Dominion or to the provinces. This state of mind was adopted perforce in wartime, and its disappearance since cannot be demonstrated.

The second factor is the continuation of the international crisis into the post-war period. The external pressure generated by the danger of war enhances the role of the federal government in two ways. It continues the importance of the defence functions and justifies a continuation of federal interest in industrial research, manufacturing capacity, the location of industry, and a wide range of other economic activities. At the same time international anarchy strengthens national unity and makes it easier for national purposes to override short-term local interests.

The third factor arises to some extent from the other two. The growth of government functions and responsibilities—particularly federal responsibilities—will be more rapid in the absence of determined opposition. The fact that there is no litigation over the terms of the constitution does not mean that change is not taking place but may mean that what change there is meets with general approval. In the past vested interests could exploit the collective indecision to prevent successful attacks on their position. Widespread fears that the determined opposition of vested interests would endanger either the wartime powers of the Dominion or the extension of some of those powers into the reconstruction period have not been borne out. On the contrary the government has retreated from its responsibilities faster than they have been attacked by any significant opposition in the courts. The reason why these expected attacks have not materialized is partly the changed attitude of the courts and partly the changed attitude of public opinion which has given pause to those who value their public relations too highly to risk being the objects of public indignation.

It is now possible to relate the rise of the Social Credit party in Alberta to this new synthesis in the Canadian federal system. Evidently the first five years of the Social Credit régime coincided with the last stage of inaction on the part of the central government in the face of problems which had ceased to be local though they were still thought of as being provincial responsibilities. The inanition of the federal government was, as we have seen, the result of a collective indecision both on the ends of state policy and on the means of achieving them. The legislative programme of the Social Credit government was the last attempt by a province to deal with the underlying causes of cyclical disturbance.

The Aberhart programme contributed positively in two ways to the resurgence of the Dominion as an agency of major economic policy. In the first place it demonstrated the limited nature of provincial action in this realm of policy. It demonstrated that provincial actions to mitigate the effects of the business cycle are one-sided and discriminatory. They shift the burden but do singularly little to reduce it or to induce recovery. At the same time the character of the Aberhart programme, which attacked powerful vested economic interests, produced insistent demands for the reassertion of the veto powers of the Dominion over discriminatory provincial economic policy, and created a litigious pressure in favour of Dominion legislative power over economic policy. The burden of proof of jurisdiction which had rested on an unenthusiastic Dominion in the Bennett New Deal cases, was thus shifted to the provinces.

Thus the conflict between the Dominion and the province of Alberta was a significant contributing factor in the shift in the balance of power between the provinces and the Dominion. Nevertheless it has been made clear that this conflict was not the underlying cause of the shift. The underlying causes were external and arose partly from the war and the uncertainties of the post-war world and partly from the gradual erosion of the grip of *laissez-faire* ideas on the courts.

This study of the relation of the conflict between a single province and the Dominion to the general problem of constitutional interpretation should serve to illustrate that the Canadian constitution is not concerned with timeless abstractions, but still remains—as it always was—a vehicle for the attainment of very practical ends. It cannot long stand if, instead of fostering those ends, it obstructs their attainment.

# Index